R00903 91077

D1597679

THE IMPERIAL RUSSIAN NAVY

THE IMPERIAL RUSSIAN NAVY

ANTHONY J. WATTS

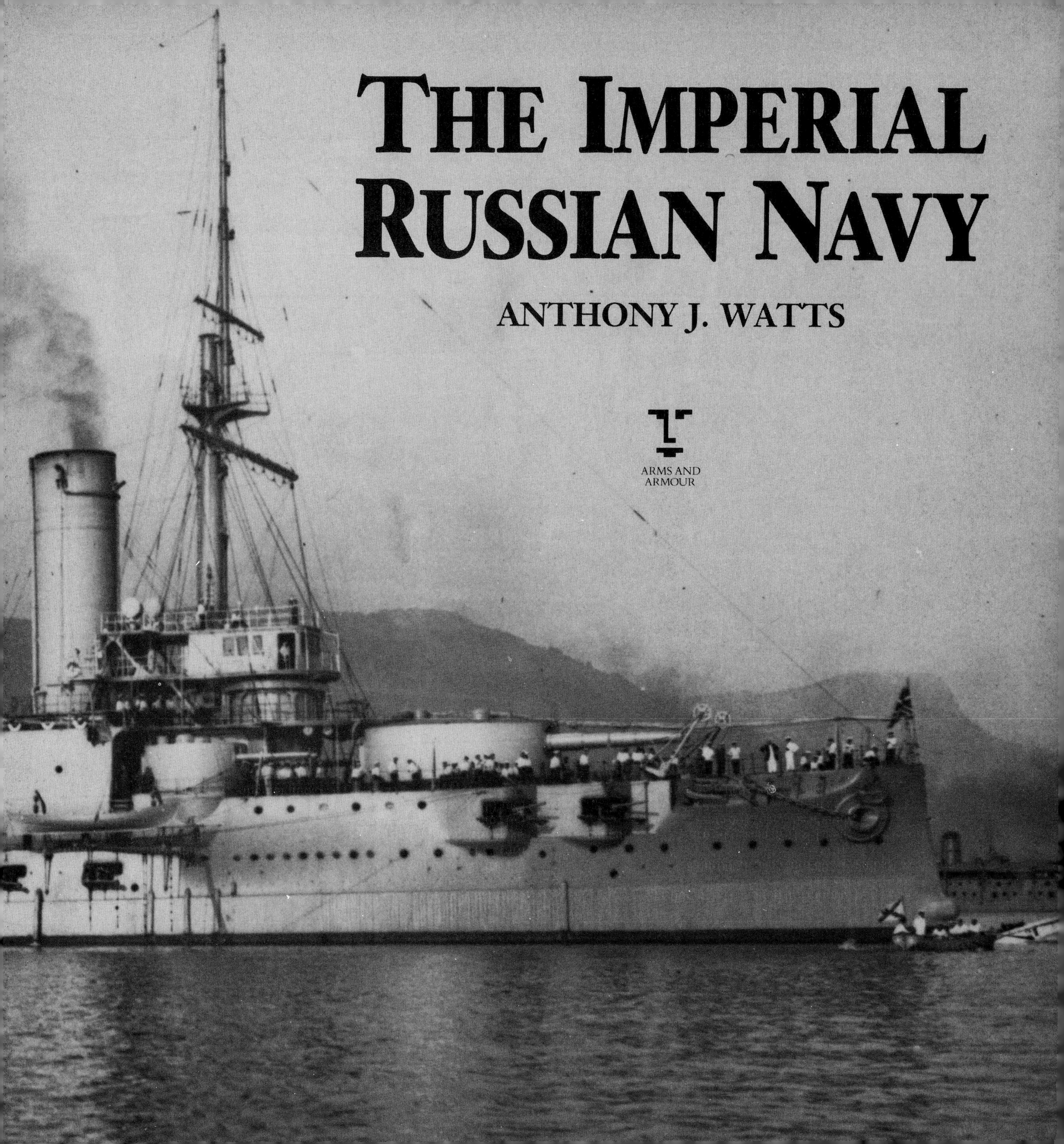

ARMS AND ARMOUR

Abbreviations and Notes Concerning Data Tables

Displacement: This is normal unless otherwise stated. Normal displacement is given in English tons and is the designed condition for older vessels, fully equipped and ready for sea with ¼ full supply of fuel, without reserve feed water, ½ to ⅔ stores and ½ to ¾ full supply of ammunition. For submarines, surfaced/submerged displacements are quoted.

Dimensions: length quoted is overall unless otherwise stated when: pp = perpendicular, wl = waterline.

Machinery
DA direct acting
HC horizontal compound
HDA horizontal direct acting
IC inverted compound
IDA inclined direct acting
IHP indicated horse power
SE single-ended
SHP shaft horse power
VC vertical compound
VTE vertical triple expansion

Armament
AA anti-aircraft
BL breech-loading
BLR breech-loading rifled
MG machine-gun
Pdr pounder
QF quick-firing
SB smooth-bore

Fate
CTL constructive total loss

First published in Great Britain in 1990 by Arms and Armour Press, Villiers House, 41-47 Strand, London WC2N 5JE.

Distributed in the USA by Sterling Publishing Co. Inc., 387 Park Avenue South, New York, NY 10016-8810.

Distributed in Australia by Capricorn Link (Australia) Pty. Ltd, P.O. Box 665, Lane Cove, New South Wales 2066.

British Library Cataloguing in Publication Data
Watts, Anthony J. (Anthony John), *1942–*
The Imperial Russian navy.
1. Russia. Fiot. Ships, history
I. Title II.
623.8250947
ISBN 0-85368-912-1

Designed and edited by DAG Publications Ltd. Designed by David Gibbons; edited by Michael Boxall; layout by Anthony A. Evans; typeset by Nene Phototypesetters Ltd, Northampton; camerawork by M&E Reproductions, North Fambridge, Essex; printed and bound in Great Britain by The Bath Press, Avon.

CONTENTS

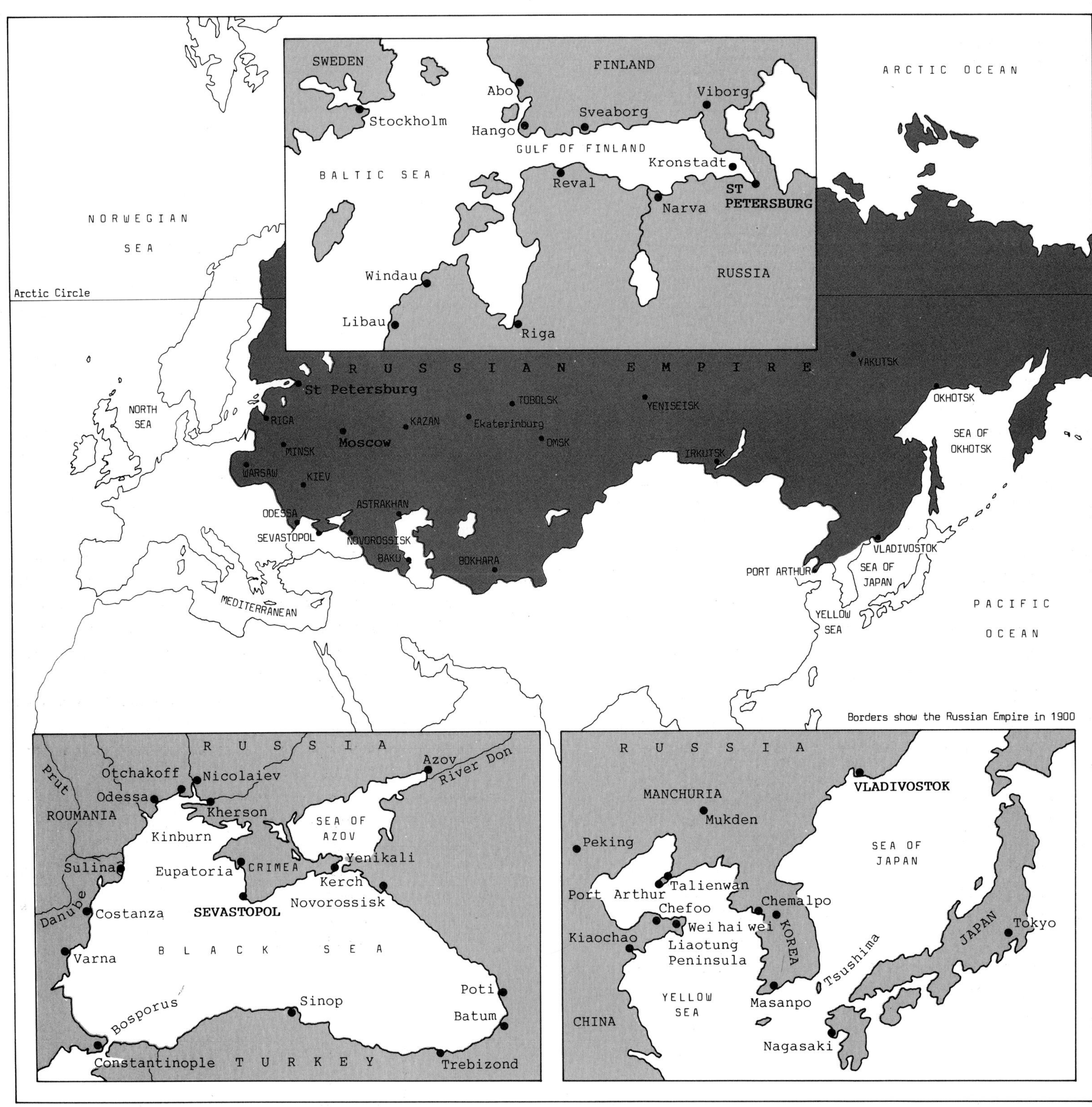
SWEDEN
FINLAND
Abo
Viborg
Stockholm
Sveaborg
Hango
GULF OF FINLAND
Kronstadt
BALTIC SEA
Reval
ST PETERSBURG
Narva
Windau
RUSSIA
Libau
Riga
ARCTIC OCEAN
NORWEGIAN SEA
Arctic Circle
RUSSIAN EMPIRE
St Petersburg
YAKUTSK
NORTH SEA
RIGA
TOBOLSK
YENISEISK
OKHOTSK
KAZAN
Ekaterinburg
Moscow
OMSK
MINSK
SEA OF OKHOTSK
IRKUTSK
WARSAW
KIEV
ASTRAKHAN
ODESSA
SEVASTOPOL
NOVOROSSISK
BAKU
BOKHARA
VLADIVOSTOK
PORT ARTHUR
SEA OF JAPAN
PACIFIC OCEAN
MEDITERRANEAN
YELLOW SEA
Borders show the Russian Empire in 1900
RUSSIA
Azov
River Don
Prut
Otchakoff
Nicolaiev
Odessa
ROUMANIA
Kherson
SEA OF AZOV
Kinburn
Yenikali
Sulina
Eupatoria
CRIMEA
Kerch
Novorossisk
Danube
Costanza
SEVASTOPOL
Varna
BLACK SEA
Poti
Bosporus
Sinop
Batum
Constantinople
TURKEY
Trebizond
RUSSIA
VLADIVOSTOK
MANCHURIA
Mukden
Peking
SEA OF JAPAN
Port Arthur
Talienwan
Chemalpo
Chefoo
Wei hai wei
KOREA
Tokyo
Kiaochao
Liaotung Peninsula
JAPAN
Tsushima
YELLOW SEA
Masanpo
CHINA
Nagasaki

PREFACE

COMPILING a reference work on the Imperial Russian Navy is fraught with difficulties. Apart from the problem of language, with the anomalies in translation arising from the Cyrillic alphabet, there remains the difficulty of reconciling those records and accounts which escaped the worst excesses of the Revolution and remain in existence, and which may be regarded as authentic and accurate, but which differ from one another. The problem is further compounded by the fact that up until 1900 the Russian calendar was 12 days behind that used by the rest of the Western world. Put together these problems can lead researchers into all sorts of confusion regarding dates, names, factual data concerning specifications and a host of other things. In compiling this work I have therefore restricted myself to a limited number of sources, which most researchers agree are to be considered as the most accurate available.

The primary sources consulted in the compilation of this reference work were *A List of the Ships of the Russian Steam and Ironclad Fleet from 1861 to 1917* by S. P. Moiseev, published in Moscow in 1948, and the researches of the late Boris Drashpil whose records and extensive photographic collection are now housed in the US Naval Historical Center in the USA. A further set of published researches which no student of the Imperial Russian Navy can ignore are those which have appeared in the American magazine *Warship International*; where doubt existed concerning the dates or specifications of Imperial Russian warships these were carefully consulted as a valuable source reference. Even so, a number of gaps still remained and to assist in filling these a number of secondary and less reliable sources were used. Lastly Conway's *All the Worlds Fighting Ships* was consulted in order to clarify a number of anomalies relating to ship classes and names. For a more complete list of sources (but excluding the very minor ones) see the Bibliography at the end.

In listing names I have generally elected to use the most familiar transliteration. Purists will doubtless disagree with some of my selections, but as there are various ways in which the Russian alphabet can be translated it seemed that to use the more familiar (but not necessarily correct) form was most suitable in order to cater for all languages.

With reference to dates, the calendar used for the more important warships has in most cases been carefully recorded in the original sources and it has therefore been relatively easy in these cases to alter this to the standard Western calendar. However, in the case of smaller warships the original sources have often neglected to note the calendar used; I have therefore assumed that most of these have used the old Russian one and changed the dates accordingly, appreciating the risk of error that entails.

This reference work only records details of ships recorded in the Imperial Fleet list up to the time of the Revolution in 1917. Subsequent fates, renamings and alterations under other flags have not been recorded in detail.

I should like to record my thanks to all those with whom I have corresponded over the years concerning the Imperial Russian Navy, and especially to Boris Lemachkov, who provided both information and photographs. I should also like to record my thanks to the various photographic sources, in particular to Marius Bar in France, and the Naval Historical Center in the USA for their help in researching little known photographs of Russian ships.

HISTORY OF THE IMPERIAL RUSSIAN NAVY

The Genesis of the Imperial Navy 1695–1815

Russian naval history has been dominated by her geography and by the fact that most of her coastline is icebound for part of the year, or else inhibited by narrow exits to the open seas. Rarely have these exits been directly under Russian control. Hence much of Russia's history has been dominated by a succession of wars in which she has striven to achieve control of those areas that will give her free access either to the Arctic Ocean, the North Sea or the Mediterranean and thence into the Atlantic, or else to ice-free bases on the Pacific coast.

One of the most important objectives which faced Russia at the end of the 17th century was the need to gain outlets in the Black Sea and the Baltic. In achieving such aims the right conditions would be created for Russia to expand her seaborne trading ties with foreign countries. At the same time such outlets would ensure the external security of the country, whose frontiers were under attack from the Tartars in the Crimea, the Turks in the south and the Swedes in the north.

Of all the coastlines controlled by Russia throughout her long history, only those bordering the Black Sea can boast of all the year round access, all the others being icebound at some time. It is not surprising, therefore, that many of Russia's endeavours to obtain free access to the open sea have concentrated on the Black Sea area. These have brought her into conflict with the other major power that borders the Black Sea, Turkey, which has almost continuously controlled that very narrow stretch of water, the Dardanelles, which forms the only outlet from the 'enclosed' Black Sea to the Mediterranean.

The end of the 17th century was, politically, an ideal time for Russia to embark on her policy of expansion, for at that time she formed part of a military alliance, which included Poland, Austria and Venice, and which was aimed at countering Turkish ambitions. It was, therefore, only a matter of time before Russia would find herself at war with Turkey. The only way in which she could wrest the Dardanelles from the Turks was to gain control of the Black Sea, and for this she would have to build a fleet of ships.

To achieve this goal the Tsar, Peter the Great, decided to attack the enemy at two points. The main thrust was aimed at the mouth of the River Don with a secondary thrust on the Lower Don. If the attacks succeeded Peter would gain bases both on the Sea of Azov and on the Black Sea and from these he could build and deploy a fleet of ships to gain dominance of the sea.

The first Azov campaign, undertaken in 1695, ended in failure, the Russian forces being unable to capture the Turkish fortress at Azov. Peter, however, was undeterred, the experience of the first campaign showing him that the fort at Azov could only be taken if it were blockaded from the sea and the garrison deprived of reinforcements and supplies. To achieve this Peter would have to build a fleet.

On 27 November 1695 he issued a decree announcing a new campaign against the Turks and the Tartars. Work immediately commenced at Preobrazhyensk, near Moscow, on the construction of fire ships and galleys. At the same time two 36-gun ships, the *Apostle Peter* and *Apostle Paul*, were laid down at Voronezh on the Don. Work also commenced on a large fleet of small craft intended for ferrying troops and equipment. A total of 1,300 river craft, 300 sea-going boats and 100 rafts were built at Kozlov, Dobrova, Sokol'sk and Voronezh. By the end of February 1696 parts for 22 galleys and four fire ships had been completed at Preobrazhyensk. The following month these were shipped to Voronezh where they were assembled and launched in April. Some 4,425 men were conscripted from the army to man the fleet which was under the command of a Swiss, Admiral Lefort. Under the combined efforts of the army and the fleet, the fort at Azov finally fell on 18 July 1696, and soon afterwards the two sides signed a truce.

Having achieved his objective of gaining a base on the Black Sea, Peter next turned his attention to the Baltic and Sweden. In 1699 he signed a secret treaty with Augustus of Saxony under which it was agreed that the two would attack Sweden and divide the spoils between them. As in the war against Turkey, Peter built a large fleet of small craft, mainly at Voronezh, which were transported north to the lakes of Ladoga and Peipus, where they engaged the Swedish vessels. Peter, however, was defeated by Charles XII of Sweden at the Battle of Narva in 1700, but continued with his efforts to gain a base on the Baltic while Charles embarked upon an ill-advised venture to invade the Russian heartland. Peter finally gained a base in the Baltic in 1703 when he captured the Swedish fort at Nyenschantz on the River Neva. Shortly after, in the first naval engagement in Baltic waters, the Russians captured two small Swedish vessels at the mouth of the River Neva. These were the first sea-going vessels to be commissioned into the Russian Navy. With the capture of Nyenschantz, Peter at once set about building up a naval base in the Baltic. A new capital was established on the site of the captured fort which was renamed St. Petersburg, a large shipyard was established for the construction of the new fleet and, in line with his vision for Russian expansion, Peter called the new capital the 'Window on the West'.[1] At the mouth of the River Neva lies the island of Kotlin, and here Peter built the large fortified naval base of Kronstadt.

In 1709 Charles and his Swedish army were defeated at the Battle of Poltava. During the following year the Russian Army moved down the Baltic coast capturing various Swedish positions, which enabled Peter to set up bases for his fleet at Reva, Riga, Elbing and Viborg. The latter base was taken by an amphibious assault led by the Commander-in-Chief, Rear-Admiral Feodor Apraxin. Under Apraxin the Russian fleet continued to achieve remarkable successes against an adversary well practised in the art of maritime warfare. So adept had the Russian fleet become that by 1714 they had gained the upper hand, the climax being reached in the summer when the fleet of Russian galleys routed a Swedish force at the Battle of Gangut (Hango Head). The Swedish fleet withdrew and the Russians were able to capture the Aland Islands from which they were able to dominate the Gulf of Bothnia. This action confirmed Russia as a major naval power and marked the eclipse of Swedish power in the Baltic although the war, known as the Great Northern War, dragged on until 1721 when the two sides signed the Treaty of Nystadt.

During this time Peter built up a considerable infrastructure for his fleet with numerous dockyards and training establishments. Previously he had been forced to rely on mercenaries and conscripted soldiers to man his fleet. With the new organization he was able to enlist the services of seamen from foreign navies to train Russian officers and men. However, the young Russian Navy was to suffer from the continuing problem of poor recruits, few seeking to enlist in a junior service with little tradition when the whole panoply of the mighty Russian Army was open to them. Simply put, Russia was and remained a continental land power with very little real pretence to acknowledging the importance of sea power and all that that entailed. It was left to visionaries such as Peter the Great to realize the importance of naval power and not even he could instil pride in such a concept throughout the vast population.

Apart from a few flashes of inspired brilliance the Russian fleet was to gain for itself the reputation of being a somewhat slovenly, inefficient force, and Peter the Great was under no illusion as to the state of his fleet. It was in the light of such knowledge that he laid down the profound requirement that the fleet should never attack a hostile force unless it had a numerical superiority of at least one-third. In spite of this rather dismal portrayal of what was one day to become the most powerful navy in the world, Dr. R. C. Anderson described its rise as '...quite unparalleled. In a few years it had not only come into existence, but had risen to the foremost place in the Baltic...'[2] While Peter was busily engaged in consolidating his gains in the Baltic, Charles XII of Sweden, who had been interned by the Turks following his defeat at Poltava, persuaded his captors to reopen hostilities against the Russians. Unable to fight a war on two such widely separated fronts, Peter agreed to negotiate for peace. Under the terms of the Treaty of Pruth, signed on 21 July 1711, Peter was forced to return Azov to Turkey, dismantle the fort at Taganrog and dispose of his Black Sea Fleet which by that time had grown to a strength of 58 ships of the line. The ships were either transferred to the Baltic via inland waterways, or handed over to the Turks.

In 1736 war again broke out between Russia and Turkey, with Azov yet again the focus of attention from the Russian forces. Lacking any naval forces, the Russians had to build up their fleet from scratch, a force of some 500 small craft being assembled on the River Don, and 400 larger vessels at Bryansk. Following the death of Peter the Great in 1725 a succession of weak rulers had neglected military matters, and although the fleet was built up in a remarkably short time, it lacked the perception of its true role and was relegated to providing inshore support for the army in its advance along the coast. Peace between the two countries was signed at the Treaty of Nissa on 3 October 1739. Under the Treaty Russia relinquished all the territory she had conquered, except Azov, which was demilitarized, and again agreed not to build a navy or merchant marine in the Black Sea.

In 1741 Sweden and Russia again found themselves at war in the Baltic. There was much manoeuvring between the two fleets, but little fighting, the Russians declining to offer battle as they did not possess the one-third superiority that Peter the Great had demanded. An attempt to achieve that superiority by transferring units from the White Sea Fleet failed, only two ships completing the journey. Peace was signed in 1743 and Russia gained some new territory in Finland.

In October 1768, with Catherine the Great on the throne, Russia once more was at war with Turkey. Britain allied herself to Russia, providing every kind of aid short of actually joining in the war. British dockyards at home and in the Mediterranean were made available to the Russians and a number of officers serving in the Royal Navy were seconded to the Russian Fleet.

Catherine ordered a force of ships to be sent to the Mediterranean from the Baltic Fleet. Seven ships of the line, a frigate and five smaller vessels, later reinforced by two ships of the line from the White Sea, sailed under command of Admiral Spiridov. Eight ships of the line were retained in the Baltic to guard against any attempt by Sweden to take advantage of the situation. However, it was deemed necessary to form a second squadron for service in the Mediterranean, the ships being drawn from those remaining in the Baltic. The force was commanded by the Scotsman Rear-Admiral John Elphinston of the Royal Navy. The Russian ships, however, were in a very poor state of repair and the men very disorganized. By 1770 only four of the ships of the line had managed to reach the British Mediterranean port in Minorca. One vessel had put into Lisbon and five other ships of the line were undergoing repairs at Portsmouth Dockyard. After a great struggle, with Britain repairing many of the Russian ships, Admiral Spiridov at last began his campaign, being joined in the Mediterranean by the Russian Commander-in-Chief, Count Aleksei G. Orlov.

In April 1770 Spiridov captured Navarino. The following month Elphinston reached the Mediterranean and concentrated his squadron off Cape Matapan. Learning of the presence of a Turkish squadron comprising fifteen ships of the line, he set off in pursuit with his three ships of the line. Action was joined on 27 May and continued throughout the day, the chase continuing during the night and the following day when the Turks retreated into the port of Nauplia. Toward evening Elphinston decided to withdraw his greatly inferior force. Throughout the action the Russian sailors had shown great courage and their tenacity was rewarded by the moral victory achieved over the vastly superior Turkish force. Russian losses amounted to fifteen killed and thirty wounded. According to one account, the action was notable for the fact that the Russians used explosive ammunition against the Turks.[3]

Having successfully defeated the Turks at Navarino, Elphinston took his four ships of the line and supporting frigates and headed for the Dardanelles, his object being to attack the Turkish Fleet in the Black Sea. Meanwhile, the main Russian fleet of nine ships of the line and eleven other vessels under Orlov came upon the Turkish fleet of fifteen ships of the line, fifteen smaller vessels and some 200 transports and storeships under the command of Hassan Bey outside the harbour at Tchesme near the island of Chios on 6 July 1770. The two flagships (*Sviatoy Yevstafy*, 66 guns and *Real Mustapha*, 84 guns) engaged each other and later both blew up, at which the Turks withdrew into the safety of the harbour. The following morning Elphinston arrived and sent a force of three ships of the line (*Europa*, *Netron Menya* and *Rostislav*) under the command of the Scottish Commodore Samuel Greig to escort four Greek coasting vessels converted to fireships into the harbour to annihilate the Turkish fleet. The Russian crews abandoned three of the fireships which ran aground, but the fourth grappled herself to a Turkish ship, setting her on fire. By the morning of the 8th only one Turkish 64-gun ship remained afloat to be captured by the Russians, together with ten small galleys. With the Turkish fleet destroyed this was the time to force the Dardanelles. But Orlov delayed, and when he finally attempted to force the Straits in October–November 1771, they had been heavily fortified by the Turks, with French assistance, and the attack failed.

On 16 July 1774 Russia and Turkey signed the Treaty of Kutchuk–Kainardji by which Russia at last gained the outlet to the Mediterranean which she had been seeking, her merchant vessels being allowed passage through the Dardanelles. In addition she was granted limited sovereignty over the port of Azov, the Kerch peninsula in the Crimea (the Crimea itself being declared independent under the Treaty), and land around the mouth of the River Dneiper and between the Dneiper and the River Bug. In return Russia had to relinquish control of some of the territory she had conquered.

In 1783 Russia annexed the whole of the Crimea and began to build up a large naval base at Sevastopol from which she could exercise command over the Black Sea. Sensing a threat to her control of the Black Sea, Turkey declared war on Russia in 1787. The Turkish fleet was greatly superior with a total of 22 ships of the line as against the Russians' five ships of the line. In frigates, however, Russia was superior with a total of twenty against the Turkish eight. In addition both fleets deployed powerful riverine flotillas of galleys, gunboats and small boats armed with field guns. Despite its superiority, the Turkish fleet was routed in a number of battles. Two battles were fought at Liman at the mouth of the Dneiper on 17 and 27 July 1788. The first action proved inconclusive, there having been rivalry in the Russian command. The situation was retrieved by the American John Paul Jones who took command and the Turkish ships withdrew. At the second battle the Russian force, under command of Jones, routed the Turks under Hassan el Ghasi. The Turks lost fifteen ships and 3,000 men, while the Russians lost one frigate and eighteen men.

With trouble having broken out in Poland, Russia was only too glad for peace and Turkey finally agreed to an armistice on 1 August 1791. The Peace Treaty of Jassy was signed on 9 January 1792, giving Russia all the territory she had conquered east of the River Dneister, including the port of Otchakov. With Otchakov and Sevastopol, Russia was now firmly in command of the northern part of the Black Sea. While Russia was occupied with Turkey in the south, the time was ripe for Gustav III of Sweden to destroy any ambitions Russia might have for the Baltic. War broke out in 1788 and the Russian fleet under command of Rear-Admiral Sir Samuel Greig joined action with the Swedish fleet at the Battle of Hogland in July 1788. Neither side gained any advantage. Sadly, Greig, one of the great architects of the Russian Navy, together with the English constructor Sir Samuel Bentham, died shortly after. During his service in the Russian Navy Greig had done much to rid the Navy and dockyards of corruption and graft. Two years later the Russian fleet of thirty ships of the line and eighteen frigates under Admirals Kruse and Tchitchagoff finally blockaded the Swedish fleet in the Bay of Viborg in June 1790. The Swedes attempted to break out of the blockade on 3 July, but a mishap with a Swedish fireship led to such confusion in the Swedish fleet that in the break-out two of the Swedish ships of the line were captured by the Russians and thirty other vessels of various types were lost. Six days later, at the Second Battle of Svenskund, the Swedes inflicted a heavy defeat on the Russian fleet which lost a third of its force of galleys and more than 9,500 dead, wounded and captured. Catherine agreed to make peace and on 14 August 1790 the Peace of Verela restored the situation to its former state.

On 6 November 1806, the Third Russo-Turkish war broke out, with Turkey declaring war on Russia. The only major naval action of the war was the Battle of Lemnos fought on 30 June 1807, in which the Russian fleet under Admiral Dmitri Seniavin defeated a slightly larger Turkish fleet.

The Greek War of Independence

The Greek War of Independence lasted from 1821 to 1829. While not being directly involved, Russia nevertheless had considerable interest in the outcome, Turkey (against whom the Greeks were fighting) being a long-standing enemy of Russia. Inevitably her support for Greek independence led to Russia declaring war on Turkey, on 26 April 1828. The war was principally one of land actions. Under the Treaty of Adrianople signed on 16 September 1829 Russia gained the mouth of the River Danube. The Greek War of Independence was notable for one major naval action in which the Russian fleet took part. Under the Treaty of London, signed on 6 July 1827, the governments of Britain, Russia and France had called for an Egyptian withdrawal from Greek territory, and an armistice between Turkey and Greece. In defiance of the Treaty an Egyptian squadron landed reinforcements at Navarino; in response Britain, France and Russia sent a naval force under command of Vice-Admiral Sir Edward Codrington. The Allied force comprised three British ships of the line, four frigates and four smaller vessels; four French ships of the line, a frigate and two smaller vessels under command of Rear-Admiral Henri Gauthier de Rigny; and a Russian squadron of four ships of the line and four frigates under the command of Rear-Admiral Count Heiden. The combined Turkish/Egyptian force under command of Admiral Ibrahim Pasha comprised seven ships of the line, fifteen frigates, 26 corvettes and some seventeen smaller craft.

The Turkish fleet was anchored in the Bay of Navarino in a horseshoe formation of three lines, with its broadsides covering the entrance to the harbour, and its flanks protected by shore batteries. Admiral Codrington's orders were to mediate between the Greeks and Turks, and force was only to be used as a last resort. It was planned that the Allied fleet would enter the Bay in two columns, the British in one followed by the French, with the Russians making a second column. In the event the Russians formed up astern of the French and the fleet entered the Bay on 20 October in a single line to anchor close to the Turkish fleet, blockading them in the Bay. A small boat from the British frigate *Dartmouth*, sent to instruct a Turkish fireship to keep its distance, was fired on by a Turkish vessel. The French flagship *Sirène* also sent a small boat to explain Allied intentions to the Turks and she too was fired on, one of her crew being killed. At this the Allied force opened fire on the Turkish fleet. Although the Turks fought resolutely, confusion reigned in their ranks. In the close-quarter fighting, which lasted for about two and a half hours, the superior training of the Allied gun crews resulted in the Turks being totally outgunned and destroyed, three-quarters of the fleet being sunk or fired by its own crews. Turkish/Egyptian losses were extremely heavy with more than 7,000 killed and wounded and some 35 vessels sunk (including one ship of the line, three 64-gun frigates, nine smaller frigates, 22 corvettes, and some smaller vessels. Allied losses in seamen were relatively light with 177 killed and fewer than 500 wounded, although the ships themselves suffered much damage.

Navarino is notable as being the last great battle between sailing ships in which the action was a simple gun duel between floating batteries. Henceforth major naval actions would involve the new technologies of the 19th century – ironclad warships armed with guns in revolving turrets.

The Crimean War

The Crimean War, which lasted from 1853 to 1856, was overtly caused by a dispute between Catholic France and Orthodox Russia as to who should be responsible for the Holy sites in Turkish-ruled Jerusalem. Seeing in this situation yet another opportunity to intimidate Turkey and thus secure her long-sought entry to the Mediterranean through the Bosphorous and Dardanelles, the Russian Army occupied the Turkish-controlled area north of the Danube. On 4 October 1853 Turkey declared war on Russia. At the opening of war the Russian Black Sea Fleet comprised sixteen ships of the line and nineteen frigates and corvettes, some of which were steam powered; the Turkish fleet, although similar in strength, was poorly equipped and no match for the Russians. During November 1853 a Turkish squadron comprising seven frigates, three corvettes and three steam vessels, under command of Vice-Admiral Osman Pasha, anchored in the Roads of Sinope. The Russians detected the Turkish squadron and blockaded them while awaiting reinforcements from Sevastopol. With the arrival of the reinforcements the Russian commander, Vice-Admiral Pavel Stepanovich Nakhimov, attacked the Turkish squadron on 30 November with six ships of the line, two frigates and a brig. Between them the Russian ships carried 38 of Paixhans smooth-bore 8¾in shell guns which had been introduced into the fleet the previous year, and possibly fired shells from their 36pdr long guns as well.

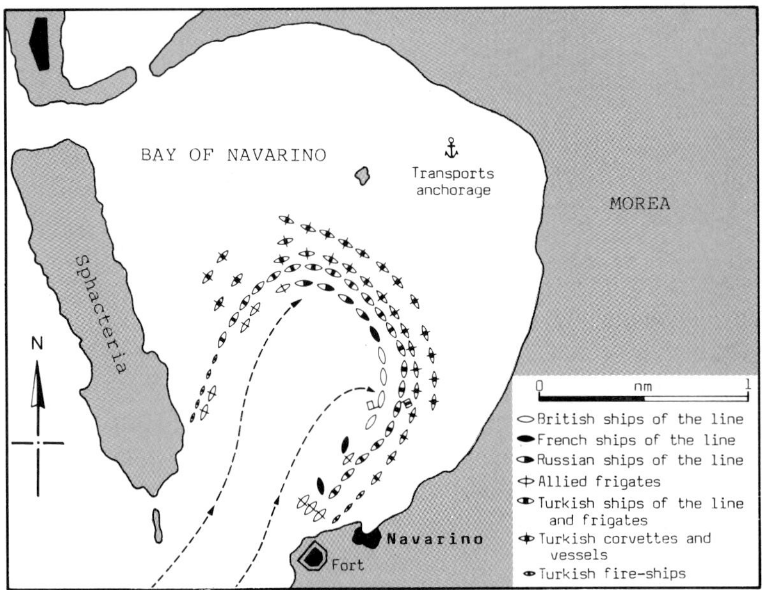

Above: The Battle of Navarino, 20 October 1827. Disposition of the fleets at the start of the battle.

Outnumbered and outgunned after two hours of intense bombardment using the new hollow spherical explosive shells, one of the Turkish frigates blew up while three others had been set on fire. After six hours the Turkish squadron had been annihilated, leaving some 2,960 Turks dead, while only the small steamer *Taif* managed to escape.

Britain and France sent warships to Constantinople to support the Turks in a move to forestall any Russian attempt to gain control of the passage of the Straits to the Mediterranean. The combined fleet entered the Black Sea on 3 January 1854. Two months later, on 28 March, Britain and France declared war on Russia. An Allied expeditionary force was sent to Varna on the Black Sea, and on 16 April the British frigate *Furious* was fired on while trying to enter Odessa under a flag of truce. Following this the Franco-British squadron bombarded the shore batteries and inflicted serious damage on them. Up to this point the enterprise had managed to achieve part of the objective, the Russians being forced to evacuate the Balkans. However, to ensure that there would be no further threat to the Dardanelles, France and Britain decided that Russian power in the Black Sea could only be broken by destroying the naval base at Sevastopol. This could only be achieved by landing an army in the region of Sevastopol and investing the base. The expeditionary force of some 60,000 men was re-embarked in a fleet of 400 warships and transports and sent to the Crimea where it set up base at Eupatoria.

The Allied army advanced on Sevastopol supported by the fleet, which followed it along the sea coast. The Russians declined to react to the impending threat, their fleet remaining in Sevastopol where a number of units were sunk to strengthen the harbour's defences, effectively blocking the channel and rendering naval co-operation in any assault from the north impossible. While the army laid siege to Sevastopol, the fleet, under Admiral Sir Edmund Lyons, blockaded the port. On 17 October the Allied warships commenced a bombardment of Sevastopol which began at midday and lasted six hours. The bombardment was a failure. Once again the new Russian shells highlighted the vulnerability of wooden ships to the more powerful new explosive, two of the Allies' 27 ships being so badly damaged that they had to be towed back to Constantinople for repair. In all the Allied fleet suffered some 340 dead and wounded in return for very little damage suffered by the Russian defences. Following this the investment settled into a long, bloody land campaign with minor skirmishes against the Russians' lines of communication in the Sea of Azov by shallow-draft Allied gunboats. It was not for nearly another year before Sevastopol finally fell to the Allies on 9 September 1855. The Russian Black Sea fleet of fourteen ships of the line and about 100 other warships was scuttled before the capitulation.

The damage suffered on 17 October 1854, combined with the effects of the action at Sinope, resulted in a major development in warship design and construction leading to the appearance of the first ironclad warships. Kinburn, at the mouth of the River Bug, was the site of the first action involving the new ironclads, three new French armoured batteries, the *Dévastation*, *Lave* and *Tonnante*, forming part of the Allied bombarding force of ten ships of the line and some eighty other vessels. The bombardment commenced on 16 October 1855 and made history. The guns of the three French steam batteries fired off some 3,000 rounds, easily demolishing the heavy masonry of the fort, while the Russian explosive shells were deflected or broke up harmlessly against the 4in wrought iron plates of the French ships at ranges of 1,000 yards or less.

The Crimean War has nearly always been regarded as a predominantly land campaign, but from a naval point of view it must be regarded as one of the turning-points in the development of the warship. It ushered in the new explosive shell, for whose introduction the Russians must be given full credit, which in turn led to the development of the armoured ship and the race between gun and armour which occupied the second half of the 19th century. The Crimea also heralded another major development in warship design, steam propulsion.

Despite having to encompass new ideas and technology, the Allies achieved their objective in preventing the Russians from gaining control of the Dardanelles, and their yearned-for egress into the Mediterranean. While the major effort at sea took place in the Black Sea, the Baltic too saw important developments in naval technology, although not a great deal of action. The Russians possessed a powerful fleet in the Baltic, and to prevent its egress into the North Sea, where it could dominate merchant shipping bringing vital raw supplies from Scandinavia to Britain and the continent, a joint expedition under the command of Vice-Admiral Sir Charles Napier was mounted. Operations in the Baltic were very low key, the only major action being the Allied bombardment of the fortress at Sveaborg controlling the approaches to Helsinki. The bombarding force under Vice-Admiral Dundas comprised 32 British gunboats and mortar vessels and 10 French gunboats together with a number of small craft armed with rockets. The bombardment began on 9 August, and at once a new menance appeared in the form of the Russian mine, one of which damaged a British sloop. The bombardment continued throughout the day, and was maintained by the rocket-armed boats after the main force withdrew at night. The next day the bombardment continued, at the end of which the Russians were thought to have lost 23 ships sunk at their moorings and 2,000 men for the loss of one Allied seaman killed and 15 wounded. Before the Allies could dispatch a much larger fleet to the Baltic in 1856, the Russians agreed to peace. The Treaty of Paris was signed on 1 April 1856, and laid down the principle of 'free ships and free merchandise'. Once again the Russians were forbidden to maintain a fleet in the Black Sea. The Treaty set limits on the size of ships Russia could possess as six warships of no more than 800 tons and four of no more than 200 tons.

Naval expansion and the Russo-Turkish War

While Russia was again forbidden to build a Fleet in the Black Sea, no such imposition was placed on the Baltic Fleet. No sooner had the Crimean War ended than the Russians began to build up their naval forces in the Baltic.

Already, in 1855, the Russians had seen the potential of underwater warships. The Bavarian inventor Wilhelm Bauer, having had his services rebuffed by a number of countries, eventually went to Russia where he was provided with funds to build *Le Diable Marin* in which he made more than 100 successful dives. He even took a party of musicians underwater to play the Russian National Anthem at the coronation of Tsar Alexander II in September 1858.

Under the Grand Duke Constantine, brother of Tsar Alexander II, the Baltic Fleet underwent a transformation. A tremendous effort was made to recover Russia's maritime position and a new shipbuilding programme laid down the foundations of a steamship navy. Ten screw, line-of-battle ships, seventeen frigates and a large number of coastal gunboats were planned. The introduction into the British and French navies of ironclads led Russia to convert two wooden ships, *Sevastopol* and *Petropavlovsk*, then under construction, to armoured frigates, fitting them with 4½ in iron plate. But innovative technology on its own does not make a modern, efficient navy. If technology is to be of any value the men responsible for controlling and operating it must have a thorough knowledge of what they are doing. Hence the Grand Duke also instituted a major reorganization of training with a new scheme of naval education and training affecting the whole fleet from newly joined boys right up to flag officer level.

According to one source[4] the total strength of the Russian fleet in 1859 was seven screw ships of the line, eleven screw frigates, twelve screw corvettes and a number of smaller screw ships, as well as twelve sailing ships of the line, seven frigates and seven corvettes, all obsolete. Assisting the Grand Duke in his reorganization and build-up at the Ministry of Marine was Likhavchev who in 1859 went to command the Russian forces in the Far East at the time of the Opium Wars. Under the terms of the Treaty of Peking, signed on 18 October 1860 at the end of the Second Opium War, China was forced to cede the province of Amur to Russia and the site where the Russians began to build the port of Vladivostock, founded in 1860–1. Likhavchev also annexed the island of Tsushima, but the Russian Government rejected the annexation and the island came under Japanese rule.

The next ten years were relatively peaceful for Russia and she was able to build up her new navy and train the men to operate the new technology. The new fleet made its first appearance in 1863 when two small squadrons were sent into the Atlantic and Pacific. The danger of war with the West convinced the Russians both of the need to build up alliances and, more importantly, to ensure her fleet was on the high seas and could not be bottled up in a sea with only one exit, as had happened so many times before.

The Russians watched with close interest the events of the US Civil War and, in particular, the action between *Monitor* and *Merrimac*. When it appeared that the European nations might become involved in Poland, the Russians decided that the capabilities of this type of craft would be well suited to operations along the Baltic coast. As a result ten monitor-type ships were ordered in 1863 to plans drawn up by the Swedish builder, Ericsson.

During the late 1860s and 1870s the Russians began to lay down battery ships either built entirely of iron, or having wooden hulls with side armour. Battery ships, although heavily armed, suffered from limited firepower because only half of the armament could fire on one broadside or the other. To overcome this deficiency, and to obtain maximum firepower available from the armament carried, guns began to be mounted in revolving turrets. The concept for the Russian turret ships can be traced back to the Crimean War, where the Royal Navy mounted revolving turrets designed by Captain Coles on rafts for use in the Sea of Azov. The Russians' turret ship, *Minin*, was designed with a tripod mast and sail rigging similar to the British *Captain*. Following the disaster to *Captain*, however, *Minin* was re-designed and completed as a broadside armoured cruiser.

The Russians quickly copied the British concept of the mastless turret ship, epitomized by HMS *Devastation*, and in 1872 launched *Piotr Veliki* at Kronstadt. *Veliki* carried four breech-loading 12 in guns in two turrets forward and aft.

Under the terms of the Treaty of Paris Russia was forbidden to possess a fleet in the Black Sea. Accordingly all new vessels built were for service in the Baltic. With the defeat of France in the 1870–1 Franco-Prussian War, however, the Russians denounced the Treaty

Right: The first turret ship in the Imperial Navy was the *Minin*. After the disaster to the British turret ship *Captain*, however, she was re-designed and completed as a broadside armoured cruiser. (Author's collection)

and work began on building units for a new Black Sea Fleet. The first two vessels completed were the unusual circular *Popovka* class built for use as floating forts.

In April 1877 Russia was again at war with Turkey. Although principally characterized by a series of land campaigns, the war was notable for the introduction of a number of new naval systems. However, the fleet construction programme begun in 1870 was not completed, and when war broke out the fleet comprised two circular batteries, four old corvettes and a number of gunboats and sloops with which to face the Turkish fleet of seven large armoured frigates and eight smaller armoured corvettes. Lacking any major Black Sea Fleet, Russia was forced, as so often in the past, to improvise some form of naval capability with which to counter the Turkish fleet. One of these ideas involved requisitioning nineteen fast merchant ships which were fitted out to carry a number of small steam launches built in the Baltic and transported overland to the Black Sea. These launches were armed with various forms of early torpedo, such as the spar (a long pole with an explosive charge at the end fitted in the bow of the launch). The spar torpedo was detonated by lowering the end over the bow of the launch so that it exploded underwater when it came in contact with the enemy ship's hull. Other types of torpedo used included a towed torpedo dragged by the launch across the bows of the enemy ship, and the 'fish' torpedo, the first real torpedo with its own compressed air propulsion system, which was fired from a tube attached to the side of the hull of the launch (the launches were very tiny) or dropped over the side of the launch. Tactics using these early torpedoes put the crews of the steam launches at considerable risk because they were only effective against the new armoured ships at very short range.

The first torpedo attack took place on 25 May 1877 when four launches under command of Lieutenant Dubasov attacked the Turkish river gunboats *Seife* and *Fethul Islam* moored at the mouth of the Danube. In pouring rain and following numerous breakdowns in the slow (maximum speed was about 5 kts), primitive craft, Dubasov in *Tsarevitch* closed the Turkish vessel *Seife* and detonated his spar torpedo under her stern. An enormous explosion shook the

Turkish vessel and almost swamped the small torpedo-boat with water. The second torpedo-boat *Xenia* (Lieutenant Tchestakov) then attacked *Seife*, exploding her torpedo against the Turkish ship's hull. The third boat, *Djigit*, was damaged as she approached and had to be run aground, to be retrieved the following day in full view of the Turks. *Seife* was last seen sinking as the Russians withdrew.

One historian has noted that: 'May 25 is memorable in the history of sea warfare as the first successful use of a weapon destined to make great ravages when developed and perfected.'[5] It foreshadowed the Japanese attack on Port Arthur and the destruction of many thousands of merchant ships in two world wars by a weapon which was almost to paralyse naval operations at sea. A second attack, mounted on 10 June, involved the merchant ship *Veliki Kniaz Constantine* carrying six torpedo-boats and escorted by the converted merchant vessel *Vladimir*. The six boats (five of them armed with spar torpedoes) were launched off the Sulina mouth of the Danube against four Turkish ironclads, protected by a rope boom defence. The first to attack is believed to have been Lieutenant Rozhdestvensky (later to lead the Baltic Fleet on its ill-fated journey to the Pacific in the Russo-Japanese War), but his attack was frustrated, his boat suffering bow damage from the boom defences. None of the boats achieved a successful attack, and one was lost after colliding with the boom defence and being shelled by the Turks.

The Russians followed up this operation with other bold attacks using torpedo-boats against targets at Batum and Sukkum Kale. The Russians cleverly camouflaged their torpedo boats in these attacks, painting them a sea-green colour so that they would merge with the sea as they made their attack. On the night of 23/24 August 1877 four torpedo-boats (*Navarin*, *Sinop*, *Tchesma*, *Torpedoist*) from *Veliki Kniaz Constantine* attacked the Turkish central battery ship *Assar-i-Chevket*. Further attacks were carried out by the torpedo-boats, and their persistence was finally rewarded on the night of 25/26 January 1878 when *Tchesma* and *Sulina*, by now fitted with proper torpedo tubes, attacked and sank the 2,000-ton Turkish gunboat *Intikbah* in Batum harbour. Fred T. Jane, the famous naval historian and founder of *Jane's Fighting Ships*, wrote of these exploits: 'They [the Russians] had no fleet to start with, and they used an almost unknown weapon.... [they] had to invent tactics... Nor, because their loss of life was small and insignificant, can this be held to detract from the individual bravery of the Russian torpedoists; on going into action there were absolutely no reasonable prospects of such an extraordinary survival.'[6]

Naval Programmes and the lead-up to the Russo-Japanese War

The last two decades of the 19th century witnessed a number of major developments within the Russian Navy. By far the most important was the preparation of the first systematic plan for a large increase in naval strength. Drawn up in 1880, the plan provided for a 20-year programme of construction aimed at building up the Russian Navy into an important naval power which, in alliance with another fleet, would be capable of meeting any possible adversary on more or less equal terms. The main threat perceived during this period was Germany, hence Russia's endeavours to build such an alliance with France.

Under the programme the fleet, which at that time boasted only four capital ships, was to be strengthened by fifteen battleships, ten cruisers and eleven gunboats. The programme ran into unavoidable delays and eventually commenced in 1882. Subsequently the figures were revised upwards to provide for twenty battleships, and 24 cruisers. While it was considered essential to built up strength in capital ships, the main emphasis in the programme lay on the construction of fast, powerful raiding cruisers (a stratagem begun in the 1870s) designed to interfere with an enemy's seaborne commerce. These were epitomized by *Admiral Kornilov*, a 5,000-ton cruiser armed with two 8 in and fourteen 6 in guns and, for the time, a high speed of 18.5 knots.

In 1880 the British shipbuilding yard of Yarrow completed the first successful sea-going or first-class torpedo-boat, *Batum*, for the Russian Navy. This type of vessel proved to be an extremely important element in all the major navies, not least the Russian, which by 1884 lead the world with a total of 115 such craft.

In 1887, following a successful demonstration at the Spithead Naval Review in England, a Nordenfelt submarine built at Barrow-in-Furness was sold to the Russian Navy. She was wrecked on the coast of Jutland while on passage to Russia. In 1890 Admiral Makaroff revived an earlier idea of developing an armour-piercing shell. Successful tests were carried out in 1894, using a French Holtzer chrome-steel shell with hard envelope and soft core fitted with a cap to penetrate face-hardened steel. The shell was subsequently adopted by the Russian Navy. Also in 1890 the Navy carried out comparative trials between plain steel, nickel steel and compound armour. These trials showed that Vickers'-manufactured plain steel plate was rather better than the nickel steel containing only 3 per cent of nickel.

Right: The launch *Tchesma* armed with a spar torpedo in 1878. She was a modified steam launch carried on davits on the requisitioned steamer *Veliki Kniaz Constantine* (seen in the background). (US Naval Historical Center)

Below: The first true torpedo boat in the Navy was the *Vzruiv*. The photograph was taken from a chromo-lithograph from La Marine Russe, St. Petersburg, 1892. (US Naval Historical Center)

Towards the end of the 19th century Russian naval ambitions in the Far East were given a major boost when the power of Imperial China was finally broken by the Treaty of Shimonoseki. Signed on 17 April 1895, the Treaty forced China to recognize the independence of her former adversary, Korea. In order to maintain a check on Japanese ambitions in the Chinese region, Russia, France, Germany and Great Britain forced concessions from supine China. As part of these concessions Russia gained control of Port Arthur and the Liaotung Peninsula in 1898, together with rights for the Chinese eastern railway which would link Port Arthur with the trans-Siberian railway. Port Arthur was developed into a major base and formed a focal point for Russian ambitions in the Far East. A powerful fleet was built up in the Far East until by 1904 it rivalled the entire Japanese Navy, or so it seemed on paper. In 1898 another naval programme was drawn up providing for the construction of eight battleships, seventeen cruisers, and fifty destroyers and torpedo-boats. When completed these units were to form the backbone of the Russian Navy during the Russo-Japanese War.

In 1901 two lieutenants in the Imperial Navy, Kolbasieff and Kuteinoff, designed an electric submarine boat, *Piotr Koschka*. The boat enjoyed limited success, but the design was not repeated. She was followed in 1903 by the 175-ton *Delfin*, a petrol-engined boat of the Holland type, built by Bubnov, later to be responsible for designing many of Russia's submarines. Five further boats of this type were built in 1904. After this the Russians contracted the Krupp Germania yard to build three small 200-ton boats (*Karp*, *Kambala*) for service in the Black Sea.

Left: Following a successful demonstration at the Spithead Naval Review the Russians purchased a Nordenfelt submarine from Barrow. She is seen here on the stocks ready for launching. (Author's collection)

Right: The First Pacific Squadron at Port Arthur in 1904. From left to right: the cruiser *Aurora*, gunboat *Chihyric*, cruiser *Variag* and battleship *Peresviet*. (P. A. Vicary)

The Russo-Japanese War

The Russian occupation of the Liaotung Peninsula and Port Arthur following the ending of the Sino-Japanese War (1894–5) and the Treaty of Shimonoseki, together with the build-up of the Far East Fleet, posed an open threat to the Japanese Empire. In an effort to settle the question peaceably and curtail Russian expansionism in the region, Japan concluded the Nishi-Rosen Agreement with Russia. At the same time she prepared for war, building up her armed forces. Disputes between the two powers continued, with the Koreans fomenting further unrest between them. In 1901 Russia reached an Agreement with China by which she would take over Manchuria. Britain, America and Japan brought pressure to bear on China to withhold approval for the Agreement. As it appeared that the Russo-Japanese Agreement was failing, Japan entered into negotiations with Britain for a formal alliance which was concluded early in 1902. In April 1902 Russia agreed to demands by which she was to have completed evacuation of Manchuria by October 1903. The Russians then demanded further concessions from China and early in 1903 re-occupied the evacuated territories. Japan still hoped to settle the dispute peaceably, negotiations continuing at St. Petersburg. Russian aggression continued, however, spreading from Manchuria to Korea. Having exhausted all means of settling the dispute peaceably and alarmed by the continual delays in the discussions, the Japanese minister responsible for negotiations left St. Petersburg on 5 February and returned to Japan. Japan severed diplomatic relations with Russia on 6 February 1904.

To deploy her army on the mainland, and transport reinforce-

ments to fight the Russians in Manchuria, Japanese command of the sea was essential. The first pre-requisite, therefore, was to destroy the Russian Pacific Fleet and capture its base of Port Arthur. This was the Russian Fleet's only port on the Pacific coast that was free of ice all the year round. Its capture would also deprive the Russians of any winter naval base should they send the Baltic Fleet to the Pacific. Having gained command of the sea the Japanese Army would be free to destroy Russian land forces in Manchuria forcing Russia to capitulate.

Since 1898 Russia had been building up her strength in the Far East and in January 1904 the Pacific Fleet comprised seven elderly battleships with another (*Osliabia*) *en route* from the Mediterranean. With five more powerful battleships completing, the Russian Pacific Fleet could have reached at least thirteen battleships by the end of 1905. Also included in the Russian order of battle were nine armoured cruisers, 25 destroyers and about 30 smaller craft. The main fleet was based on Port Arthur, with two cruisers at Chemulpo (Inchon), Korea and four more cruisers at Vladivostock. In addition the trans-Siberian railway would soon be completed, ahowing the Russians to send reinforcements to the Far East much more quickly. The Japanese fleet consisted of six up-to-date battleships armed with 12 in guns, one older battleship, eight fine armoured cruisers, 25 lighter cruisers, nineteen destroyers and 85 torpedo-boats, plus sixteen smaller craft. In all respects the Japanese fleet was superior to the Russian both in doctrine, training and leadership.

On 3 February 1904, the Russian First Pacific Squadron in Port Arthur assumed a preliminary degree of readiness and put to sea. Russia's war plan envisaged a fleet action as soon as possible after the declaration of war. No Japanese warships were sighted, and the fleet returned to Port Arthur. The fleet was forced to anchor in the roadstead outside due to the state of the tide. At low tide the depth of water at the entrance to Port Arthur was insufficient to allow the battleships to leave harbour, which would have meant that should the Japanese appear, the ships would have been trapped. While the fleet anchored outside the harbour, two destroyers were told off to patrol offshore as a precautionary measure. Both the Russian naval commanders, Admiral Alexiev, the Governor-General of Siberia and Commander-in-Chief, together with Vice-Admiral Stark, commanding the First Pacific Fleet, were lulled into a false sense of security as they considered that war would be signalled by a formal declaration rather than merely breaking off diplomatic relations. This was not to be the case, however, and the first Japanese move involved a pre-emptive strike on the Russian Pacific fleet before a formal declaration of war had been made. As the Russian Fleet lay at anchor outside Port Arthur on the night of 8 February 1904, it was attacked by ten Japanese destroyers. The Fleet had taken no precautions against a surprise attack, except to surround its ships with crinoline torpedo nets. Ships had steam available only for running emergency systems and for maintaining power sufficient for lighting, pumps, dynamos, etc. Two ships had been detailed to maintain a searchlight guard and the two destroyers were on picket duty twenty miles out to sea. Even the guns in the shore batteries were still under their protective coverings.

The night was calm and cool and despite some confusion in the darkness and running into the Russian destroyers, which did not suspect their presence, the Japanese destroyers pressed home their attack, firing nineteen torpedoes at the anchored Russian ships from ranges varying between 700 and 1,600 yards. Only three torpedoes struck targets, the Russian battleship *Tsessarevitch* and *Retvisan* (which were temporarily put out of action) and the cruiser *Pallada*. All but the leading Japanese destroyer division were caught in the Russian searchlights and hotly engaged by many quick-firing guns, but suffered only minor damage and returned safely to harbour.

The failure of this and a subsequent attack by forty Japanese destroyers and torpedo-boats, which failed to score any hits, did little to minimize the threat of the torpedo which, for the remainder of the short war, almost paralysed Russian naval strategy.

It was, however, to the anticipated clash between the opposing squadrons of armoured warships that most eyes turned. The first encounter took place on the morning after the torpedo attack on Port Arthur, 9 February 1904. The Japanese Admiral Togo in his flagship *Mikasa* led his fleet into Port Arthur roads in the hope of catching the Russians in disarray following the night attack. The Russian fleet had already sailed, however, and the two fleets passed each other at a range of 7,000 yards. The Japanese squadron was led by a homogeneous group of six battleships of the First Division, followed by a squadron of five armoured and four protected cruisers. The Russian fleet consisted of five battleships led by *Petropavlovsk* followed by a mixed cruiser squadron comprising one armoured cruiser, three protected cruisers, and two light cruisers. The battle was confused and indecisive, the mixed gun batteries confusing the spotting of fall of shot and hampering the primitive fire-control arrangements. Furthermore, the short-range action imposed a flat trajectory on the projectiles with the result that those that did manage to hit a target did so on the side armour which they failed to penetrate. As the fleets drew apart it was seen that the Russian cruisers had drawn most of the Japanese fire and suffered a number of hits, although none had been put out of action. The Russian battleships had also been hit repeatedly; *Pobieda* had received fifteen hits, mostly from secondary armament, but not a single shell had penetrated the armour or inflicted serious damage. Russian casualties amounted to twenty-one killed and 101 wounded. Four Japanese ships were hit, but suffered only superficial damage, and casualties were lighter than the Russians'.

While Togo was engaging the Russians at Port Arthur, the Japanese armoured cruiser squadron, escorting transports carrying the Japanese expeditionary force, entered Chemulpo, Korea and attacked the Russian cruiser *Variag* and the gunboat *Korietz* at anchor. The cruiser was sunk and the gunboat so severely damaged that she was eventually scuttled by her crew. During the following weeks the Japanese fleet carried out long-range bombardment of Port Arthur to which the Russian gunners replied with unexpected accuracy. Vice-Admiral Stephen Ossipovitch Makarov (the torpedo-boat commander who won distinction during the Russo-Turkish war) was appointed Commander-in-Chief of the First Russian Pacific Squadron in March. Admiral Makarov galvanized the Russians into action, and from 8 March to 13 April the ships carried out a number of sorties to harass the Japanese blockading ships and to carry out tactical minelaying. Returning from one of these sorties, Admiral Makarov's flagship *Petropavlovsk* struck a Japanese mine and sank with all hands, Russia losing her one commander capable of inspiring action. *Pobieda* also struck a mine in the same field, but was not seriously damaged.

Port Arthur was now blockaded, and with the Russian fleet neutralized the Japanese Army was free to carry out operations against Russia. Under Admiral Vitgeft (who had succeeded Makarov) the Russians made a final serious attempt to break the blockade on 10 August 1904, sailing from Port Arthur at dawn to meet the Japanese later in the day at the Battle of the Yellow Sea (also called the Battle of Shantung). The Russian squadron comprised the battleships *Tsessarevitch*, *Perseviet*, *Pobieda*, *Poltava*, *Retvisan* and *Sevastopol*, four cruisers and fourteen destroyers. The Japanese fleet comprised the battleships *Asahi*, *Fuji*, *Mikasa*, and *Shikishima*, the armoured cruisers *Kasuga* and *Nisshin*, eight other cruisers, and 48 destroyers and torpedo-boats. The object was for the Port Arthur squadron to join forces with the Vladivostock squadron. By midday the Japanese fleet had manoeuvred itself into position off the Shantung Peninsula to block further progress of the Port Arthur squadron. Action was joined at 1300 hours and the Russians managed to break away from the Japanese, who immediately took up the chase. Steaming up from the south-west, the fast Japanese ships gradually overhauled the Russians and at 1600 action recommenced with a long-range gunnery duel between opposing 12 in guns at ranges between 8,000 to 9,000 metres. This proved to be much more effective than the short-range engagement using mixed calibre guns. It also demonstrated that in an action between armoured ships only large-calibre weapons were of any value. The shells from 8 in and 6 in guns failed to inflict any serious damage.

Early in the action the Russians scored two hits on *Mikasa* causing serious damage and many casualties. The Japanese failed to score any significant hits on the Russians, despite engaging all their guns from 6 in calibre upwards. The Russian ships remained virtually unharmed. At 1800, however, just as the action seemed about to end in favour of the Russians, two 12 in shells struck the Russian flagship *Tsessarevitch* and detonated, throwing her out of control and killing all the personnel on the bridge, including Admiral Vitgeft. The rest of the Russian line was thrown into confusion and in the gathering darkness the Japanese broke off the action, allowing their torpedo-boats to carry out night attacks. These were repulsed by the Russians who managed to escape, five battleships, a cruiser and nine destroyers returning to Port Arthur. Of the remaining ships, *Tsessarevitch* and three destroyers went to Tsingtao, the cruiser *Askold* and a destroyer to Shanghai and the cruiser *Diana* to Saigon where they were all interned. The small cruiser *Novik* made for Vladivostock, but was intercepted by the Japanese cruisers *Chitose* and *Tsushima*, and forced aground at Sakhalin. Meanwhile the Russian armoured cruisers *Gromoboi*, *Rossia* and *Rurik* and the cruiser *Bogatyr* had sailed south from Vladivostock to support the breakout of the Port Arthur squadron. On 14 August, at the Battle of the Japanese Sea, this squadron was intercepted by four Japanese armoured cruisers. In a four-hour fight *Rurik* was sunk, and the other vessels returned to Vladivostock to take no further part in the war.

Finally, after a five-month siege during which most of the Russian ships were struck by Japanese Army artillery and severely damaged, sunk or scuttled, Port Arthur fell. The final weeks of the siege witnessed the first operational use of a submarine in war when unsuccessful attempts were made to operate *Piotr Koschka*, built in 1901 (see above). She had originally been powered by two pairs of bicycle pedals, but these were replaced by a motor car engine.[7]

Then, on 27 May 1905 came the Japanese Trafalgar. The Russian Baltic Fleet, which had been built up since the outbreak of war with four battleships (one other battleship could not be completed in time) and four cruisers being hurriedly completed and a number of obsolete vessels overhauled, sailed to reinforce the Pacific

Right: The remains of the First Pacific Fleet at Port Arthur. On the left the battleship *Poltava* and to the right *Peresviet*. (Author's collection)

Fleet before the latter was scuttled in Port Arthur. Strenuous but unsuccessful efforts were also made to build up naval strength by acquiring second-hand warships, principally from Argentina, Brazil and Chile. Diplomatic efforts were also made to gain exits through the Dardanelles, but these too failed.

Under Admiral Rozhdestvensky the Baltic Squadron, which was referred to as the Second Pacific Squadron, sailed for the Pacific on 14 October 1904. On its way through the North Sea the crews on board the motley squadron of obsolete, just completed or worn-out ships became so jittery as a result of torpedo scares from Japanese torpedo-boats that, in the darkness, they opened fire on a British fishing fleet on the night of 21/22 October, sinking four trawlers.

The squadron took the long route round the Cape of Good Hope, refuelling frequently at sea from colliers specially sent to rendezvous points by the Russians, all neutral ports being closed to the Squadron because of the war. By December the Squadron, after many vicissitudes, reached Madagascar where it was able to carry out a short 2-month refit preparatory to sailing on the next stage of its long journey to the Far East. While at Madagascar, on 2 January, Port Arthur fell. Rozhdestvensky's Second Pacific Squadron sailed from Madagascar in March and reached Korea at the end of May. Here, on 27 May, off the Island of Tsushima between Japan and Korea, the brave Second Squadron having been joined by a third squadron of coastal defence ships which had sailed from the Baltic through the Mediterranean and Suez Canal, was annihilated by the Japanese Fleet.

The fact that the squadron ever reached Tsushima has been a constant cause for wonderment by historians, particularly when one considers how ill prepared the squadron was for such a long voyage, the generally poor state of repair and the age of the ships, the sub-standard training of the crews and the fact that it was unable to use virtually any sheltered anchorage to refuel and carry out repairs on its long voyage to the Far East.

The Battle of Tsushima

27 May 1905 is a day that will long be remembered by both the Russian and Japanese Navies. During the night the Russian Second and Third Pacific Squadrons under Admiral Rozhdestvensky steamed slowly in line ahead through the mist in the Straits of Tsushima. Rozhdestvensky had hoped to pass through the Straits unobserved, but, obeying the rules of war, two hospital ships at the rear of the Russian column continued to burn all their lights and these were spotted in the early morning by the Japanese. The morning dawned grey and damp and through the mist the Russians spotted Japanese ships steaming on a parallel course to the north-west. Led by the armed merchant cruiser *Shinano Maru*, a squadron of Japanese light cruisers and the armoured cruiser *Idzumo* heralded the appearance of the Japanese battle fleet.

At about 1340 the Japanese First Division, led by the flagship *Mikasa*, followed by the battleships *Shikishima*, *Fuji* and *Asahi* and the armoured cruisers *Nisshin* and *Kasuga* came up with the Russian fleet. The Japanese first steamed across the bows of the Russian line from east to west and then reversed course to steam west to east, a manoeuvre which took some fourteen minutes. The armoured cruiser squadron comprising *Idzumo*, *Yakumo*, *Asama*, *Adzuma*, *Tokiwa* and *Iwate* then took station astern of the First Division, the long line of Japanese warships steaming on a north-easterly course in attempt to cross the Russian T. To avoid being raked by the Japanese fleet, the Russians also altered course to the north-east, away from their intended course to Vladivostock. The two fleets were now steaming on nearly parallel courses.

Below: The Battle of Tsushima, 27 May 1905. Disposition of the fleets at the moment of opening fire.

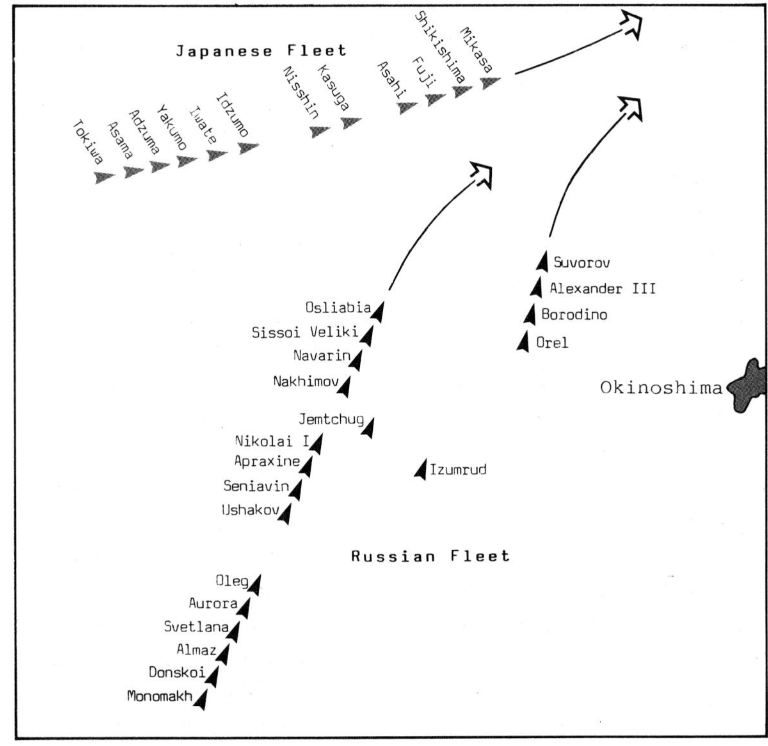

The Russians were first to open fire at 1408 at a range of about 7,000 yards, a number of hits being recorded on the Japanese flagship *Mikasa*. Togo, steaming at 15 knots, soon overhauled the Russians whose best speed was no better than 9 knots. The Japanese soon began to register on the Russian flagship *Suvarov* (the leading ship) and *Osliabia* (the fifth ship in the line). The two battleships were soon severely damaged, *Osliabia* being abandoned to capsize at about 1500, and *Suvarov*, a mass of flames, being disabled to be sunk by Japanese destroyers at about 1930. As the Japanese drew ahead of the Russians the latter attempted to double back on their track and resume their course for Vladivostock. The Japanese conformed and with their superior speed and firepower forced the Russians to manoeuvre on a useless circular course to the south.

With their two flagships crippled, and in the face of the superior speed, firepower and manoeuvrability of the Japanese, the Russian fleet began to lose all sense of cohesion and singly or in small groups the surviving ships endeavoured to escape.

Despite the devastation and horror as ship after ship was pounded into a wreck by the Japanese guns or blew up when a magazine ignited, the Russian seamen continued to fight their ships and man the guns, firing whenever they could sight a Japanese ship through the smoke and flames. At times the range dropped to no more than 2,500 yards at which point the destruction was terrible.

In less than two hours two Russian battleships and a cruiser had been put out of action. By nightfall, with Rozhdestvensky severely wounded, and three battleships (including the flagship) sunk, the surviving ships under Admiral Nebogatov fled in confusion. During the night Japanese armoured cruisers, destroyers and torpedo-boats continued to harry the Russians and by dawn the next day all that was left of the Second and Third Russian Squadrons were the battleships *Orel*, *Imperator Nikolai I*, *General Admiral Apraxin* and *Admiral Seniavin*, the light cruiser *Izumrud* and some destroyers. As the Japanese recommenced action, Admiral Nebogatov, who had commanded the Third Squadron, ordered the surviving Russian ships to surrender. The cruiser *Izumrud*, two destroyers and the armed yacht *Almaz* managed to escape. The destroyers and the yacht managed to reach Vladivostock, but *Izumrud* ran aground before she could reach the port. The old cruiser *Dmitri Donskoi* also escaped, but was scuttled off Matsushima after expending all her ammunition in action with a Japanese squadron. One other destroyer managed to escape and was later found drifting by a British merchant ship, having used up all the fuel and wood on board. She was subsequently interned in Shanghai. Three other destroyers managed to reach Manila where they were interned. In addition to their ships, the Russians suffered some 5,000 killed, 500 wounded and 6,000 prisoners compared to 600 Japanese dead.

At Tsushima Japanese battleships had an almost three to one hit advantage over the Russians and were easily able to out-manoeuvre them. Again it was 12 in guns firing at long range which dominated the action, Japanese gunnery and command proving far superior to the vainglorious efforts of the Baltic Fleet.

On 5 September 1905 the Portsmouth Treaty was signed, ending the Russo-Japanese War. Under the terms of the Treaty Russia ceded North Sakhalin and the Liaotung Peninsula to Japan and recognized Japanese interests in Korea.

The Russo-Japanese war principally involved two types of ship – the pre-dreadnought and the armoured cruiser. These were supported by the much feared and recently developed torpedo-boats and destroyers. The striking power of high-velocity guns was impressive even against modern chrome-steel armour, but the ability of the antagonists to take advantage of this at anything but a very short range was extremely limited, the weapons having outstripped the means of control and direction which were still confined to small rangefinders and simple telescope sights on guns. That the Russian ships were able to withstand such punishment was due mainly to the fact that the Japanese ships used high-explosive shells which burst on impact. Thus, while they caused considerable damage to upper decks and exposed positions, they rarely penetrated the armour of the Russian ships, except when their trajectory caused them to hit the relatively weak Russian decks. In contrast the Russian ships carried armour-piercing shells which, while they carried less explosive, were able to penetrate the Japanese armour before detonating. The real danger to warships during the war, however, lay in the torpedo and its devastating effects; its very potential paralysing Russian operations. The torpedo was largely responsible for reducing the effectiveness of Russian operations during the early days of the war.

During the war the Russians had made strenuous efforts to acquire warships from other countries. At one point they attempted to acquire from Chile *Constitucion* and *Libertad* under construction in Britain for the Chilean Navy. Britain considered this would upset the balance of power in the Far East and refused to allow the sale to proceed, the ships then being purchased for the Royal Navy.

Mutiny and the Rebuilding of the Fleet

Even before the end of the Russo-Japanese war events in Russia were taking an ominous turn. In January 1905 the country was torn by riots and strikes. Then in June there was a mutiny in the Black Sea Fleet. Because the Russians were unable to gain access to the Mediterranean, the Black Sea Fleet was the only one that was unable to take part in the Russo-Japanese War. However, during the War the best officers and ratings were transferred to the Pacific to make good the losses suffered there. This left the Black Sea Fleet manned only by raw recruits and the less able officers. As a result morale slumped and reached an all time low when the outcome of the War was known. On 27 June, a month after the Battle of Tsushima, matters came to a head on board *Kniaz Potemkin Tavricheski* when there was a complaint about bad food. It seems that overbearing officers who had little regard for the wellbeing of the ratings lost their heads and some ratings were killed. At this the ratings killed the senior officers on the ship and took command, sailing her to the port of Odessa. There on 28 June, riots broke out during which some 5,000 to 6,000 people were killed, *Potemkin* firing two shells into the town in support of the rioters.

To quell the munity the battleships *Georgi Pobiedonosets*, *Dvienadsat Apostolov* and *Tri Sviatitelia* sailed from Sevastopol for Odessa. They were joined by *Sinop* and the flagship of the Black Sea Fleet, *Rostislav*, with the Commander-in-Chief, Vice-Admiral Krieger on board. Having only just ended a disastrous war in which the major portion of the navy had been sunk or captured, the authorities were loath to risk having any more of their warships sunk. There was little the fleet could do, therefore, in the face of the defiant sailors in *Potemkin*. Likewise, *Potemkin*'s mutineers failed to persuade any of their comrades in other ships to join them. The only ship that did make a half-hearted attempt to join the rebels was *Georgi Pobiedonosets*, but her crew changed their mind and she attempted to return to the main fleet, only to see the guns of *Potemkin* trained on her. In attempting to comply with the threat from *Potemkin* she ran aground and took no further part in the affair. *Potemkin* left Odessa and sailed for Rumania but failed to achieve anything. She then sailed for Theodosia and finally to Constanza where the mutineers scuttled the ship in shallow water.

She was raised and refitted, but was again involved in mutiny at Sevastopol in November 1905. After putting down the revolt the authorities renamed the ship *Panteleimon*, together with the cruiser *Ochakov* which had also mutinied and which was renamed *Kagul*. These November mutinies also involved units in the Baltic Fleet where *Pamiat Azova* mutinied. She was subsequently renamed *Dvina*.

By the end of 1905 Russia's internal problems seemed to have been overcome, but the seeds of later troubles which grew into the 1917 Revolution had already been sown, and the end of Imperial Russia was at hand.

The defeat at Tsushima led to a number of far-reaching changes in the organization of the Imperial Navy. The post of General Admiral was abolished in June 1905 and replaced by a new position – Minister of the Navy. In April 1906 a Naval General Staff (GENMOR) was set up to replace the autocratic control previously exercised by the single head of the Navy – the General Admiral. GENMOR was given full responsibility by the Tsar for establishing and formulating naval strategy and for the reconstruction and mobilization of the fleet.

Under the new Minister of the Navy, Birilev, the Navy was reorganised. By 1906 the active fleets comprised the following units.

Baltic:	5 battleships (4 new, 1 obsolete)
	4 armoured cruisers
	6 cruisers
	85 torpedo-boats
	32 torpedo-boat destroyers
Black Sea:	6 battleships
	2 cruisers
	19 torpedo-boat destroyers
	6 obsolete gunboats
Siberian Flotilla:	2 cruisers
	13 torpedo-boats

During 1907 GENMOR proposed a construction programme designed to redress Russian naval imbalance *vis-à-vis* potential enemies in the Baltic, Black Sea and Pacific. The Baltic and Pacific Fleets were to have two squadrons each of eight battleships, four battlecruisers, nine light cruisers and 36 destroyers, while the Black Sea would have one squadron of eight battleships, four battlecruisers, nine light cruisers and 36 destroyers. In the event Parliament (the Duma) was asked to approve only the construction of units for the Baltic Fleet. After considerable argument the Duma agreed in spring 1908 to provide funds for the construction under the 1909 Programme of four dreadnoughts (*Gangut*, *Petropavlovsk*, *Poltava* and *Sevastopol* armed with twelve 12 in guns, three submarines and a depot ship for the Baltic, and fourteen destroyers and three submarines for the Black Sea.

As soon as the 1909 Programme was approved GENMOR, in the summer of 1909, set about preparing a 10-year naval programme. Had this programme ever been completed, it would have given the Russian Navy eleven new battleships, four battlecruisers, twelve light cruisers, 72 destroyers, 45 torpedo-boats, 38 submarines, six minelayers and four gunboats.

The government, however, asked GENMOR to modify this very ambitious plan and it was re-submitted with a request for funds for nine destroyers for the Black Sea Fleet (instead of the eighteen of the previous plan), six minelayers and four gunboats for the Pacific (the previous plan provided for eighteen destroyers, nine torpedo-boats and twelve submarines in addition to these units), and eight battleships, four battlcruisers, four light cruisers, eighteen destroyers and some submarines for the Baltic Fleet (the original plan proposed in addition to these units, another five light cruisers, eighteen destroyers, 36 torpedo-boats and twenty submarines). Finally in 1911 the Duma approved funds for the construction of three battleships, nine destroyers and three submarines for the Black Sea.

In April 1911 a new Minister of the Navy was appointed and under his direction the Duma was finally persuaded to vote the necessary funds for a much more ambitious building programme approved in July 1912. This provided for the construction of four super battlecruisers, *Borodino*, *Kinburn*, *Ismail* and *Navarin* (laid down during the First World War, these ships were abandoned before completion) – four armoured cruisers, eight light cruisers, 36 destroyers, faster and much more powerful than anything in the British fleet (they were designed to carry up to fifteen torpedoes), the prototype of which was *Novik*, which achieved a remarkable speed of 37 knots, and twelve submarines as well as many other smaller vessels and auxiliaries. It was intended that this massive building programme would be completed between 1912 and 1916. The Programme was authorized in July 1912 and came to be known as the 'Little Programme'.

It was at this point that the authorities decided that the future threat lay in continental Europe and decided to revert to a continental rather than a maritime strategy. As the situation in Europe deteriorated the need to deny the German fleet the coastal waters of the Baltic became a priority in the minds of the Russian planners. This resulted in the Baltic Fleet being placed under the command of the northern army and a general who had little understanding of the meaning of maritime power. The Baltic Fleet therefore came to be regarded as a coastal defence force, despite the powerful new capital ships which were under construction for it. To improve coastal defence still further a new mine was developed which remained superior to other mines developed by the Allies until 1917. Ever since the Crimean War Russia had been pre-eminent in the use and tactics of mine warfare, and once war broke out they were not slow to make good tactical use of their new weapon.

As part of the new construction programmes Russia laid down the world's first minelaying submarine, *Krab*. She took so long to build, however, that both Germany and Britain had minelaying submarines operational by the time she was completed. *Krab* operated successfully in the Black Sea during the First World War.

While the new construction programmes in themselves were well balanced, Russian industry was totally incapable of meeting the challenge. As a result much material and equipment, in particular machinery (especially diesels for submarines), heavy steel fabrication and other specialized items, had to be purchased abroad and, incomprehensibly, much of it was ordered from Germany. However, these large construction programmes had been instituted too late for the vessels to be ready at the outbreak of war and Russia had perforce to rely on obsolete capital ships, many of them dating from before the Russo-Japanese War. Likewise, the cruisers had all seen service in the Pacific at the turn of the century while the destroyers and torpedo-boats were inferior to new units completing in Germany.

The situation for Russia was not quite as bad as it might have been, however, for Germany was forced to station the bulk of her fleet, including the most modern units, where they could menace the British Grand Fleet. The Baltic, for the Germans, was very much a backwater where five obsolete and two more modern cruisers were stationed, together with eleven destroyers and torpedo-boats and three very old submarines.

First World War – The Baltic

Although at the outbreak of war the Baltic Fleet found itself equipped with largely obsolescent ships, it did, nevertheless, achieve some remarkable successes. The Commander-in-Chief of the Baltic was the energetic Admiral Essen, a distinguished captain and hero of the Russo-Japanese War. Perhaps the Fleet's greatest success was the capture of two copies of the German secret signal-book from the light cruiser *Magdeburg* which had grounded on the island of Odensholm during a minelaying operation and bombardment of Russian coastal towns in the Baltic. One of the code-books was forwarded to the British Admiralty where it helped to provide advance warning of German naval movements.

Actions in the Baltic, however, principally involved minelaying and submarine operations. On 11 October, *U 26* sank the Russian armoured cruiser *Pallada*, and on 17 November a Russian mine sank the German cruiser *Friedrich Carl*. Control of the Baltic was vital to the German war effort, for Sweden supplied most of the iron ore on which the giant Krupp works relied for armament production. In an effort to block this vital trade, Russia appealed to Great Britain for help and British submarines entered the Baltic to assist the Russians.

Minelaying in winter in the Baltic becomes almost impossible once the ice has set in. As the winter of 1914 wore on, the Russians were forced to abandon the use of their lightly hulled destroyers in the inhospitable conditions and resort to the use of cruisers. On one such sortie on 13 February 1915, the cruiser *Rurik* grounded on the Swedish island of Gotland in a heavy snowstorm. With two of her three boiler rooms flooded and with 2,700 tons of water on board, the ship managed to free herself and make for Reval for repairs. At a maximum speed of no more than 2 knots the trip took three days, during which the Germans, themselves hampered by snow and fog, were unable to make contact with the seriously damaged ship. Following temporary repairs at Reval, and at the express command of Admiral Essen, *Rurik*, with the aid of two icebreakers, made the almost impossible journey to Kronstadt for permanent repairs. At this point tragedy struck the Baltic Fleet when Admiral Essen died, to be replaced by a much less able officer, Admiral Kanin.

With the melting of the ice in April 1915 naval activities could recommence, the Russians continuing minelaying operations and British submarines carrying out attacks against the iron ore trade. The main German objective in northern Russia in 1915 was the port of Riga, a valuable jumping-off point for an attack on Petrograd (formerly St. Petersburg, renamed at the start of the war). To counter these moves a powerful squadron comprising *Admiral Makarov* (flying the flag of Rear-Admiral Bakhirev), *Bayan*, *Bogatyr*, *Oleg*, *Rurik* and a number of destroyers sailed south to bombard the port of Memel. During the night of 30 June/1 July 1915, the force split up in the fog, *Rurik* and *Novik* continuing on course. The following morning the remainder of the force fell in with the German minelayer *Albatros* which they drove aground on the Swedish island of Ostergarn. While the crew of *Albatros* were being rescued by the Swedes, the German cruisers *Lübeck*, *Roon* and four torpedo-boats appeared. By this time the Russian ships had expended a considerable amount of their ammunition, and although superior to the German force, were forced to ask for help from *Rurik*. Salvoes were exchanged at long range, *Rurik* being struck by an 8in shell from *Roon*. At the same time *Rurik*'s forward turret broke down, and she was forced to turn away in order to engage her after turret. Almost immediately she scored a hit on *Roon* which started a fire. *Rurik* scored a number of hits on *Roon* which retreated, closely followed by *Rurik*, which abandoned the chase at the report of U-boat sightings. Meanwhile the German cruisers *Prinz Adalbert* and *Prinz Heinrich* had been detached to go to the assistance of *Roon*, but *Adalbert* was torpedoed by the British submarine *E 9*.

As Germany intensified her military efforts in the east and the Russians lost ground, the German fleet in the Baltic increased its endeavours to contain the Russian Baltic Fleet and reduce it to impotency. As part of this plan, a powerful German force of eleven battleships and twelve cruisers protected by a number of destroyers and minesweepers entered the Gulf of Riga to attack the Russian fleet. Defending the Gulf was the Russian battleship *Slava*, the gunboats *Korietz* and *Sivutch*, supported by British submarines.

On 8 August 1915 the Germans began their attack with a long-range bombardment of *Slava*. The results were inconclusive and the Germans withdrew, losing two torpedo-boats and the light cruiser *Thetis* damaged. The attack was renewed on 16 August, and as the German ships slowly advanced the Russians retreated farther back into the Moon Sound. During the gunnery duel *Sivutch* was set on fire and *Koreetz* ran aground and was wrecked.

The Germans attacked again on the night of 16/17 August, the large destroyers *V99* and *V100* pursuing *Slava* further up the Sound. They were intercepted by *Novik*, however, and *V99* was sunk and *V100* damaged. The following day, 18 August, the main German force entered the Sound. The British submarine *E 1* also entered the Sound and torpedoed the battlecruiser *Moltke* on 20 August. At this *Moltke*, supported by the rest of the German fleet, gave up the attempt to force Moon Sound and withdrew. British submarines continued to operate against German forces in the Baltic, forcing Germany to withdraw all her large obsolete units, retaining only light forces in the area.

With command of the Baltic Sea secure in Russian hands, plans were drawn up in September 1915 for a sortie by the battleships. The sortie was interrupted, however, by a mutiny aboard *Gangut* – again bad food being the cause. Shortly after this, the crew of *Imperator Pavel* also mutinied. *Gangut* and *Petropavlovsk* were later able to leave the Gulf of Finland, on 11 November, and sailed as far south as Gotland, the operation being used to mask further extensive minelaying operations in the Gulf of Riga.

The submarine force, meanwhile, was built up, a number of boats being built in Russia and six others being assembled in the Baltic from parts supplied by Canada and sent across to Europe via the trans-Siberian railway from the Pacific.

As the ice began to melt in the spring of 1916 the Russians set

Above: The wreck of the battleship *Slava* in the Baltic in 1917. (P. A. Vicary)

about building up their strength in Moon Sound. As before, the mainstay of the defences was the battleship *Slava*. On 27 April 1916, *Slava* had the ignominious distinction of being the first capital ship in history to be hit by bombs dropped from an aircraft. In order to get her back to Russia where repairs could be carried out a new route had to be dredged out of Moon Sound. The completion of the new channel allowed the larger Russian ships to enter the Gulf of Riga from the Gulf of Finland without having to make the long passage by open sea.

Minelaying and submarine operations continued to dominate Russian naval activity in the Baltic, and in particular the British submarines were very active against the German iron ore trade from Sweden. As a result the Germans were forced to introduce the convoy system for their merchant ships, against which the British submarines had no counter. It was thereafter left to Russian naval forces to continue action against this trade, and Russian destroyers attacked convoys whenever they passed near Russian bases.

At long last *Slava* was reinforced by *Tsessarevitch*, *Diana* and *Admiral Makarov*, making use of the new channel dredged through Moon Sound. Intensive minelaying operations continued. In November 1916 the field off Baltic Port achieved a major success. On the night of 9/10 November a force of eleven destroyers from the German 10th Flotilla entered the mouth of the Gulf of Finland to carry out a bombardment of Baltic Port. During the operation the force ran on to the minefield and two destroyers were sunk. On the way out five more destroyers were sunk on the same minefield, a total of seven of the eleven being sunk during the operation.

First World War – The Black Sea

An uneasy peace settled over the Black Sea during the first three months of the war. The main enemy force in the Black Sea comprised the German battlecruiser *Goeben* and light cruiser *Breslau* which operated under the Turkish flag.

The Russian Black Sea Fleet was in many respects superior to the German/Turkish forces, certainly outclassing the latter in firepower, and it was certainly much better trained and equipped than the Baltic Fleet. It was, however, inferior to the German ships in one major aspect – that of speed. This was to have a considerable impact on operations throughout the war, for the Russians were never able to manoeuvre the two German ships into a position where they could be outgunned. The Russian fleet comprised five pre-dreadnought type battleships, three cruisers, seventeen destroyers and four submarines, all obsolete.

The gunnery of the Black Sea Fleet proved to be exceedingly accurate, a factor which owed much to the introduction of short-wave radio-telecommunication within the ships to transmit range and bearing from the central control position by bridge to the main armament, an early form of fire control. That this innovation was introduced at all was due principally to the Commander-in-Chief of the Black Sea Fleet, Vice-Admiral A. A. Eberhardt, who recognized its importance.

Operations in the Black Sea commenced on 29 October when German and Turkish ships carried out a bombardment of Russian ports. *Goeben* bombarded Sevastopol, *Breslau* Novorossisk, the Turkish cruiser *Hamidieh*, Theodosia and Turkish destroyers Odessa. With the bombardment of October any hope of Russia obtaining diplomatic sanctions to use the Dardanelles vanished. This in itself was a serious blow, for the Straits were the only reasonable route by which Russia could be supplied by her Allies. This was essential in view of the parlous state of Russian industry, which could not hope to maintain the country's vast war effort on its own. The only other practicable route by which the Allies could support Russia was the trans-Siberian railway. Use was also made of the limited route through the White Sea and the northern port of Murmansk, but this was often iced up during winter. It was principally because of this that in 1915 the Allies embarked on the ill-fated Dardanelles campaign.

In spite of being cut off from the outside world, the Black Sea Fleet operated more or less continuously during the war, and achieved the greatest successes.

A vigorous mine warfare campaign was conducted to blockade the Anatolian coast. All the coal for Constantinople and the German and Turkish warships had to be transported by ship from the Anatolian port of Zonguldak. To counter this traffic the Russians fitted out a number of small fast passenger steamers as seaplane carriers. These were to carry out some of the earliest bombing attacks from the air.

In the Caucasus the left flank of the Turkish Army found itself harried by Russian destroyers. In an attempt to force the Russians to withdraw their forces from the area *Breslau* carried out a bombardment of the Russian base at Poti on 7 November 1914. The Russian fleet, led by the flagship *Evstafi*, followed by *Ioann Zlatoust*, *Penteleimon*, *Tri Sviatitelia* and *Rostislav*, put to sea on 15 November to intercept *Breslau*. *Goeben*, meanwhile, had sailed to support *Breslau*. Some 30 miles south of Cape Saritch *Almaz* sighted *Goeben* through patches in the fog. Visibility was good enough to engage and the Russian ships, in line ahead, opened fire at a range of 8,000 yards. The action lasted only ten minutes before *Goeben* disappeared into the fog. During the brief action *Evstafi* was hit in the forward starboard 6in gun battery and four officers and thirty men were killed.

An attempt was made to close the port of Zonguldak with blockships, but the Russian force was intercepted by *Goeben* and *Breslau* and two of the blockships were sunk and the others driven off. On her return *Goeben* struck two mines and was badly damaged.

In the summer of 1915 the Russian Black Sea Fleet was considerably strengthened by the completion of *Imperatritsia Maria* and *Imperatritsia Ekaterina II*. Although they were the latest battleships to enter service with the fleet, they were still too slow to catch *Goeben* and *Breslau*. The new ships had a chance to prove their capability on 8 January 1916. In misty weather *Imperatritsia Ekaterina II*, covering an attack on Turkish coastal shipping by Russian surface forces, fell in with *Goeben*. *Ekaterina* opened fire at a range of 20,000 yards, her first salvo straddling *Goeben*. *Ekaterina*, however, had only just completed her trials and one after another her turrets broke down. She continued to engage *Goeben* until the range opened out to 24,000 yards. During the action *Ekaterina* fired a total of 96 rounds at *Goeben*. The Russians carried out a number of similar attacks against coastal shipping transporting coal to Turkish bases,

Left: The Black Sea Fleet surrendered at Sevastopol in 1918. (Author's collection)

and so successful did these prove that the operations of *Goeben* and *Breslau* were very severely curtailed.

On 20 October 1916 the Black Sea Fleet was dealt a major blow when *Imperatritsia Maria* suffered an explosion in her forward secondary armament magazine. A serious fire broke out which threatened to ignite the main magazine which, if it blew up, would cause very serious damage to the port and shipping. To prevent this, the new Commander-in-Chief, Admiral Kolchak, ordered that the sea cocks be opened and the ship scuttled.

The First World War – The Pacific Fleet

Sine the end of the Russo-Japanese war the Russian Pacific Fleet had been but a shadow of its former self. At the start of the war only a remnant of a once proud fleet remained at the base of Vladivostock. The fleet comprised two obsolete cruisers – *Askold* and *Jemtchug* – and some old destroyers and submarines used for local defence around the base. During the early months of the war the two cruisers took part in the hunt for the German Far East Squadron of Admiral von Spee. While in Penang on 28 October 1914, *Jemtchug* was surprised by the German light cruiser *Emden*, disguised as a British cruiser. *Emden* fired torpedoes at *Jemtchug* which rolled over and sank. After von Spee had left Far Eastern waters and the remaining German light cruisers in the Far East had been rounded up, *Askold* left for the Mediterranean. After a spell there she sailed for Northern Russia where plans had been formulated to organize a White Sea Fleet to help protect ships sailing for the northern port of Murmansk, this being the only lifeline still open through which Russia could be supplied from the West.

The White Sea Fleet was formed from three ex-Russian battleships captured by the Japanese during the Russo-Japanese War, *Askold*, and some half-dozen obsolete destroyers which sailed from the Pacific for the White Sea. These were: *Tango* (ex-*Poltava*, subsequently renamed *Tchesma* when she re-entered Russian service), and *Sagami* (ex-*Peresviet* which was given back her old name) and *Soya* (ex-*Variag*, also given back her old name). The obsolete battleship *Peresviet* was also to have been included in the White Sea Fleet order of battle, but she was mined off Port Said on 1 January 1917 while on her way to the north. On 12 March 1917, Imperial Russia – and with her the Imperial Russian Navy – ceased to exist.

Conclusion

The impression may be gained that during the First World War the Russian Navy took little part in naval operations. Quite the contrary is true. Although space here precludes listing all the operations undertaken by the Russian Navy, it was heavily involved throughout the war, and even after the Revolution warships under the new regime carried out a number of operations against German forces. While for the Western Powers the Baltic and Black Sea were largely regarded as backwater theatres, such was not the case as far as the Germans, Turks and Russians were concerned. In fact it was in these areas that the Russians developed many of their concepts of maritime strategy which have been so forcefully instituted since the end of the Second World War.

During the First World War the foundation of co-operation between all three services was laid down and gradually built on post-war, while in other countries the services continued jealously to guard their 'empires'. The use of force against merchant shipping, particularly in the Baltic against the Swedish iron ore trade, forced the Germans to institute the convoy system and employ large numbers of escorts to ensure the safe arrival of a few merchant ships. Likewise, in the Black Sea small Russian craft completely disrupted the transport of coal from the Turkish mines. In the Black Sea the Russians laid down the foundations of maritime air power and integrated carrier battle groups using seaplane carriers screened by forces of destroyers and the latest battleships. In the Dardanelles the British found that amphibious operations required meticulous planning and specialized ships, backed up by carefully controlled naval gunfire support to achieve a successful landing in the face of enemy opposition. The Russians conceived special, purpose-built ships for amphibious operations in the Black Sea and also constructed an artificial harbour. In a number of important operations the Russians developed the strategy and tactics of amphibious warfare, transporting strong forces of troops across the sea and landing them safely on hostile shores without loss. Finally there were the incredibly successful Russian mining operations, conducted in both the Baltic and Black Sea. This form of warfare was developed to such a degree that the Russians have been able to build on this knowledge and develop their present-day extensive capability in mine warfare.

Notes

1. Warner, Oliver. *Fighting Sail.* Cassell, 1979, p. 71
2. Anderson, Dr. R. C. *Naval Wars in the Baltic.* C. Gilbert Wood, London, 1910
3. 'An Authentic Narrative of the Russian Expedition Against the Turks.' Anon.
4. Busk, Hans. *The Navies of the World: Their Present State and Future Capabilities*
5. Mordal, Jacques. *25 Centuries of Sea Warfare.* Futura, 1976, p. 233
6. Jane, Fred T., *The Imperial Russian Navy.* W. Thacker & Co., London, 1904, p. 200
7. Woodward, David. *The Russians at Sea.* p. 139

CAPITAL SHIPS

PETR VELIKI TURRET SHIP

The iron-hulled turret ship *Petr Veliki* is considered by most authorities to be the first true battleship in the Russian Navy, all previous vessels either being predecessors of the cruiser type or more closely related to the monitor type of coast defence vessel. She joined the Baltic Fleet in 1876.

She was fitted with Hughes compound armour comprising 22 in of wood sandwiched between two 7 in wrought iron plates. In service the horizontal coompound engines gave considerable trouble and in 1881 she was given an extensive refit at Glasgow during which she was re-engined with more powerful double expansion engines developing 5,500 IHP. The rectangular boilers were removed and replaced by oval boilers. Although with more powerful engines, maximum speed in fact dropped by just over one knot to 12.9 knots.

During this refit the armament was modified, four 8.4 in guns being added and the number of quick-firers reduced to thirteen. Two submerged 15 in torpedo tubes were also added. The alterations led to an increase in displacement to 9,790 tons. In 1905 the ship underwent a major reconstruction to a gunnery training ship. During the conversion the upper deck and superstructure were completely altered. The number of masts was reduced to two and a new superstructure was built in front of the forward mast. The single funnel previously fitted was replaced by two funnels spaced forward and aft of the previous funnel's position. To equip the vessel for her gunnery training role the armament was completely altered, four 8 in, six 6 in, twelve 3 in, four 57 mm, four 47 mm and two machine-guns being fitted. As a result of the reconstruction the length had increased to 339 ft 8 in (oa) and draught to 27 ft 2 in with a resulting increase in displacement to 10,406 tons.

After the Revolution, she was renamed *Respublikanets* (although some sources quote the name as *Barrikada*). She was hulked and subsequently scrapped, although some sources state that she survived until after the Second World War.

NAME	BUILDER	LAID DOWN	LAUNCHED	COMPLETED	FATE
Petr Veliki	Galernii Island	1 June 1869	27 Aug 1872	14 Oct 1876	Scrapped 1922

Displacement:	9,665 tons
Dimensions:	328 ft 2 in (oa) × 62 ft 3 in × 23 ft 9 in (99.94 m × 18.95 m × 7.23 m)
Machinery:	reciprocating horizontal return connecting rod; 2 shafts; 12 rectangular boilers; IHP 8,258; 14 kts
Bunkers:	1,200 tons coal
Protection:	belt 11½/14 in (amid) reducing to 8/10 in (ends) (292/355 mm 203/254 mm) deck 1½/3 in (38/76 mm) citadel 14 in (355 mm) turrets 14 in (355 mm)
Armament:	four (2×2) 12 in/20 cal (305 mm) six 3.4 in (86 mm)
Complement:	432

Left: *Petr Veliki* was one of the earliest turret ships in the world. She is shown here nearing completion. (P. A. Vicary)

Right: *Petr Veliki* following modernization in 1881. A small bridge has been added together with extra armament. The ship was divided into sixteen watertight compartments. (Author's collection)

EKATERINA II Class BARBETTE SHIPS

NAME	BUILDER	LAID DOWN	LAUNCHED	COMPLETED	FATE
Ekaterina II	Nicolaiev	Nov 1883	22 May 1886	1889	Stricken 1907–8
Georgi Pobiedonosets	Ropit	July 1889	9 Mar 1892	1894–6	To Bizerta 1920
Sinop	Ropit	April 1883	1 July 1887	1889–90	Scrapped 1922–3
Tchesma	Ropit	Nov 1883	18 May 1886	1889	Stricken Aug 1907

Once the restrictions concerning development of a Black Sea Fleet had been lifted after the Crimean War, Russia designed a new class of barbette ship which would match the capital ships in the Turkish Navy. When completed these ships were among the most powerful in the world, only the British *Anson* type being more powerful. They were fitted with several different sets of machinery, those of *Ekaterina* being supplied by Cockerill of Belgium, those for *Sinop* by Napier of Glasgow, while *Tchesma*'s engines were built in Russia. *Sinop* was the world's first warship to be fitted with triple expansion engines; at some time during her career she had an extra four cylindrical boilers fitted. Compound armour was fitted except in *Pobiedonosets* which had steel.

The siting of the main armament was unique in that the two forward mounts were placed on each beam at the forward end of the redoubt abreast the foremast and superstructure, while the after turret was sited on the centreline. In *Sinop* the guns were mounted in pairs on three turntables in a single armoured enclosure. The guns in *Ekaterina* were carried on hydraulic disappearing mountings. *Georgi Pobiedonosets* was one of the first ships to be fitted with electric hoists. Her guns were fitted with hoods, while those in *Sinop* were in open mounts. In *Tchesma* the barbettes were sponsoned. The quick-firing guns in all three ships were mounted in sponsons. The design suffered from the fact that the secondary battery was unarmoured. By 1914 the ships had been re-armed with four 8in, eight 6in, four 47mm and four machine-guns, and the torpedo tubes had been removed. The increasing use of aircraft against ships during the First World War led to both *Sinop* and *Pobiedonosets* being fitted with a number of 3pdr AA guns. The various alterations to the ships during their life resulted in displacement increasing to between 11,032 and 11,396 tons.

Tchesma was stricken from the Navy List in August 1907 and was sunk as a floating target in 1908. In 1914 *Sinop* was re-armed with four 8in 50cal and eight 6in 45cal guns, and four of the 3pdrs were removed; *Pobiedonosets* was re-armed

Above: The *Ekaterina II* class barbette ships were designed to build up Russian strength in the Black Sea to counter Turkey. When completed they were among the most powerful ships afloat. The photograph shows *Ekaterina II* as completed. (Author's collection)

Left: *Georgi Pobiedonosets.* Note the quick-firing guns in the fighting top. (Author's collection)

Right: *Imperator Alexander II* as completed. (Author's collection)

with eight 6 in guns. Both ships were then used as guardships: *Sinop* at Odessa in September 1914 and at Sevastopol in October 1914; *Pobiedonosets* at Sevastopol. The only occasion on which her guns were fired in anger was on 29 October 1914 when *Goeben* was bombarding Sevastopol. In the spring of 1917 *Sinop* was used as a convoy escort in the Black Sea.

During the Revolution the engines in *Sinop* and *Pobiedonosets* were destroyed (19 April 1919) by British forces supporting the White Russians to prevent their use by the Bolsheviks. When the White Russians evacuated the Crimea in 1920, *Pobiedonosets* with other Russian warships was towed to Bizerta in Tunisia where she was interned. *Sinop*, virtually a wreck, was left behind and was scrapped in 1923–4.

Displacement:	10,181/10,280 tons
Dimensions:	339 ft 6 in (oa) × 69 ft × 27 ft 10 in/28 ft 9 in (103.4 m × 21.01 m × 8.48/8.76 m)
Machinery:	reciprocating (VC) (*Sinop* VTE); 2 shafts; 14 (*Pobiedonosets* & *Sinop* 16) cylindrical boilers; IHP 9,100 (*Pobiedonosets* & *Sinop* 13,000); 15 (*Pobiedonosets* & *Sinop* 16/16+) kts
Bunkers:	700/870 tons coal
Protection:	belt 8/18 in (*Sinop* 16 in) (amid) reducing to 6/8 in (ends) (203/457 (406) mm 152/203 mm) bulkheads 9/10 in (228/254 mm) deck 2 in (*Ekaterina* 1½)/2.25 in (25 (38)/57 mm) redoubt 12 in (305 mm) CT 8/9 in (*Pobiedonosets* 12 in) (203/228 (305) mm)
Armament:	Six (3×2) 12 in/30 cal (35 cal in *Pobiedonosets* & *Tchesma*) (305 mm) seven (7×1) 6 in/35 cal (152 mm) eight 3 pdr QF (not in *Pobiedonosets*) (47 mm) four (*Pobiedonosets* ten) 1 pdr QF (37 mm) seven (above water) 15 in TT (381 mm) 100 mines
Complement:	650/674

IMPERATOR ALEXANDER II Class BARBETTE/TURRET SHIPS

NAME	BUILDER	LAID DOWN	LAUNCHED	COMPLETED	FATE
Imperator Alexander II	New Admiralty	Nov 1885	23 July 1887	June 1891	Scrapped 1922
Imperator Nikolai I	Galernii Island	23 July 1886	20 May 1889	July 1891	Stricken 1918

The two ships in this class differed when completed, principally in the main armament. In *Imperator Alexander* the 12 in guns were mounted in a barbette with a shield, while those in *Imperator Nikolai* were carried in a turret. Secondary armament was mounted on the main deck, the 6 in guns being in unarmoured mounts.

Both ships were modernized in the early 1900s, *Nikolai* undergoing a major reconstruction in 1900. During this she was reboilered with sixteen Belleville cylindrical boilers. The quick-firing weapons were replaced with sixteen 3 pdr weapons. *Alexander* underwent a major refit in the French yard at La Seyne from 1902 to 1904. During this refit the 9 in and 6 in guns were replaced by five 8 in/45 cal weapons in single mounts, and eight 6 in/45 cal guns. Her quick-firing guns were replaced by ten 3 pdr weapons, and the torpedo tubes were removed. After reconstruction length had increased to 346 ft 7 in and displacement to 9,900 tonnes. *Imperator Alexander*: 1914 gunnery training ship Baltic Fleet. Crew took part in Oct–Nov 1917 Revolution. Renamed *Saria Svobodia* by Soviets. 1919 accidentally sank. 1921 salvaged. 1922 broken up. *Imperator Nikolai I*: 15 Feb 1905 sailed with Second Pacific Squadron for Pacific. 27 May 1905 suffered minor damage at Battle of Tsushima. 28 May 1905 surrendered to Japanese forces. Refitted by Japanese and renamed *Iki*.

Displacement:	8,440 tons
Dimensions:	333 ft 6 in (wl); 346 ft 6 in (oa) × 67 ft × 25 ft 10 in (101.57/105.53 m × 20.4 m × 7.87 m)
Machinery:	reciprocating (VC) (*Imperator Nikolai* – HTE); 2 shafts; 12

	cylindrical boilers; IHP 8,500; 15.3 kts
Bunkers & Radius:	1,200 tons coal; 4,000 nm at 10 kts
Protection:	belt 14/16 in closed by 6 in bulkheads (355/406 mm 152 mm) barbette/turret 10 in (254 mm) casemates 3/6 in (76/152 mm) deck 2½ in (63 mm) CT 10 in (*Imperator Nikolai* 8 in) 254 (203) mm)
Armament:	two (1×2) 12 in/30 cal (305 mm) four (4×1) 9 in/35 cal (228 mm) eight (8×1) 6 in/35 cal (152 mm) ten 3 pdr QF (47 mm) eight 1 pdr QF (37 mm) five (*Imperator Nikolai* six) (above water) 15 in TT (381 mm)
Complement:	611

Above: *Imperator Nicolai I* differed from her sister ship in a number of ways. Note the more pronounced ram bow and the 12in guns mounted in turrets. Those in *Imperator Alexander II* were carried in a large barbette with a shield. (Author's collection)

Right: *Imperator Alexander II* following her 1904 refit. Note the removal of the fighting tops and the addition of searchlight platforms on the masts, together with a lattice mast amidships for searchlights. The 9in guns on each beam at the fore and after ends of the citadel have been replaced by 8in weapons. (Dr L. Accorsi)

Right: *Imperator Nicolai I.* (Author's collection)

DVIENADSAT APOSTOLOV BARBETTE SHIP

Although similar to the *Imperator Alexander II*-class ships, *Apostolov* was a much better fighting ship. She was fitted with a heavier armament, both sets of guns being mounted in barbettes, one forward and one aft. Secondary armament was improved, being of only one calibre which greatly assisted in spotting the fall of shot. The main armour belt was of the compound type, but the battery and conning tower were fitted with steel armour. She was still afloat at the start of the First World War, but was classified as a hulk, being relegated to harbour duties and of no fighting value.

Displacement: 8,709 tons

NAME	BUILDER	LAID DOWN	LAUNCHED	COMPLETED	FATE
Dvienadsat Apostolov	Nicolaiev	Feb 1888	23 Sept 1890	Dec 1892	Scrapped

Dimensions: 342 ft (oa) × 60 ft × 27 ft 6 in (104.16 m × 18.29 m × 8.38 m)
Machinery: reciprocating (VTE); 2 shafts; 8 cylindrical boilers; IHP 8,750; 15.7 kts
Bunkers: 800 tons coal
Protection: belt 6/14 in closed by 9/12 in bulkheads (152/355 mm 228/305 mm)
deck 2/2½ in (51/63 mm)
barbettes 10/12 in (254/305 mm)
battery 5 in (127 mm)
CT 8 in (203 mm)
Armament: four (2×2) 12 in/30 cal (305 mm)
four (4×1) 6 in/35 cal (152 mm)
twelve 3 pdr (47 mm)
ten 1 pdr QF (37 mm)
six (above water) 15 in TT (381 mm)
Complement: 599

Left: *Dvienadsat Apostolov circa* 1905. Note the 12in gun in the large open barbette. (Author's collection)

GANGUT BARBETTE SHIP

Gangut was designed as a smaller, shallow draught version of the *Imperator Alexander II* class, and was built primarily for coastal operations in the Baltic.

NAME	BUILDER	LAID DOWN	LAUNCHED	COMPLETED	FATE
Gangut	New Admiralty	1889	18 Oct 1890	1892–4	Wrecked on rock 12 June 1897

Displacement: 6,590 tons
Dimensions: 289 ft 9 in (wl) × 62 ft × 21 ft (88.24 m × 18.9 m × 6.4 m)
Machinery: reciprocating (VTE); 2 shafts; 8 cylindrical boilers; IHP 6,000; 14.7 kts
Bunkers: coal 650 tons
Protection: belt 10/16 in closed by 9 in bulkheads (254/406 mm 228 mm)
deck 2 in (51 mm)
barbette 7/9 in (178/228 mm)
battery 5 in (127 mm)
CT 10 in (254 mm)
Armament: one 12 in/30 cal (305 mm)
four (4×1) 9 in/35 cal (228 mm)
four (4×1) 6 in/35 cal (152 mm)
four 3 pdr (47 mm)
ten 1 pdr (37 mm)
six 1 pdr QF (37 mm)
six (above water) 15 in TT (381 mm)
Complement: 521

Right: *Gangut* was much smaller and lighter than previous capital ships and with her shallower draught was principally designed for coastal bombardment operations. The 12in gun, which had a very short barrel, was mounted in a barbette protected by an armoured shield 4 in thick. (Author's collection)

NAVARIN TURRET SHIP

Like *Gangut*, *Navarin* was designed for coastal operations. She was distinguished by her four funnels mounted in pairs abreast and the high superstructure which allowed the secondary armament to be mounted in an upper deck battery. Mounting the secondary guns higher up overcame the problem experienced in earlier ships of the secondary battery being unusable in heavy seas. She was well protected with compound armour which was well sited, but it could not withstand the effect of torpedo hits at the Battle of Tsushima.

She sailed for the Pacific as part of the Second Pacific Squadron on 15 October 1904, gaining notoriety as being the ship which 'spotted Japanese torpedo-boats' in the North Sea. She opened fire on the unfortunate fishing fleet. At the Battle of Tsushima she suffered a number of hits which did only superficial damage. During the night of 27/28 May a steam pipe broke which reduced her speed to about 4kts. At about 2300 hours she was attacked by a number of Japanese torpedo-boats and was struck by a torpedo which flooded the forward 6in magazine. She listed to starboard and at about 0200 was again attacked by torpedo-boats, being hit by two more torpedoes. She turned turtle and sank, only three of her crew of 622 being saved after spending some time in the water.

NAME	BUILDER	LAID DOWN	LAUNCHED	COMPLETED	FATE
Navarin	Galernii Island	1889	20 Oct 1891	1896	Sunk at Tsushima 28 May 1905

Displacement:	9,476 tons
Dimensions:	357ft 8in (oa) × 67ft × 27ft 6in (109m × 20.4m × 8.38m)
Machinery:	reciprocating (VTE); 2 shafts; 12 cylindrical boilers; IHP 9,140; 15.5kts
Bunkers:	700 tons coal
Protection:	belt 8/16in closed by 12in bulkheads (203/406mm 305mm) deck 2/2½in (51/63mm) turrets 12in (305mm) battery 5in (127mm) CT 10in (254mm)
Armament:	four (2×2) 12in/35cal (305mm) eight (8×1) 6in/35cal (152mm) eight 3pdr (47mm) fifteen 1pdr (37mm) six (above water) 15in TT (381mm)
Complement:	622

TRI SVIATITELIA TURRET SHIP

In general *Tri Sviatitelia* followed the same design principles as *Navarin*, being fitted with Harvey nickel steel armour. The secondary armament was very cramped, the 4.7 in and some of the 3 pdrs being mounted in an unarmoured battery above the secondary battery. She was fitted with wireless telegraph in 1899, the first ship in the world to be so equipped. In 1911–12 she underwent a major refit and modernization, the superstructure being reduced in size and the 6 in, 4.7 in and 3 pdr guns being removed. Ten 6 in were fitted in the armoured casemates and four 6 in guns in shields mounted above the battery at the corners. The torpedo tubes were also removed during the refit and subsequently four 3 in AA guns were mounted on top of the main gun turrets. New boilers were fitted during the modernization and IHP increased to 11,400. Displacement increased to 13,318 tonnes.

In June 1905 the ship formed part of the detachment sent to Constanza to deal with the *Potemkin* mutiny, and on 11 July she towed *Potemkin* back to Sevastopol for repairs.

During the First World War she was frequently involved in providing cover for minelaying operations at the entrance to the Bosphorous, and was in action with *Breslau* and *Goeben* on 18 November 1914. On 12 July 1915, with other battleships, she escorted *Imperatritsa Maria* from the builder's yard to Sevastopol. On 5 April 1916 she escorted a troop convoy. She was gradually relegated to less important tasks as newer battleships entered service in the Black Sea. With her engines worn out from continuous steaming, gun barrels worn smooth from numerous gunfire support operations, and with lack of spare parts, materials and labour shortages, she spent more of her time swinging at anchor in Sevastopol. Morale fell and her crew were active in supporting the Bolshevik cause. As the White Russian forces retreated, the British destroyed her engines and when she was eventually captured by the Soviets she was a mere rusting hulk.

NAME	BUILDER	LAID DOWN	LAUNCHED	COMPLETED	FATE
Tri Sviatitelia	Nicolaiev	27 Aug 1891	13 Nov 1893	1898	Scrapped 1922

Displacement:	12,480 tons
Dimensions:	370 ft 8 in (pp)/377 ft 9 in (wl) × 73 ft × 28 ft 5 in (112.89/115.05 m × 22.25 m × 8.65 m)
Machinery:	reciprocating (VTE); 2 shafts; 14 cylindrical boilers; IHP 11,300; 17 kts
Bunkers:	1,000 tons coal
Protection:	belt 9/18 in closed by 14/16 in bulkheads (228/457 mm 355/406 mm) deck 2/3 in (51/76 mm) turrets 16 in (406 mm) casemates 5 in (127 mm) CT 12 in (305 mm)
Armament:	four (2×2) 12 in/40 cal (305 mm) eight (8×1) 6 in/45 cal (152 mm) four (4×1) 4.7 in/45 cal (120 mm) ten 3 pdr (47 mm) thirty 1 pdr (37 mm) ten 1 pdr QF (37 mm) six (above water) 15 in TT (381 mm)
Complement:	753

Left: The turret ship *Navarin* differed from previous capital ships in having a very low freeboard. Note the mushroom-type ventilators on top of the main turret, and the 3pdr guns at the corners of the superstructure. She was notable for carrying four funnels in pairs abreast. She gained notoriety as being the vessel which opened fire on 'Japanese torpedo-boats' in the North Sea as the Second Pacific Squadron sailed for Port Arthur. (Marius Bar)

Right: The *Tri Sviatitelia* seen in the Black Sea sometime between 1905–9 prior to her major refit. (Boris Drashpil/US Naval Historical Center)

SISSOI VELIKI BATTLESHIP

The general layout of *Sissoi Veliki* followed that of the previous two ships, but on a much smaller length. Although the freeboard was relatively high, the upper superstructure was reduced in height, all the secondary 6in armament being mounted in a large casemate on the main deck battery. The main armament was of the French centre pivot type, and was carried in very high closed turrets.

After completion in 1896 *Veliki* was posted to the Far East and between 16 and 19 March 1898 was involved in the occupation of Korea. She was also involved in the Boxer Rebellion. During gunnery drill she suffered an explosion in an after 12in gun as the result of an incompletely closed breech. She returned to the Baltic in 1902 for a major refit and sailed again for the Far East in October 1904 with the Second Pacific Squadron. At the Battle of Tsushima she suffered a number of hits and at about 1620 was struck in the forward starboard casemate and two 6in guns were destroyed. Fire broke out and swept the forward part of the ship. She was out of action for nearly two hours while the fire was put out. As a consequence of the amount of water pumped in to put the fire out she settled by the bow, bringing some of the previously sustained shell holes under water, which allowed yet more water to enter the ship. She joined with the group of ships led by *Nikolai I*, but the speed of the formation was such that the resulting pressure caused her forward bulkhead to collapse. She was left behind and during the night Japanese torpedo-boats made a number of attacks. She fought back resolutely and two torpedo-boats were sunk in the third attack. During that attack she was struck aft by a torpedo. The steering compartment flooded, the rudder jammed, and the blades of a propeller were stripped off. The ship headed for Tsushima Island in a sinking condition. At 1030 the following day she surrendered to a group of Japanese ships and was taken in tow, but sank with the Russian flag still flying at 1106 when the sea cocks were opened.

NAME	BUILDER	LAID DOWN	LAUNCHED	COMPLETED	FATE
Sissoi Veliki	New Admiralty	May 1892	1 June 1894	1896	Scuttled at Tsushima 28 May 1905

Displacement:	10,400 tons
Dimensions:	351ft 10in (oa) × 68ft × 25ft 6in (107.15m × 20.71m × 7.77m)
Machinery:	reciprocating (VTE); 2 shafts; 12 Belleville boilers; IHP 8,500; 15.7kts
Bunkers:	800 tons coal
Protection:	belt 4/16in closed by 9in bulkheads (102/406mm 228mm) deck 1.75/3in (44/76mm) turrets 12in (305mm) casemates 5in (127mm) CT 8in (203mm)
Armament:	four (2×2) 12in/40cal (305mm) six (6×1) 6in/45cal (152mm) twelve 3pdr (47mm) eighteen 1pdr (37mm) six (above water) 18in TT (457mm)
Complement:	586

Left: *Sissoi Veliki* (shown here as completed) escorted Japanese troops to China to take part in suppressing the Boxer Rebellion. (Author's collection)

Right: *Admiral Seniavin* and her two sister ships were designed for coastal operations in the Baltic. (Author's collection)

ADMIRAL USHAKOV Class COASTAL DEFENCE BATTLESHIPS

These small battleships were designed as a counter to the Swedish coast defence ships, and were intended solely for duty in the Baltic. *General Admiral* differed from the other units in having only three 10in guns, the after turret mounting a single gun and was fitted with Harvey armour in place of the compound armour of *Ushakov*.

All three ships sailed round the world with the Second Pacific Squadron to take part in the Battle of Tsushima. *Ushakov* was sunk, and the other two vessels surrendered to the Japanese who repaired them and put them into service with the Imperial Japanese Navy.

NAME	BUILDER	LAID DOWN	LAUNCHED	COMPLETED	FATE
Admiral Seniavin	Baltic Works	June 1892	22 Aug 1894	1896	Scrapped 1928
Admiral Ushakov	New Admiralty	1892	Nov 1893	1895	Sunk at Tsushima 28 May 1905
General Admiral Graf Apraxine	New Admiralty	1894	12 May 1896	1899	Scrapped 1926

Displacement: 4,971 tons
Dimensions: 286ft 6in (oa) × 52ft × 19ft 6in (87.25m × 15.85m × 5.94m)
Machinery: reciprocating (VTE); 2 shafts; 8 (*Admiral Ushakov* 4) cylindrical boilers; IHP 5,750; 16kts
Bunkers: 450 tons coal
Protection: belt 4/10in (102/254mm)
turrets 8in (203mm)
deck 3in (76mm)
CT 8in (203mm)
Armament: four (2×2) (*General Admiral Graf Apraxine* three) 10in/45cal (254mm)
four (4×1) 4.7in/45cal (120mm)
six 3pdr (47mm)
ten 1pdr (37mm)
six 1pdr QF (37mm)
four (above water) 15in TT (381mm)
Complement: 404

Below left: This picture of *Admiral Ushakov* clearly shows the low freeboard supporting a massive superstructure and very tall funnels typical of Russian coast defence warships. This, together with the very shallow draught, made them very unstable vessels in any kind of seaway. The fact that they negotiated the Atlantic and Indian Oceans to take part in the Battle of Tsushima was a remarkable feat. (Author's collection)

Below: *General Admiral Graf Apraxine.* (Author's collection)

PETROPAVLOVSK Class BATTLESHIPS

NAME	BUILDER	LAID DOWN	LAUNCHED	COMPLETED	FATE
Petropavlovsk	Galernii Island	May 1882	9 Nov 1894	1899	Mined 13 April 1904
Poltava	New Admiralty	May 1882	25 Nov 1894	1899	Scrapped 1923
Sevastopol	Galernii Island	May 1882	1 June 1895	1899	Scuttled 2 Jan 1905

These were the first flush deck battleships in the Russian Navy and were distinguished by an extensive tumblehome. *Sevastopol* was distinguishable from her two sisters by having shorter funnels. The main armament was mounted in Russian-built, French-style turrets equipped with electric hoists and electrically controlled. Four of the secondary 6in were carried in twin turrets on each beam abreast the funnels on the main deck while the remaining 6in guns were mounted close together in a battery on the second deck between the turreted 6in.

All the ships served in the First Pacific Squadron and were based in the Far East. At the start of the Russo-Japanese war they were at Port Arthur. *Petropavlovsk* was sunk when her magazine detonated after striking a mine outside Port Arthur. *Poltava* was severely damaged at the Battle of the Yellow Sea on 10 August, being struck by fourteen shells of 12in to 8in calibre. She was blockaded in Port Arthur and was again heavily damaged by howitzer shells from the Japanese Army, which set

Above: *Poltava* before the Battle of Tsushima. (P. A. Vicary)

the ship on fire. The ship was flooded with water to put the fires out and she settled in shallow water (5 December 1904). She was raised on 21 July 1905, repaired and refitted by the Japanese and renamed *Tango*. The cylindrical boilers were replaced by sixteen Miyabara large water-tube boilers. The 3pdr and 1pdr guns and the bow and stern torpedo tubes were removed, ten 76mm guns were added and the ship served as a gunnery training ship. She served with the Japanese Navy until 1916 when she was sold back to the Russian Navy and renamed *Tchesma*. After a short refit at Vladivostock she sailed for the White Sea where she arrived in January 1917. Some of her guns were dismounted for use during the Revolution and after the failure of Soviet operations in August 1918 she was manned by a White Russian crew and carried out a number of operations. She was captured by the Soviets and remained on the Navy List until 1922.

Sevastopol was damaged by a mine on 23 June 1904. She was present at the Battle of the Yellow Sea 10 August 1904, suffering a number of hits. She too was blockaded in Port Arthur and was also struck by a number of howitzer shells. She was taken to the outer roads and protected by nets and booms. A number of torpedoes were fired at the ship; some were detonated in the nets while others struck the ship. When Port Arthur surrendered she steamed out to deep water and was scuttled.

Above: The battleship *Tchesma* (ex-*Poltava*) after having been returned to Russia by the Japanese in 1916. (P. A. Vicary)

Displacement:	11,354 (*Sevastopol* 11,842) tons	Protection:	belt 5/16 in (*Sevastopol* 5/14½in) closed by 8/9 in bulkheads (127/406 mm (127/355 mm) 203/228 mm)	Armament:	four (2×2) 12 in/40 cal (305 mm)
Dimensions:	369 ft (oa) × 70 ft × 25 ft 6 in (designed mean) (112.38 m × 21.31 m × 7.77 m)		deck 2½/3½ in (63/89 mm)		twelve (4×2, 4×1) 6 in/45 cal (152 mm)
Machinery:	reciprocating (VTE); 2 shafts; 12/16 cylindrical boilers; IHP 11,250; 16.5 kts		turrets 6/10 in (152/254 mm)		twelve 3 pdr (47 mm)
Bunkers & Radius:	1,500 tons coal; 4,000 nm at 10 kts		6 in turrets and casemates 5 in (127 mm)		twenty-eight 1 pdr (37 mm)
			CT 12 in (305 mm)		six (4 submerged) 14 in TT (360 mm)
					60 mines
				Complement:	632

Above: *Petropavlovsk* showing marked tumblehome aft. (Marius Bar)

ROSTISLAV BATTLESHIP

Rostislav was originally designed as a sister ship to *Sissoi Veliki*, but differed in a number of ways when completed. She mounted a smaller calibre main armament than *Veliki* which was mounted in French-style turrets. The 6in secondary armament was mounted in twin turrets amidships on each beam. Armour protection also differed, *Rostislav* being completed with a thinner belt of Harvey armour. The bulkheads were protected by compound armour. *Rostislav* was notable as being the first battleship in the Black Sea Fleet to be fitted for oil burning, but this was rarely used, the ship normally burning coal which she consumed at a prodigious rate. On trials she made 18kts using oil.

Rostislav was involved in suppressing the mutinies in the Fleet in 1905, taking part in the search for *Potemkin*. On 15–28 November 1905 she was attacked by torpedo-boats whose crews had mutinied. She fired on *Ochakov* which caught fire and sank. She was considered to be a weak ship and consequently was usually stationed at the rear of the Russian battleship squadron. Despite her weakness, however, she performed valiant service during the First World War. She carried out numerous sorties with the battleship squadron in support of minelaying operations, bombarding shore installations and generally supporting the Russian Army along the coast. At the Armistice she was taken over by the Germans and used as a barracks ship, and then by the British intervention forces who destroyed her engines on 19 April 1919. Finally she was taken over by White Russian forces who used her as a floating battery in the Sea of Azov, before being run aground on 16 November 1920 and her breech-blocks removed. She was subsequently scrapped by the Soviets.

NAME	BUILDER	LAID DOWN	LAUNCHED	COMPLETED	FATE
Rostislav	Nicolaiev	1895	2 Sept 1896	1898	Run aground 16 Nov 1920

Displacement:	8,880 tons
Dimensions:	345ft (pp)/351ft 10in (oa) × 68ft × 22ft (105.07/107.15m × 20.71m × 6.7m)
Machinery:	reciprocating (VTE); 2 shafts; 12 cylindrical boilers; IHP 8,700; 15.6kts
Bunkers:	800 tons coal
Protection:	belt 5/14in closed by 5/9in bulkheads (127/355mm 127/228mm) upper belt 5in (127mm) deck 2/3in (51/76mm) turrets 5/10in (127/254mm) casemates 5in (127mm) CT 6in (152mm)
Armament:	four (2×2) 10in/45cal (254mm) eight (8×1) 6in/45cal (152mm) twenty 3pdr (47mm) sixteen 1pdr (37mm) six (2 submerged) 18in TT (457mm)
Complement:	650

Left: *Rostislav* carried out numerous sorties in the Black Sea during the First World War. She is seen here in company with another unit of the Black Sea Fleet sometime during the War. (Author's collection)

Above: *Rostislav* was the first oil-fired ship to serve with the Black Sea Fleet. (Author's collection)

Above: The *Rostislav* seen at Constantinople in 1912. See data on previous page. (Boris Drashpil/US Naval Historical Center)

Right: *Osliabia* seen at La Spezia in October 1903. (Author's collection)

PERESVIET Class BATTLESHIP

This class of pre-dreadnought battleships, which was an intermediate design between battleships and armoured cruisers, was distinguished by a high forecastle deck extending for two-thirds the length of the ship to the after main turret, and a steep tumblehome. Although very habitable ships with plenty of freeboard they offered a large target. Advances made in armament during the lengthy period the ships were under construction were not incorporated into the design. As a result the design proved to be most unsatisfactory, being unstable, inadequately armed and protected and having a poor speed. The secondary 6in armament was divided between the main deck (4 guns in casemates) and the upper deck (6 guns). *Peresviet* was the first of the Russian battleships to be fitted with rapid-firing 6in guns. The majority of the light armament of 3in guns was sited in unprotected batteries on the main and upper decks. The ships were protected by a mixture of Krupp and Harvey armour, *Pobieda* being fitted with all Krupp armour, except for the deck which was of alloy steel. *Pobieda* had a complete belt of Krupp armour which reduced to only four inches at the ends and had no bulkheads. The armour belt of *Peresviet* ended some thirty feet from the ends where it was closed by bulkheads.

NAME	BUILDER	LAID DOWN	LAUNCHED	COMPLETED	FATE
Osliabia	New Admiralty	21 Nov 1895	Nov 1898	1901	Sunk at Tsushima 27 May 1905
Peresviet	New Admiralty	21 Nov 1895	19 May 1898	July 1901	Mined 4 Jan 1917
Pobieda	Baltic Works	1 Aug 1898	24 May 1900	June 1902	Disarmed April 1922, broken up 1945

All three ships took part in the Russo-Japanese War. On 8 February 1904 *Peresviet* was struck by three torpedoes during the night attack on Port Arthur, but suffered only slight damage. On 13 April 1904 she sortied with the Fleet to intercept the Japanese. On 15 April she scored a notable success when, using indirect fire, she scored a hit on the Japanese cruiser *Nisshin*. During the abortive sortie to reach Vladivostock on 10 August 1904, she suffered a number of hits from heavy land battery shells which severely damaged her superstructure, and put the forward 12in turret out of action. During the siege she was hit a number of times by Japanese Army shells and on 6

Above: *Pobieda* seen here shortly after completion. Note the gun mounted in the stem. (Author's collection)

Right: The first ship in the Imperial Navy to carry quick-firing 6 in guns in her secondary battery was *Perseviet*. (Author's collection)

December was scuttled in shallow water to prevent further damage from enemy shelling. The Japanese found her relatively undamaged and refloated her on 3 July 1905 when she was taken to Japan, renamed *Sagami* in April 1908 and incorporated into the Imperial Japanese Navy. She was sold back to Russia in March 1916 and handed over on 5 April, reverting to her original name, *Peresviet*. She was assigned to the White Sea Fleet and sailed via the Mediterranean where, on 4 January 1917, she struck a mine laid by *U73* off Port Said and sank.

Pobieda was slightly damaged by *Mikasa* off Port Arthur on 9 February 1904. She sailed with Admiral Makarov on the disastrous sortie of 13 April 1904 in which *Petropavlovsk* was mined. *Pobeida* struck a mine shortly after *Petropavlovsk* had sunk, but managed to reach Port Arthur where repairs were affected. She suffered a number of hits during the siege and finally succumbed on 7 December, after being struck by a number of 11 in shells from land batteries. She was raised by the Japanese in October 1905 and towed to Japan for repairs, being commissioned into the Imperial Japanese Navy as *Suwo*.

Osliabia developed engine trouble on her way to the Far East and had to return to Europe for repairs thence returning to the Baltic. On 14 October 1904 she finally joined the Second Pacific Squadron for its journey to the Far East and the Battle of Tsushima. There she was struck and severely damaged early on in the action, and finally capsized at 1505 on 27 May 1905.

Displacement:	12,683 tons
Dimensions:	401 ft 3 in (pp) 434 ft 6 in (oa) × 71 ft 6 in × 26 ft (*Pobieda* 26 ft 3 in) (122.21/132.33 m × 21.77 m × 7.92 m) (*Pobieda* 8.00 m)
Machinery:	reciprocating (VTE); 3 shafts; 32 (*Pobieda* 30) Belleville boilers; IHP 15,000; 18/18.5 kts
Bunkers & Radius:	coal 2,100 tons, oil 250 tons; 10,000 nm at 10 kts
Protection:	main belt 5/9 in reducing to 4/6 in at ends and closed by 8/9 in bulkheads (127/228 mm 102/152 mm 203/228 mm) lower belt 5 in (127 mm) deck 2/3 in (51/76 mm) turrets 5/9 in (*Pobieda* 5/10 in) (127/228 mm 127/254 mm) casemates 5 in (127 mm) CT 6 in (*Pobieda* 8.25 in) (152 mm 209 mm)
Armament:	four (2×2) 10 in/45 cal (254 mm) eleven (11×1) 6 in/45 cal (152 mm) twenty (20×1) 3 in (75 mm) twenty (20×1) 3 pdr (47 mm) eight (8×1) 1 pdr (37 mm) five (3 submerged) 15 in TT (381 mm) ? mines
Complement:	752

KNIAZ POTEMKIN TAVRITCHESKY BATTLESHIP

This ship gained notoriety for her part in the mutiny of 27 June 1905. Failing to gain support for her cause the crew, after sailing the ship to various ports in the Black Sea, finally surrendered to the Rumanians in Constanza. She was towed back to Sevastopol and was renamed *Penteleimon* on 9 October 1905. She was involved in a number of operations in the Black Sea during the First World War, sailing with the battleship squadron, carrying out shore bombardment in support of the army, and escorting coastal convoys. After the 1917 Revolution she was renamed *Potemkin* and a month later *Boretz Za Svobodu*. On 19 April 1919 British interventionist forces damaged her engines to prevent her being of any further use.

NAME	BUILDER	LAID DOWN	LAUNCHED	COMPLETED	FATE
Kniaz Potemkin Tavritchesky	Nicolaiev	Dec 1898	9 Oct 1900	Nov 1903	Scrapped 1922–4

Displacement:	12,582 tons
Dimensions:	370 ft 8 in (pp)/378 ft 6 in (oa) × 73 ft × 27 ft (112.89/115.28 m × 22.23 m × 8.22 m)
Machinery:	reciprocating (VTE); 2 shafts; 22 Belleville boilers; IHP 10,600; 16.6 kts
Bunkers:	870 tons coal
Protection:	main belt 5/9 in (127/228 mm) upper belt 6 in (152 mm) turrets 5/10 in (127/254 mm) battery 5 in (127 mm) casemates 6 in (152 mm) CT 9 in (228 mm)
Armament:	four (2×2) 12 in/40 cal (305 mm) sixteen (16×1) 6 in/45 cal (152 mm) fourteen 3 in (75 mm) six 3 pdr (47 mm) five (submerged) 15 in TT (381 mm)
Complement:	750

Left: *Kniaz Potemkin Tavritchesky* gained notoriety as being the ship at the centre of the October 1905 Revolution. After the Revolution she was renamed *Panteleimon.* (Author's collection)

RETVISAN BATTLESHIP

NAME	BUILDER	LAID DOWN	LAUNCHED	COMPLETED	FATE
Retvisan	William Cramp	Dec 1899	23 Oct 1900	Dec 1901	Sunk as target July 1924

For her next battleship Russia turned to the United States of America. With a long history of indigenous warship construction it is hardly surprising that *Retvisan* has been described as the finest ship in the Russian Navy at that time. The design naturally reflected American practice, although the armament followed the pattern laid down in previous Russian battleships. In particular the main armament continued to be the 12 in gun carried in a French-style turret. As before, the secondary armament was arranged in a main deck battery and upper deck casemates, eight guns in the lower battery, and four in the upper. All the guns were electrically controlled, hoists being either hand or hydraulically operated. On completion the ship crossed the Atlantic and joined the Baltic Fleet. Following a year of trials and work-up she sailed to join the First Pacific Squadron in late 1902, arriving in May 1903.

On the night of the Japanese surprise attack on Port Arthur, 9 February 1904, *Retvisan* was struck by a torpedo under the main armour belt abreast the forward 12 in turret. A number of compartments were flooded and she shipped a large quantity of water – so much so that when she tried to enter harbour, she stranded on a sand bar. She was refloated on 8 March and towed into Port Arthur where repairs were carried out. On 27 July she supported Russian troops with gunfire.

During the Battle of the Yellow Sea on 10 August 1904 she was again damaged, being struck by eighteen heavy shells. Many of these were sustained when *Retvisan* interposed herself between the damaged *Tsessarevitch* and the Japanese squadron. She later led the fleet back into Port Arthur. During the siege of Port Arthur she was again struck by a number of howitzer shells (1 October), suffering heavy damage, being sunk on 6 December 1904. After the fall of Port Arthur she was refloated by the Japanese on 22 September 1905 and towed to Japan for repairs, after which she was commissioned into the Imperial Japanese Navy as *Hizen* in November 1908. In 1923 she was removed from the effective list and was expended as a target in July 1924.

Displacement:	12,700 tons (full load)
Dimensions:	376 ft (wl)/382 ft 3 in (oa) × 72 ft × 28.25 ft (114.6/116.5 m × 21.92 m × 8.6 m)
Machinery:	reciprocating (VTE); 2 shafts; 24 Niclausse boilers; IHP 16,000; 18 kts
Bunkers & Radius:	2,000 tons coal; 8,000 nm at 10 kts
Protection:	main belt 5/9 in (amid) reducing to 2 in (ends) and closed by 9 in bulkheads (127/228 mm 102 mm 228 mm) upper belt 6 in (152 mm) deck 2/4 in (51/102 mm) turrets 9/10 in (228/254 mm) casemates 6 in (152 mm) battery 5 in (127 mm) CT 10 in (254 mm)
Armament:	four (2×2) 12 in/40 cal (305 mm) twelve (12×1) 6 in/45 cal (152 mm) twenty (20×1) 3 in (75 mm) twenty-four (24×1) 3 pdr (47 mm) eight (8×1) 1 pdr (37 mm) six (2 submerged) 18 in TT (457 mm) 45 mines
Complement:	738

Right: *Retvisan*, seen here in about 1903, was the first major warship to be built in America for a foreign navy. She was distinguished by three funnels with very tall cowls. (Author's collection)

TSESSAREVITCH BATTLESHIP

Under the terms of the 1891 Franco-Russian Treaty the French Navy was to provide technical assistance to Russian shipyards. The next battleship, *Tsessarevitch*, was ordered from the La Seyne shipyard in Toulon. She was distinguished by having only two funnels, and a pronounced tumblehome which had become the hallmark of Russian battleships of the late 1890s. She was extremely heavily armed, and both secondary and main armament were mounted in turrets. The secondary 6 in gun turrets were sited on each beam high up abreast the fore and mainmasts, with the centre turrets mounted on sponsons extending out from the sloping sides. Armour protection followed a pattern tested in Toulon in 1890, with two armoured decks, the lower one sloping down to form a torpedo bulkhead extending from just forward of 'A' turret to just abaft 'Y' turret. The high freeboard and extensive superstructure carrying turreted secondary armament resulted in the light armament being mounted low down in the hull where it was subject to flooding and resultant instability.

Tsessarevitch joined the First Pacific Squadron in December 1903 with defective main armament and engines, problems which were never put right. She was torpedoed abaft the new torpedo bulkhead in the night attack on Port Arthur on 9 February 1904 and grounded when she tried to re-enter harbour, but was refloated the next day. She was again damaged on 10 August during the Battle of the Yellow Sea when a 12 in shell struck the conning tower, killing the First Pacific Squadron C-in-C and jamming the helm, putting the ship out of control. Severely damaged she managed to stagger to Kiao-Chau where she was interned.

Tsessarevitch returned to the Baltic in 1906 and served with the Baltic Fleet. By the start of the First World War she was considered obsolete and relegated to minor duties. At the time of the Revolution she was renamed *Grazhdanin*, and on 17 October 1917 was involved in the action off Moon Sound when she engaged the German dreadnought *Kronprinz*, suffering slight damage. She was scrapped in 1922.

Displacement:	12,915 tons
Dimensions:	388 ft 9 in (oa) × 76 ft 1 in × 26 ft (118.4 m × 23.17 m × 7.92 m)
Machinery:	reciprocating (VTE); 2 shafts; 20 Belleville boilers; IHP 16,500; 18.5 kts
Bunkers:	1,350 tons coal
Protection:	belt 7/10 in (amid) reducing to 4.75/6.75 in (ends) (178/254 mm 121/171 mm) decks 2½ in and 1½ in (63 mm 38 mm) turrets 10 in (254 mm) 6 in turrets 6 in (152 mm) CT 10 in (254 mm)
Armament:	four (2×2) 12 in/40 cal (305 mm) twelve (6×2) 6 in/45 cal (152 mm) twenty 3 in (75 mm) twenty 3 pdr (47 mm) four (2 submerged) 15 in TT (381 mm) 45 mines
Complement:	782

NAME	BUILDER	LAID DOWN	LAUNCHED	COMPLETED	FATE
Tsessarevtich	La Seyne	June 1899	23 Feb 1901	Aug 1903	Scrapped 1922

Far right: The French-built *Tsessarevtich* (shown as completed) sailed immediately for the Far East on completion and was suffering from a number of defects which were never put right before the Battle of the Yellow Sea. (P. A. Vicary)

Right: *Tsessarevitch* interned at Kiao-Chau after the Battle of the Yellow Sea. The picture shows the considerable tumblehome aft and some of the damage suffered during the battle. (P. A. Vicary)

BORODINO Class BATTLESHIPS

This was the largest class of battleships ever built by Russia, and the design followed closely that of *Tsessarevitch*. The design itself was prepared by the Russian Chief Constructor, Koutejnikoff, who incorporated certain modifications to the *Tsessarevitch* design, the most important relating to protection. The thickness of the main belt was reduced by 2½in and the width by 12in. The upper armour belt protecting the 3in casemates was of only 3in thickness and afforded little protection against large shells filled with modern explosive, a fact brought home only too vividly during the Battle of Tsushima. The torpedo bulkhead was also modified and, unlike *Tsessarevitch*, was joined to the lower deck by a narrow flat section rather than the pronounced slope used in *Tsessarevitch*. The reduction in thickness and width of the armour belt gave rise to other problems, notably that of stability. With massive top hamper and secondary turrets mounted high up, the ships

NAME	BUILDER	LAID DOWN	LAUNCHED	COMPLETED	FATE
Borodino	New Admiralty	July 1899	8 Sept 1901	Aug 1904	Sunk at Tsushima 27 May 1905
Imperator Alexander III	Baltic Works	July 1899	3 Aug 1901	Nov 1903	Sunk at Tsushima 27 May 1905
Kniaz Suvarov	Baltic Works	July 1901	25 Sept 1902	Sept 1904	Sunk at Tsushima 27 May 1905
Orel	Galernii Island	11 June 1900	19 July 1902	Oct 1904	Scrapped 1924–5
Slava	Baltic Works	Oct 1902	29 Aug 1903	June 1905	Scuttled off Moon Sound 17 Oct 1917

were found to be unstable in service and noted for rolling.

The first four ships completed sailed with the ill-fated Second Pacific Squadron for Tsushima where three of them were sunk and one captured. Such was the haste and urgency with which the Squadron was prepared that these ships had not even completed trials when they sailed. *Borodino*, constantly beset by mechanical breakdowns during her voyage to Tsushima, was so heavily damaged by gunfire on 27 May 1905 that she capsized and sank when her forward magazines exploded. Likewise *Imperator Alexander III* was gunned into a wreck and towards the end of the day capsized taking her entire crew with her. *Kniaz Suvarov* was flagship of the Second Pacific Squadron and led the squadron into battle at Tsushima. She was soon severely damaged by Japanese gunfire and lost control when her steering was put out of action. Steering by engines alone was a hazardous and slow business and the ship became an easy target for the Japanese. She was gunned into a blazing wreck and finally capsized and sank after being torpedoed by Japanese destroyers. The severely injured Admiral Roshestvensky had been taken off, but the rest of the crew were lost when she sank. In spite of the appalling damage the gun crews of the three battleships continued to fight all serviceable guns until the ships sank. *Orel* was somewhat luckier than her sisters, and although like them severely damaged by Japanese gunfire, survived the night to surrender to the Japanese the following day. She was taken to Japan, repaired (30 May 1905–June 1907), and recommissioned into the Imperial Japanese Navy as *Iwami*. She was rerated a coastal defence ship 1 September 1912; disarmed in 1921; stricken in 1923; scrapped in 1924–5.

Slava took no part in the Russo-Japanese War and was soon considered to be obsolete, and relegated to a training role. Towards the end of the decade she carried out a cruise in the Mediterranean, but on her way home in July 1910 developed engine trouble and had to return to Toulon for repairs and a major refit. *Slava* returned to the Baltic in 1911 and during the early part of the First World War she operated in the Gulf of Riga, on a number of occasions engaging German battleships. She was principally involved in providing gunfire support for Russian troops. Although of little fighting value *Slava* proved such a source of irritation to German naval forces in the Baltic that by 1916 they put a high priority on her destruction, carrying out a number of air attacks on the battleship. In October 1917 she was in action again with German battleships in Moon Sound. During this action she was severely damaged and was ordered to be scuttled in the entrance to the Sound. Although her magazines were blown up, the ship failed to sink, and destroyers were ordered to complete her destruction with torpedoes. She finally sank in shallow water with her upper deck above water; the wreck was eventually broken up in 1935.

Displacement:	13,516 tons (as designed) (15,275 tons full load)
Dimensions:	397 ft (oa) × 76 ft 2 in × 26 ft 2 in (120.91 m × 23.19 m × 7.97 m)
Machinery:	reciprocating (VTE); 2 shafts; 20 Belleville boilers; IHP 15,800; 17.5/17.8 kts
Bunkers & Radius:	1,520 tons coal; 5,000 nm at 10 kts
Protection:	main belt 6/7.5 in (amid) reducing to 4/5.75 in (ends) (152/190 mm 102/146 mm) upper belt 3 in (76 mm) decks 1½/2½ in (38/63 mm) turrets 4/10 in (102/254 mm) 6 in turrets 6 in (152 mm) 3 in battery 3 in (76 mm) CT 8 in (203 mm)
Armament:	four (2×2) 12 in/40 cal (305 mm) twelve (6×2) 6 in/45 cal (152 mm) twenty (20×1) 3 in (75 mm) twenty (20×1) 3 pdr (47 mm) four (2 submerged) 15 in TT (381 mm)
Complement:	835

Left: *Borodino* as completed. (Author's collection)

Right: *Kniaz Suvarov* was completed without caps on the funnels (compare with *Borodino*). See data on previous page. (Marius Bar)

Left: The last unit of the *Borodino* class to be completed was *Slava*. In service the ships were shown to be unstable resulting from excessive top hamper. (Marius Bar)

EVSTAFI Class BATTLESHIPS

NAME	BUILDER	LAID DOWN	LAUNCHED	COMPLETED	FATE
Evstafi	Nicolaiev	Dec 1903	3 Nov 1906	5 Aug 1910	Scrapped 1922
Ioann Zlatoust	Sevastopol	Nov 1903	13 May 1906	11 Aug 1910	Scrapped 1922

Although laid down before the start of the Russo-Japanese War, to a design similar to *Kniaz Potemkin Tavritcheski*, these ships were under construction for such a long time that the Russians were able to modify the design to incorporate lessons learned from the War. The severe punishment inflicted on the Russian ships at Tsushima led to an improvement in the scale of protection incorporated in the ships. The ends of the main belt and the region around the upper deck battery of 3 in guns was given 3 in armour protection, while the armoured deck was increased in thickness, the slopes over the area between main and upper belts being increased to 3 in, a reflection of the damage suffered at Tsushima from plunging shells. The limitation in range and power of the secondary armament of the ships which fought at Tsushima was also reflected in a heavier secondary battery. The four 6 in guns that were to have been mounted on the upper deck were replaced by 8 in guns sited at the fore and after ends of the upper deck battery.

The ships spent their entire career in the Black Sea, *Evstafi* being the Flagship of the Black Sea Fleet. During the First World War both ships were involved in actions against *Goeben* and *Breslau*, *Evstafi* suffering slight damage on 18 November 1914, and again in January 1915. By the outbreak of the Revolution both ships had spent so much time at sea that they were worn out and badly in need of repair and refit. In April 1919 British Interventionist Forces destroyed the machinery in both ships to prevent their use by the Bolsheviks.

Displacement: 12,840 tons
Dimensions: 387 ft 3 in (oa) × 74 ft × 27 ft (117.94 m × 22.54 m × 8.22 m)
Machinery: reciprocating (VTE); 2 shafts; 22 Belleville boilers; IHP 10,800; 16.5 kts
Bunkers: 800 tons coal
Protection: main belt 5/9 in (amid) reducing to 3 in (ends) (127/228 mm 76 mm)
upper belt 4/6 in (102/152 mm)
deck 2.25/3 in (57/76 mm)
turrets 4/10 in (102/254 mm)
battery & casemates 5 in (127 mm)
3 in battery 3 in (76 mm)
CT 9 in (228 mm)
Armament: four (2×2) 12 in/40 cal (305 mm)
four (4×1) 8 in/50 cal (203 mm)
twelve (12×1) 6 in/45 cal (152 mm)
fourteen 3 in (75 mm)
six 3 pdr (47 mm)
three (submerged) 18 in TT (457 mm)
Complement: 879

IMPERATOR PAVEL Class BATTLESHIPS

NAME	BUILDER	LAID DOWN	LAUNCHED	COMPLETED	FATE
Andrei Pervoswanni	Galernii Island	April 1903	20 Oct 1906	27 July 1910	Torpedoed and sunk 18 Aug 1919
Imperator Pavel	Baltic Works	April 1904	7 Sept 1907	7 Sept 1910	Scrapped 1922

These two units were laid down just before the outbreak of the Russo-Japanese War as part of the plan to modernize the Baltic Fleet. Construction was delayed in order to incorporate lessons learned as a result of the War. The need for improved protection extending the full length of a ship was introduced in this class, but to meet design criteria had to be thinner than in previous designs. The extensive flooding resulting from shell splinters and the scuttles in hulls at the Battle of Tsushima led to a decision to dispense with all scuttles in this class, and the ships were fitted with forced ventilation using deck-mounted ventilators. This was not successful in practice and the crew's health suffered as a result. The hull was flush decked with a sheer forward and aft.

The War had also shown the need for improvements to the armament. The main turrets were re-designed allowing the guns to achieve an elevation of 35 degrees. In addition 'Y' turret was sited as far aft as possible to improve the arcs of fire. The 8 in gun turrets were sited closer together to achieve a better concentration of fire and make sighting the fall of shot easier against the firing of the 12 in guns. The remaining 8 in guns were sited in an upper deck battery amidships with improved quick-firing 4.7 in guns superimposed above and

Above: The first 'modern' battleships to enter service with the Imperial Navy were the two units of the *Imperator Pavel* class. The design of these flush-decked fully armoured ships was considerably modified in the light of experience gained during the Russo-Japanese War. The photograph is of *Andrei Pervozvanny* as completed. (Author's collection)

protected by 3½in armour. The ships were originally fitted with lattice cage masts of US design. These were later cut down level with the funnels and pole tops installed when excessive vibration was experienced during trials. The ships were already obsolete when completed and no match for German dreadnoughts. As a result they took little part in the fighting in the Baltic during the First World War. *Andrei Pervoswanni* was torpedoed and sunk by a British CMB (coastal motor boat) on 18 August 1919. The wreck was scrapped between 1922 and 1924. *Imperator Pavel* was renamed *Respublika* in 1917 and scrapped in 1922.

Displacement:	17,400 tons (18,580 full load)
Dimensions:	460 ft (oa) × 80 ft × 27 ft (140.1 m × 24.36 m × 8.22 m)
Machinery:	reciprocating (VTE); 2 shafts; 22 Belleville boilers; IHP 18,000; 17.5 kts
Bunkers:	1,500 tons coal
Protection:	belt 5/8.5 in (amid) reducing to 3.5/5 in (ends) (127/215 mm 88/127 mm)
	upper belt 3/5 in (76/127 mm)
	decks 1½/3 in (38.76 mm)
	turrets 4/8 in (102/203 mm)
	8 in turrets 4/6 in (102/152 mm)
	battery 5/6.5 in (127/165 mm)
	CT 8 in (203 mm)
Armament:	four (2×2) 12 in/40 cal (305 mm)
	fourteen (4×2, 6×1) 8 in/50 cal (203 mm)
	twelve (12×1) 4.7 in/45 cal (120 mm)
	four 3 pdr (47 mm)
	three (submerged) 18 in TT (457 mm)
Complement:	933

Left: The launch of *Imperator Pavel.* (Courtesy A. Fraccaroli)

GANGUT Class BATTLESHIPS

The block obsolescence of Russian battleships after the Russo-Japanese War, and the introduction of the dreadnought-type battleship into other navies forced the Russians to give serious consideration to their own main battle fleet. As a result plans were drawn up for a new class of dreadnought-type battleship with a speed of 21.5 knots and armed with twelve 12 in guns in triple turrets, the first to be fitted in Russian warships, and sixteen 4.7 in casemate guns. There was strong opposition from the Duma to the new shipbuilding programme, but this was overridden by the Tsar himself when in 1908 he personally authorized the construction of the new battleships. Warship design experience was sadly lacking in Russia and in view of the specialized requirements for the new battleships Russia invited tenders. A total of 51 designs were submitted by 27 yards, for which only six Russian yards offered solutions. Within the Russian Command there was a divergence of opinion regarding the designs, the Naval Technical Committee favouring a design submitted by Blohm & Voss of Germany, while the Naval General Staff favoured the Italian Cuniberti design. However, as Cuniberti proposed to mount the 4.7 in guns in turrets rather than the casemates requested, his design was turned down. This left the Blohm & Voss design as favourite contender. By this time, however, there was a considerable body of opinion which regarded Germany as a potential adversary and political opposition to the choice grew both from within Russia and from France, Russia's ally. In the end it was decided to buy the German design and build the ships in Russia to a design prepared by the Baltic Yard. As a result the Russian design had to be completely reworked, with assistance from John Brown of Britain, and incorporating various features from the other designs. The end result was a hybrid ship, neither battleship nor battlecruiser, but which in its general arrangement followed closely the design concepts of Cuniberti.

On the armament side the ships were certainly a major improvement on anything the Russians had had previously. The four centreline triple turrets with their Obukhov 12 in guns gave a broadside more powerful than any British or German ships then operational. The same, however, could not be said of the siting of the 4.7 in guns. The casemates for these weapons were sited immediately beneath the muzzles of the 12 in guns, and were thus to a large degree unserviceable when the main guns were firing broadsides.

Machinery was also considerably improved on that in earlier ships. The boilers were sited amidships in two boiler rooms, one forward of 'C' turret and the other aft. Instead of the heavy

Above: The first dreadnoughts built for the Imperial Navy were the *Gangut* class. *Gangut* is seen here during the early part of the First World War. (Author's collection)

Belleville boilers mounted in previous ships a change was instituted and light Yarrow boilers were fitted. These enabled the ships to achieve an increase in speed of 1.5 knots, some 2–3 knots better than any other dreadnought of the time. To achieve this advantage in power, however, resulted in a substantial weight penalty, which inevitably involved armour protection. Following the Russo-Japanese War it had been agreed that all future armoured ships would have to carry an armour belt extending the full length of the ship. This idea was introduced in the previous class and continued with the *Gangut* class. However, because of the penalties already noted above, and following the practice of the previous class, this armour belt was reduced in thickness compared to earlier ships by some 1 in to 3 in. Underwater protection against mines and torpedoes consisted of a double bottom which extended up to the level of the armoured deck.

To enable the ships to operate in the Baltic throughout the year they were completed with specially strengthened ice-breaking bows. They were also to have been fitted with cage masts, but following the trials of the previous class these were replaced with pole masts before the ships were completed. Not only were Russian designers completely lacking in dreadnought design experience, but Russian yards were also totally inadequate to the task of constructing such complicated warships. The use of longitudinal hull strengtheners, allied with the use of high-tensile steel for the entire construction gave rise to considerable problems for the constructors. Work ceased in 1910 when doubts were raised as to the strength of the hull. Design improvements were incorporated and poor workmanship rectified. These difficulties, together with the abysmal administrative and bureaucratic system, delayed completion of the ships by two years, by which time the design had been outclassed by the 13.5 in-gunned ships of other European powers.

The ships saw little action during the First World War, and were not employed in any major operation because the Navy command, crippled by the memory of the heavy losses sustained at the Battle of Tsushima, was fearful that the ships might be lost or seriously damaged. Operations were therefore restricted to the Gulf of Finland and the ships were employed on minor missions such as protecting *Slava* and escorting minelaying operations.

The ships were demobilized on 29 January 1918 and remained inactive at Kronstadt. *Petropavlovsk* was used during the Civil War, but was torpedoed by the British CMBs *CMB 31* and *CMB 88* in the raid of 18 August 1919. She was renamed *Marat* on 31 May 1921 and recommissioned in 1922. *Poltava* suffered a serious fire in her forward boiler room on 24 November 1919 and was so severely damaged that it was decided not to repair her. She was to have been used as a test bed in 1925, but was renamed *Frunze* on 7 January 1926 and subsequently repaired and recommissioned. She was finally sunk in Leningrad in 1941, raised in 1944 and broken up in the mid-1950s. *Sevastopol* was renamed *Parizhkaya Kommuna* on 31 March 1921, and *Gangut* became *Oktyabrskaya Revolutsiya* on 27 May 1925.

Displacement:	23,360 (normal), 25,850 (full load) tons
Dimensions:	549 ft 6 in (wl)/590 ft 6 in (oa) × 87 ft 3 in × 27 ft 6 in/30 ft 2 in (179.85/181.2 m × 26.57 m × 8.38/9.2 m)
Machinery:	geared Parsons turbines; 4 shafts; 25 Yarrow boilers; SHP 42,000; 23 kts
Bunkers:	coal 3,000 tons, oil 1,170 tons
Protection:	main belt 4/9 in closed by 4/5 in bulkheads (102/228 mm 102/127 mm)
	decks 1/3 in (25/76 mm)
	turrets 5/8 in (127/203 mm)
	barbettes 8 in (203 mm)
	CT 10 in (254 mm)

Opposite page: *Petropavlovsk.* (Author's collection)

Above: *Sevastopol* during the First World War. (Author's collection)

Armament:	twelve (4×3) 12 in/52 cal (305 mm)
	sixteen (16×1) 4.7 in/50 cal (120 mm)
	four 47 mm
	four (submerged) 18 in TT (457 mm)
Complement:	1,126

NAME	BUILDER	LAID DOWN	LAUNCHED	COMPLETED	FATE
Gangut	Admiralty Yard	16 June 1909	7 Oct 1911	Dec 1914	Scrapped 1959
Petropavlovsk	Baltic Yard	16 June 1909	9 Sept 1911	Dec 1914	Constructive total loss 23 Sept 1941
Poltava	Admiralty Yard	16 June 1909	10 July 1911	17 Dec 1914	Stricken 1925
Sevastopol	Baltic Yard	16 June 1909	27 June 1911	17 Nov 1914	Scrapped 1957

Left: The stern of *Sevastopol* showing the massive 12in turret. See data on previous page. (Author's collection)

Below: *Imperatritsa Maria* in May 1916. (Author's collection)

IMPERATRITSA MARIA Class BATTLESHIPS

Designed by Professor N. Krylov just after the *Gangut* class, and authorized under the 1911 Programme, these three dreadnoughts were similar to the *Gangut*s, but carried heavier armament and were better protected, being true battleships as opposed to the hybrid *Gangut*. It had been intended that the ships should mount new 14in guns then under development, and achieve a speed of 22 knots in order to counter the new Turkish *Resadiye* class dreadnoughts then under construction in Britain. However, the 14in guns could not be developed in time and the ships were completed with 12in guns. In the event the Turkish ships were taken over by the British Government. The increase in weight occasioned by the improvements in the design resulted in a 2-knot decrease in speed. Russian shipyards had many contacts in Europe, particularly with British yards, and John Brown, Thornycroft and Vickers were all employed as technical consultants in the design.

The first ship to be completed, *Imperatritsa Maria*, was heavily involved in convoy escort work in the Black Sea, and in support of land operations, providing gunfire support. She was destroyed on 20 October 1916 when one of her secondary magazines ignited setting fire to the ship. To prevent the main magazines detonating, which would have destroyed Sevastopol, the order was given to scuttle the ship. The wreck was subsequently raised, but found to be so badly damaged

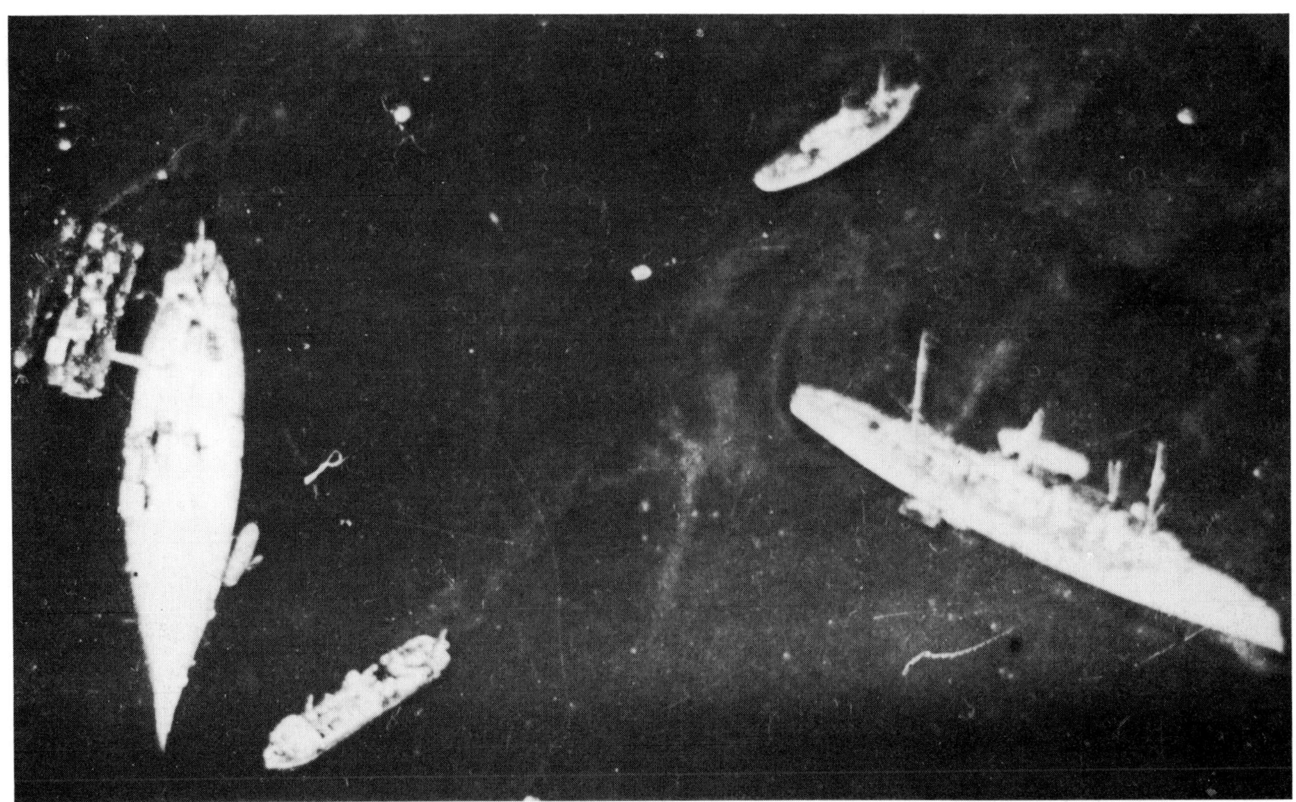

Left: The upturned wreck of *Imperatritsa Maria* seen in Sevastopol in 1918. (Author's collection)

Right: *Volya.* (P. A. Vicary)

NAME	BUILDER	LAID DOWN	LAUNCHED	COMPLETED	FATE
Imperatritsa Ekaterina Velikaya (ex-*Ekaterina II*)	Nicolaiev SB & Engineering Co	30 Oct 1911	6 June 1914	18 Oct 1915	Sunk by destroyer *Kertch* 18 June 1918
Imperatritsa Maria	Nicolaiev SB & Engineering Co	7 July 1912	1 Nov 1913	6 July 1915	Lost 20 Oct 1916
Volya (ex-*Imperator Alexander III*)	Russud Yard	30 Nov 1911	15 April 1914	28 June 1917	Sold 1924

as to be not worth repairing, and the hulk was finally scrapped in 1926–7.

Like her sister, *Imperatritsa Ekaterina Velikaya* (she had been renamed 27 June 1915) was involved in convoy escort duties in the Black Sea, and on a couple of occasions engaged the German warships. She was renamed in 1917 and after escaping from the German advance on Sevastopol in May 1918, sailed to Novorossisk where the Bolsheviks finally decided to scuttle her, the destroyer *Kertch* firing torpedoes into the ship.

Imperator Alexander III was renamed *Volya* before she was commissioned in the summer of 1917. She was finally handed over to the Germans in Sevastopol and flew the German ensign for three months from September to November 1918. After the Armistice she fell into British hands and was then handed over to the White Russian Wrangel Squadron in October 1919 and renamed *General Alekseiev*. On the collapse of White Russian resistance, the Wrangel Squadron, including *Alekseiev*, sailed from Sevastopol on 31 October 1920 for Bizerta and internment with a large number of refugees. The Cross of St Andrew was finally lowered on 29 October 1924. The French finally decided that the Wrangel Squadron should be returned to the new Soviet administration whom the French had recognized. The ships were in such a bad state of repair, however, that none of them ever returned to the Soviet Union. *Alekseiev* was finally broken up where she lay between 1926 and 1937. The main armament was kept by the French at Bizerta, the remainder being handed over to Finland where it was used against the Russians in 1939. The four 12in guns were captured by the Germans and used to fortify German coastal batteries on Guernsey in the Channel Islands.

Displacement:	22,600 (normal) (*Ekaterina II* 23,783), 24,000 (full load) tons
Dimensions:	550ft 6in (*Ekaterina II* 557ft) (oa) × 89ft 6in (*Ekaterina II* 91ft 6in) × 27ft 6in (167.66m (169.64m) × 27.26m (27.86m) × 8.38m)
Machinery:	Parsons (*Volya* Brown-Curtiss) geared turbines; 4 shafts; 20 Yarrow boilers; SHP 26,500 (*Ekaterina II* 27,000); 21kts
Bunkers:	coal 3,000 tons, oil 720 tons
Protection:	belt 4/10.5in (102/266mm) turrets 12in (305mm) barbettes 8in (203mm) decks 3in (76mm) CT 12in (305mm)
Armament:	twelve (4×3) 12in/52cal (305mm) twenty (*Volya* 18) (20×1) 5.1in/55cal (130mm) eight 75mm four 47mm four MG four (submerged) 18in TT (457mm)
Complement:	1,220

IMPERATOR NIKOLAI I BATTLESHIP

Designed as an improved *Imperatritsa Maria*-type battleship to counter the third Turkish dreadnought purchased from Brazil, armour protection was considerably increased over the previous class. War experience led to a decision to improve the light armament. However, the ship was given a low priority when it became apparent that the Turks were not going to increase the strength of their fleet. She had still not been completed when the Revolution began. She was renamed *Demokratia* on 29 April 1917 and fell, incomplete, into German hands in February 1918 when they overran Nicolaiev. She was again recaptured by the Allies, and the hulk finally wrecked by the White Russians to prevent her completion by the Soviets.

NAME	BUILDER	LAID DOWN	LAUNCHED	COMPLETED	FATE
Imperator Nikolai I	Russud Yard	28 Jan 1915	18 Oct 1916	–	Broken up incomplete 1923–4

Displacement:	27,300 (normal) tons
Dimensions:	597 ft (wl)/616 ft 9 in (oa) × 94 ft 9 in × 29 ft 6 in (181.82/187.84 m × 28.86 m × 8.98 m)
Machinery:	Brown-Curtis geared turbines; 4 shafts; 20 Yarrow boilers; SHP 27,300; 21 kts
Bunkers:	coal 2,300 tons, oil 720 tons
Protection:	belt 4/10.5 in (102/266 mm) turrets 12 in (305 mm) barbettes 8 in (203 mm) decks 4 in (102 mm) CT 16 in (406 mm)
Armament:	twelve (4×3) 12 in/52 cal (305 mm) twenty (20×1) 5.1 in/55 cal (130 mm) eight 75 mm four 47 mm four 18 in TT (457 mm)
Complement:	1,252

BORODINO Class BATTLECRUISERS

Under the Little Programme authorized by the Duma on 10 June 1912, four battlecruisers were projected. The design for the new class allowed for extensive armour protection together with nine of the new 14 in guns in triple turrets and a speed of 28 knots. The design was later amended with a fourth turret added and speed reduced by 1.5 knots, the ships being in essence battleships rather than battlecruisers. Appearance was to be the same as the *Gangut* class so that the two types would be almost indistinguishable, except at close quarters. Because of the higher speed, the flush deck of the *Ganguts* was abandoned and an extra forecastle deck added. Although the class was better armoured than *Gangut*, they were still not as powerful as the German battlecruisers. As with the *Ganguts*, the casemate guns were again badly sited beneath the broadside muzzles of the main turrets.

To speed up construction, machinery for two of the units (*Navarin* and *Izmail*) was ordered from Vulkan in Germany, a fatal decision as it turned out, for with war about to break out it was most unlikely that the engines would ever be delivered. The turbines for the other ship were ordered from

NAME	BUILDER	LAID DOWN	LAUNCHED	COMPLETED	FATE
Borodino	Admiralty Yard, St. Petersburg	13 Dec 1912	7 July 1915	–	Broken up incomplete 1923
Izmail	Admiralty Yard, St. Petersburg	19 Dec 1912	22 June 1915	–	Broken up incomplete 1931
Kinburn	Baltic Yard	19 Dec 1912	30 Oct 1915	–	Broken up incomplete 1923
Navarin	Baltic Yard	19 Dec 1912	11 Nov 1916	–	Broken up incomplete 1923

Parsons in Britain. In the end the turbines for both ships had to re-ordered from the Franco-Russian Works. Continual shortages of material and labour severely delayed construction, and development of the new 14in guns continued to be held up despite technical assistance from Vickers in the UK. It was later proposed to fit the already tried and tested 12in mounts. Construction was suspended in 1917, the most advanced of the four ships being *Izmail*. Work on *Izmail* also ceased on the outbreak of the Revolution and she was laid up. The three sister ships were sold to German shipbreakers in 1922. Various proposals were made concerning the fate of *Izmail*, including completion as a modernized battlecruiser and even conversion to an aircraft carrier. None of these plans were ever implemented and she too was broken up.

Displacement:	32,500 (normal), 38,000 (full load) tons
Dimensions:	728ft (pp)/750ft (oa) × 100ft × 33t 6in (221.72/228.43 m × 30.45 m × 10.2 m)
Machinery:	Parsons geared turbines; 4 shafts; 25 Yarrow boilers; SHP 68,000; 26.5kts
Bunkers & Radius:	coal 1,950 tons, oil 1,575 tons; 3,830nm at 16kts
Protection:	belt 4/12in (102/305mm) turrets 12in (305mm) decks 2.5in (63mm) CT 12in (305mm)
Armament:	twelve (4×3) 14in/52 cal (355mm) twenty-four (24×1) 5.1in/55cal (130mm) eight 75mm four 63 mm AA four MG six (submerged) 21in TT (533mm)
Complement:	*c.*1,250

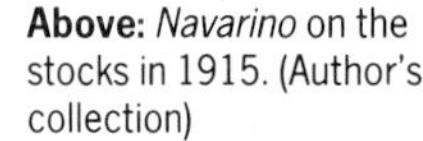

Above: *Navarino* on the stocks in 1915. (Author's collection)

Left: The battlecruiser *Borodino* on the slip in 1914. In the background is *Navarino*. (Author's collection)

Right: The central battery *Kniaz Pojarski* as completed with single funnel. Awnings have been furled and canvas ventilators raised to air the ship while at anchor. (Marius Bar)

CRUISERS

SEVASTOPOL BROADSIDE IRONCLAD

Originally laid down as an unarmoured wooden frigate, *Sevastopol* was converted to an ironclad while under construction and completed with wrought iron side armour extending to 5 ft 2 in below the waterline and extending to within 50 ft of the ends of the battery deck. Fourteen of the 8 in guns were mounted in the armoured battery, while the 6 in gun fired over the bows. The ship was fitted with a ram bow and carried a light three-masted schooner rig.

NAME	BUILDER	LAID DOWN	LAUNCHED	COMPLETED	FATE
Sevastopol	Kronstadt	16 Mar 1862	12 Aug 1864	9 July 1865	Scrapped 1887

Displacement: 6,130 tons
Dimensions: 295 ft × 52 ft × 26 ft (89.84 m × 15.84 m × 7.92 m)
Machinery: reciprocating horizontal return connecting-rod; 1 shaft; rectangular boilers; IHP 3,090; 12 kts
Bunkers & Radius: ?
Protection: belt 4½ in (114 mm) battery 4½ in (114 mm)
Armament: eighteen (18×1) 8 in/22 cal (203 mm) one 6 in/22 cal (152 mm) ten 3.4 in (86 mm)
Complement: 607

PETROPAVLOVSK BROADSIDE IRONCLAD

Originally laid down as a sister ship to *Sevastopol*, *Petropavlovsk*, like her sister, was converted to an ironclad while under construction, being fitted with a wrought iron belt. *Petropavlovsk* carried twenty of her 8 in guns in the armoured battery.

NAME	BUILDER	LAID DOWN	LAUNCHED	COMPLETED	FATE
Petropavlovsk	New Admiralty	9 Sept 1861	1865	16 Aug 1867	Scrapped 1892

Displacement: 6,040 tons
Dimensions: 293 ft 3 in × 56 ft × 24 ft 6 in (89.31 m × 17.05 m × 7.46 m)
Machinery: reciprocating horizontal return connecting-rod; 1 shaft; rectangular boilers; IHP 2,800; 11.9 kts
Bunkers & Radius: ?
Protection: belt 4½ in (114 mm) battery 4½ in (114 mm)
Armament: twenty-one 8 in/22 cal (203 mm) one 6 in/23 cal (152 mm) ten 3.4 in (86 mm) Harvey torpedoes
Complement: 680

KNIAZ POJARSKI CENTRAL BATTERY SHIP

With the full-rigged iron-hulled *Kniaz Pojarski*, the Russian Navy adopted the central battery idea for mounting the main armament, rather than the broadside battery featured in the previous ship. To provide a certain degree of axial fire, the hull was recessed forward and aft, the 9 in guns being mounted in a short battery, with the 6 in guns sited forward and aft on the upper deck. In 1885 the ship underwent a major refit and modernization when she was reboilered and two funnels were added. The armament was also modified, the 9 in guns being replaced by 8 in/35 cal weapons, and two 6 in/23 cal guns, eight 4 pdr and four quick-firing guns being added. The ship was later again re-armed with light weapons when four 4 pdr QF, four 47 mm and six 1 pdr QF and two above water 15 in torpedo tubes were mounted. The ship was relegated to a training role in March 1906, carrying various armaments.

NAME	BUILDER	LAID DOWN	LAUNCHED	COMPLETED	FATE
Kniaz Pojarski	Mitchell, Galernii Island	30 Nov 1864	12 Sept 1867	1873	Stricken 1911

Displacement:	5,138 tons
Dimensions:	272 ft 8 in (wl) × 49 ft × 24 ft 6 in (83.05 m × 14.92 m × 7.46 m)
Machinery:	reciprocating (HDA); 1 shaft; 8 cylindrical boilers; IHP 2,835; 11.7 kts
Bunkers & Radius:	350/600 tons coal; 3,000 nm
Protection:	belt 4½ in (114 mm) battery 4½ in (114 mm)
Armament:	eight (8×1) 9 in/20 cal BLR (228 mm) two 6 in/23 cal (152 mm) four 3.4 in (86 mm) three spar torpedoes, three towed torpedoes
Complement:	495

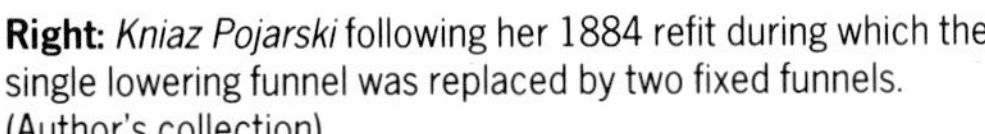

Right: *Kniaz Pojarski* following her 1884 refit during which the single lowering funnel was replaced by two fixed funnels. (Author's collection)

MININ ARMOURED CRUISER

NAME	BUILDER	LAID DOWN	LAUNCHED	COMPLETED	FATE
Minin	Baltic Works	24 Nov 1866	3 Nov 1869	1878	Mined in Baltic 16 Aug 1915

Minin was originally ordered as a sister ship to the battery ship *Pojarski*, but construction was postponed as it was considered that the armament layout in *Pojarski* was inferior and new foreign designs were considered to have made the design obsolete. The design was recast with revised armament and layout and more powerful machinery, and *Minin* was launched as a turret ship with very low freeboard and full rig, on the lines of the British *Captain*. Two twin turrets carrying 11 in guns were to be carried, together with two twin 6 in mounted on the forecastle and poop. The disaster to *Captain* led to a halt in work on *Minin* and she was again re-designed and completed as a broadside battery ship with turrets removed and revised machinery and a single funnel which could be lowered.

The ship underwent a major refit in 1886–7 during which she was reboilered with Belleville water-tube boilers and two fixed funnels which replaced the single funnel. During this refit *Minin* was also fitted with three 14 in torpedo tubes (two submerged on each broadside, and one bow submerged tube). During the 1890s the ship was refitted and relegated to a training role. She was again refitted in 1893–5 and armament altered to four 8 in, twelve 6 in, four 4 pdr and 16 quick-firers. At the same time the rig was reduced and the funnels raised. It appears that the ship was again re-armed in 1901–2, but precise details are lacking. *Minin* was renamed *Ladoga* in October 1909 and converted to a minelayer being again reboilered and fitted with one fixed funnel and two pole masts. Armament was reduced to just four 47 mm quick-firing guns, and internal alterations provided for the carriage of 1,000 mines. During the First World War she was involved in laying the mine barrier in the Gulf of Finland. She sank on a mine laid by the German submarine *UC4*.

Displacement:	6,136 tons (full load)
Dimensions:	295 ft (wl) × 49 ft 6 in × 25 ft 5 in (89.84 m × 15.08 m × 7.74 m)
Machinery:	reciprocating (VC); 1 shaft; 12 cylindrical boilers; IHP 5,290; 14 kts
Bunkers & Radius:	1,000 tons coal; 6,000 nm
Protection:	5/6 in, closed by 4½ in bulkheads (127/152 mm 114 mm)
Armament:	four (4×1) 8 in/22 cal (203 mm) twelve (12×1) 6 in/23 cal (152 mm) four 3.4 in (86 mm) eight 1 pdr QF (37 mm)
Complement:	500

Above: *Minin* as completed with a single lowering funnel. (Author's collection)

Above: *Minin* following the 1886–7 refit, with two fixed funnels and full ship rig and four 8 in and twelve 6 in guns. (Marius Bar)

Right: *Minin* in April 1891, prior to a major refit. (Official US Navy photograph)

GENERAL ADMIRAL Class AMOURED BATTERY FRIGATES

NAME	BUILDER	LAID DOWN	LAUNCHED	COMPLETED	FATE
General Admiral	Society of Metal & Mining Works	27 Nov 1870	2 Oct 1873	1875	Stricken 1938
Gerzog Edinburgski	Baltic Works	27 Sept 1870	10 Sept 1875	1877	Hulked 1915

These iron-hulled fully rigged ships, designed by Vice-Admiral Popov (famous for the unconventional circular *Novgorod* design) can be considered as the first purpose-designed armoured cruisers of the Russian Navy. Everything was sacrificed in order to achieve speed and endurance. The main armament was centrally sited on the upper deck in an open armoured redoubt, with the secondary 6in guns mounted on a lower deck.

The class had a long career during which a number of changes were effected. In about 1890 one of the 6in BL guns in *General Admiral* had been removed and six 87mm added in place of the 4pdr guns, while an extra above water torpedo tube had been added. By 1889 *Gerzog Edinburgski* had also received changes to her armament, six 6in/45 Canet guns replacing the earlier 6in guns, and six 75mm, eight 47mm QF, and two 37mm replacing the secondary and light armament. In 1886 the machinery in *General Admiral* was updated, and three double-ended cylindrical boilers fitted. In 1892 she received a further two single-ended cylindrical boilers. At about this time two fixed funnels replaced the original lowering funnel, and the original screw which could be raised or lowered was replaced by a fixed one. *Gerzog Edinburgski* was similarly refitted. After the 1892 refit *General Admiral* was officially rated as a cruiser.

By the mid-1890s both ships had been relegated to a training role. Further armament changes ensued, *General Admiral* carrying four 6in/45 Canet QF guns, six 47mm and eight 37mm. The armament in *Edinburgski* remained unaltered. From 1909 to 1911 both ships were converted to minelayers (q.v.), the sailing rig being removed together with all main and secondary armament, the ships carrying just light armament. *General Admiral* carried four 75mm and some light guns together with 900 mines, 350 of which were stowed on the deck. *Edinburgski* was similarly armed, but carried only 800 mines of which 200 were on deck. Again, *General Admiral* had her machinery system thoroughly overhauled, receiving eight cylindrical boilers which were replaced in 1913 with six Belleville water-tube boilers. On completion of the conversion the ships were renamed, *General Admiral* becoming *Narova* and subsequently *25 Oktiabrya*, and *Edinburgski* becoming *Onega*.

As *Narova*, *General Admiral* carried out a number of minelaying operations during the First World War, and after the 1917 Revolution was employed by the Soviets to lay defensive minefields off Kronstadt. She remained in service with the Soviet Navy until about 1938, but her final fate is unknown.

Left: *General Admiral* in August 1885. (Marius Bar)

Right: *General Admiral* in the 1890s. The funnel is lowered and sails are drying on the forestays. (Official US Navy photograph)

Displacement:	5,031 tons (*Edinburgski* 4,813 tons)
Dimensions:	285 ft 10 in × 48 ft × 24 ft 5 in (87.05 m × 14.62 m × 7.44 m)
Machinery:	reciprocating (VC); 1 shaft; 5 cylindrical boilers (*Edinburgski* four double-ended cylindrical); IHP 4,772 (*Edinburgski* 5,590); 12.3 kts (*Edinburgski* 11.5)
Bunkers & Radius:	1,000 tons coal; 5,900 nm at 10 kts (*Edinburgski* 5,000 nm)
Protection:	main belt 5/6 in (127/152 mm)
Armament:	six (6×1) 8 in/22 cal (*Edinburgski* four 8 in) (203 mm) two (2×1) 6 in/23 cal (*Edinburgski* five 6 in) (152 mm) two (2×1) 3.4 in (*Edinburgski* six 9 pdr) (86 mm) one (above water) 15 in TT (*Edinburgski* three) (381 mm)
Complement:	482

Left: *General Admiral* in April 1893. She has been refitted with two fixed funnels. (Official US Navy photograph)

Top: The stern of *General Admiral*. (Official US Navy photograph)

Above: *Gerzog Edinburgski* in October 1901. (Author's collection)

PAMIAT MERKURIA UNPROTECTED CRUISER

The iron and steel barque-rigged *Pamiat Merkuria* was designed as a long-range cruising vessel with an extended ram bow. Two of the 6in guns were mounted forward and aft while the remainder were carried on sponsons on the upper deck. The guns were carried in open mounts with not even a light shield to protect the crews. Light armament was later amended to four 3pdr, two 1pdr and two 1pdr quick-firing guns, and two torpedo tubes were added.

NAME	BUILDER	LAID DOWN	LAUNCHED	COMPLETED	FATE
Pamiat Merkuria	Le Havre	1878	22 May 1880	1881	Stricken 1906

Displacement: 2,997 tons
Dimensions: 295ft 3in × 40ft 8in × 19ft 7in (89.92m × 12.38m × 5.96m)
Machinery: reciprocating (HC); 1 shaft; six cylindrical boilers; IHP 3,000; 14kts
Bunkers: 300 tons coal
Armament: six (6×1) 6in/28 (152mm)
four (4×1) 4.2in/20 (107mm)
five (5×1) 2½pdr
four (4×1) 1pdr QF (37mm)
four 15in (above water) TT (381mm)
Complement: 341

Above: *Pamiat Merkuria* as completed with original barque rig. (Marius Bar)

Right: *Dmitri Donskoi* as completed. Note the torpedo-boat amidships. (Marius Bar)

VLADIMIR MONOMAKH Class ARMOURED FRIGATES

NAME	BUILDER	LAID DOWN	LAUNCHED	COMPLETED	FATE
Vladimir Monomakh	Baltic Works	21 May 1881	22 Oct 1882	13 July 1883	Sunk at Tsushima 28 May 1905
Dmitri Donskoi	New Admiralty Yard	21 May 1881	30 Aug 1883	Aug 1884	Scuttled at Tsushima 29 May 1905

These two iron-hulled full-rigged ships were very similar in design and appearance, and to all intents and purposes can be considered to be of the same class. They were ordered as an interim measure following the Russo-Turkish war of 1877–8 which highlighted the lack of ocean-going vessels in the Russian fleet. The design followed closely that of *Minin*, but with certain improvements. Completion of *Donskoi* was held up for lack of funds and the opportunity was taken to incorporate further improvements to the design following experience with *Vladimir Monomakh*. The delay allowed the builders to install new long-range 8in guns which had been developed. The 6in guns on the two ships, being of a new model, also had a much longer range than earlier 6in guns, and so the ships were much more powerful than they at first appeared, although still not as powerful as their British contemporaries. These features, together with the designed extended cruising range, so essential for Russian ocean-going ships because of lack of overseas coaling facilities, enabled these ships to carry out long cruises overseas.

From 1893 to 1895 *Dmitri Donskoi* underwent a major refit during which she was re-armed with six new 6in/45cal and ten 4.7in/45cal quick-firing guns, and six 47mm and twenty-two 37mm. The

full rig was removed and replaced by light pole masts. *Vladimir Monomakh* underwent a similar refit from 1897 to 1898 after which she carried five 6in/45cal Canet, six 4.7in Canet, sixteen 47mm, four 37mm, and three above water torpedo tubes. In 1902–3 *Dmitri Donskoi* was again re-armed to carry six 6in/45cal Canet, ten 75mm, six 47mm, twelve 37mm and four torpedo tubes.

At the Battle of Tsushima *Vladimir Monomakh* was assigned as one of the escorts to the Russian transport group. Early in the action she engaged the Japanese cruiser *Idzumo*, and during the evening of 27 May was attacked by Japanese torpedo-boats, one of whose torpedoes caused severe flooding which could not be contained. She managed to reach the shore of Tsushima Island, where she was abandoned by her crew the following morning, and sank.

Dmitri Donskoi was also assigned as escort to the Russian transport group, but during the night of 27 May became separated from *Monomakh*. She continued to evade Japanese attempts to destroy her during 28 May and although suffering severe damage towards the evening, managed to drive off the Japanese cruisers *Naniwa* and *Otowa*, which both suffered heavy damage. After disembarking the majority of her crew, together with survivors from *Osliabia* on a Japanese island, *Donskoi* was taken out to sea and scuttled.

Displacement:	5,593 tons (full load), (*Donskoi* 6,200)
Dimensions:	296ft 3in × 51ft 8in × 24ft 9in (90.23m × 15.74m × 7.54m)
Machinery:	reciprocating (VC) (*Donskoi* 3-cyl compound); 2 shafts; six (*Donskoi* eight, type unknown) cylindrical boilers; IHP 7,000; 15.2kts (*Donskoi* 16.5)
Bunkers & Radius:	900 tons coal; 6,200nm (*Donskoi* 7,000) at *c.*10kts
Protection:	main belt 4½/6in closed by 3/4in bulkheads (114/152mm 76/102mm) deck 2/3in (51/76mm) battery 3/4in (76/102mm)
Armament:	four (4×1) 8in/22cal (*Donskoi* two 8in/30) (203mm) twelve (12×1) 6in/28cal (*Donskoi* fourteen 6in) (152mm) four (4×1) 75mm six (6×1) 37mm three (*Donskoi* four) 15in (above water) TT (381mm)
Complement:	502 (*Donskoi* 515)

Left: *Dmitri Donskoi* in April 1893. Note the booms for anti-torpedo nets fitted along the hull. (Official US Navy photograph)

Top: *Dmitri Donskoi* following her 1893–5 refit. Note the added fighting top with machine-guns and the bridge amidships. (Author's collection)

Above: *Vladimir Monomakh* in about 1885. (Official US Navy photograph)

Right: *Vladimir Monomakh* following her 1896–7 refit. (Author's collection)

VITIAZ Class PROTECTED CRUISER

These steel- and iron-hulled cruisers carried only light armour protection and comments have been made that the ships exhibited signs of weakness, causing *Rynda* to have to be strengthened. By 1901 *Rynda* had been relegated to the role of training ship, armament being amended to four 6in, two 3.4in, two 3 in, ten 1 pdr quick-firing guns and four 15 in torpedo tubes.

NAME	BUILDER	LAID DOWN	LAUNCHED	COMPLETED	FATE
Rynda	Galernii Island	1883	1885	1887	Stricken 1914
Vitiaz	Galernii Island	1883	1884	1886	Wrecked May 1893

Displacement: 3,537 tons
Dimensions: 260 ft 6 in (wl) × 45 ft × 19 ft 11 in (79.34 m × 13.7 m × 6.06 m)
Machinery: reciprocating (HC); 1 shaft; ten cylindrical boilers; IHP 3,000; 14.4 kts
Bunkers: 500 tons coal
Protection: deck 1½ in (38 mm)
Armament: ten (10×1) 6 in/28 cal (152 mm)
four (4×1) 3.4 in (86 mm)
eight (8×1) 1 pdr QF (37 mm)
three (above water) 15 in TT (381 mm)
Complement: 330

Left: The protected cruiser *Rynda* as completed. (Author's collection)

ADMIRAL NAKHIMOV ARMOURED CRUISER

NAME	BUILDER	LAID DOWN	LAUNCHED	COMPLETED	FATE
Admiral Nakhimov	Baltic Works	July 1884	2 Nov 1885	15 Dec 1887	Scuttled at Tsushima 28 May 1905

Having managed to obtain drawings of the British *Imperieuse*, the Russians designed a close copy, the brig-rigged *Admiral Nakhimov*. The design was not followed exactly, however, one major difference being the re-siting of the bunkers and hatches which considerably reduced the protection afforded the machinery spaces. Although protection around the machinery spaces was weak, the rest of the ship was well armoured, even to the extent that the magazine hoists were armoured. One other weakness concerned the unprotected 6in guns sited on the main deck.

The ship was refitted in 1899 and the machinery modernized, Belleville water-tube boilers being fitted. She took part in the Battle of Tsushima, but sustained relatively little damage from the day's fighting. However, she was torpedoed during the night and the following day the crew surrendered to the Japanese, scuttling the ship to avoid capture.

Displacement: 8,524 tons
Dimensions: 333 ft (wl) × 61 ft × 27 ft 6 in (101.42 m × 18.58 m × 8.37 m)
Machinery: reciprocating (IC); 2 shafts; 12 single-ended cylindrical boilers; IHP 8,000; 17 kts
Bunkers & Radius: 1,100 tons coal; 4,200 nm
Protection: main belt 6/10 in closed by 6/10 in bulkheads (152/254 mm 152/254 mm)
deck 3 in (76 mm)
barbettes 3/8 in (76/203 mm)
CT 6 in (152 mm)
Armament: eight (4×2) 8 in/35 cal (203 mm)
ten (10×1) 6 in/35 cal (152 mm)
twelve 3 pdr QF (47 mm)
six 1 pdr QF (37 mm)
three (above water) 15 in TT (381 mm)
Complement: 570

Right: *Admiral Nakhimov* drying sails, *c.*1890. (Author's collection)

Left: *Admiral Nakhimov* early in 1893. (Author's collection)

Right: *Admiral Nakhimov* c.1889–91. Note torpedo-boat on davits amidships. (Official US Navy photograph)

Left: *Admiral Kornilov* in September 1888. (Author's collection)

ADMIRAL KORNILOV PROTECTED CRUISER

For their next cruiser the Russians turned to a French designer and builder, La Seyne. This protected steel cruiser with pronounced bow ram was originally completed as a barque-rigged ship. The 6in guns were mounted behind shields and sited on each side of the upper deck with end guns in sponsons which projected slightly over the beam. Protection was provided by a cofferdam which extended for most of the waterline.

In company with many other ships, she was refitted in 1904–5, and the armament modernized with ten 6in/45cal replacing the fourteen older guns. In 1908 she was relegated to the role of torpedo school ship.

NAME	BUILDER	LAID DOWN	LAUNCHED	COMPLETED	FATE
Admiral Kornilov	La Seyne St-Nazaire	1886	9 April 1887	1888	Stricken 1911

Displacement: 5,863 tons
Dimensions: 368ft (oa) × 48ft 8in × 25ft 6in (112.08m × 14.82m × 7.77m)
Machinery: reciprocating (HTE); 2 shafts; 8 cylindrical boilers; IHP 5,977; 17.6kts
Bunkers: 1,000 tons coal
Protection: deck 1/2½in (25/63mm) CT 3in (76mm) 3/4½in over engine room (76/114mm)
Armament: fourteen (14×1) 6in/35cal (152mm) six 3pdr (47mm) ten 1pdr QF (37mm) six (above water) 15in TT (381mm)
Complement: 479

PAMIAT AZOVA ARMOURED CRUISER

Pamiat Azova was completed as a barque-rigged ship with three closely spaced funnels and a very pronouced bow ram. The hull was sheathed and coppered. The two 8in guns were carried on sponsons behind light 2in shields in a position just aft of the first funnel. The unprotected 6in guns were all sited on the main deck.

In 1904 the cruiser underwent a major rebuild during which she was reboilered with eighteen Belleville water-tube boilers. Armament was also modernized and twelve 6in/45cal Canet QF guns replaced the original 6in guns. In addition, two 3in, ten 3pdr and two 1pdr guns were fitted and one of the torpedo tubes removed together with the 8in guns. As a result of the major reconstruction the ship was not available to take part in the Russo-Japanese War.

In 1909 the cruiser was reclassified as a training ship attached to the torpedo school and renamed *Dvina*. At this time she carried just four 3pdr and the two torpedo tubes. She served in this role until 1914. She was renamed *Pamiat Azova* on 13 April 1917 and at the end of the year was taken over by the Soviets. She was eventually torpedoed by the British *CMB 79* during the attack on Kronstadt. The hulk was broken up during the 1920s.

NAME	BUILDER	LAID DOWN	LAUNCHED	COMPLETED	FATE
Pamiat Azova	Baltic Works	24 July 1886	1 June 1888	1890	Sunk by *CMB 79* 18 Aug 1919

Displacement:	6,734 tons
Dimensions:	384ft 6in (oa) × 56ft 6in × 26ft 10in (117.11m × 17.21m × 8.17m)
Machinery:	reciprocating (VTE); 2 shafts; 6 double-ended cylindrical boilers; IHP 8,500; 17kts
Bunkers & Radius:	967 tons coal; 3,190nm
Protection:	main belt 4/6in closed by 4in bulkheads (102/152mm 102mm) deck 1½/2½in (38/63mm) CT 1½in (38mm)
Armament:	two (2×1) 8in/35cal (203mm) thirteen (13×1) 6in/35cal (152mm) seven 3pdr (47mm) eight 1pdr QF (37mm) three (above water) 15in TT (381mm)
Complement:	569

Left: *Pamiat Azova* as completed. (Author's collection)

Right: *Pamiat Azova* *c.*1895–9. (Official US Navy photograph)

RURIK ARMOURED CRUISER

Anticipating that her most likely antagonist in the late 1890s would be Great Britain, Russia faced the prospect of meeting an adversary whose strength she could not hope to match. To redress this imbalance it was decided to adopt some of the lessons learned from the recent American Civil War. During that war recourse had been made to the commerce raider as a way of interfering with the enemy's sea lines of communication. Based on such a strategy Russia contended that she could overcome any disadvantage in comparative naval strength, and so *Rurik* was laid down in 1890. At the time details and facts concerning the vessel were clouded in secrecy, and when news of her construction became known it created consternation among European navies, which led to the development of the armoured cruiser. When *Rurik* first made her appearance at the opening of the Kiel Canal in 1893, however, observers saw not a modern warship, but a three-masted full-rig ship, a design feature which had already been abandoned on cruisers as being obsolete by most other navies.

Propulsion comprised four sets of triple expansion engines mounted in pairs in longitudinally separated compartments, the arrangement allowing one of a pair of engines to be disconnected for maintenanace purposes. Speed was found to be inadequate to catch the latest type of merchant ship then entering service, a severe limitation considering that the intended role of the ship was commerce raiding. Surprisingly for a ship of that time the engineering compartments were well-ventilated with numerous air shafts and electric ventilators.

Rurik was heavily armed, although the guns were poorly sited and inadequately protected. The unprotected battery was directly responsible for the heavy loss of life suffered in her final action. Lack of protection also resulted in many of the guns being put out of action early in the fight. Protection was considered to be generally inadequate, while compartmentation left a great deal to be desired. The main armament comprised the Obukhov 8in gun, while secondary armament was provided by French Canet guns. The guns were of short calibre and low muzzle velocity. The torpedo tubes were mounted one each in the bow and stern, the remainder on the broadside. The design exhibited good sea-keeping qualities, the maximum roll being such that the vessel retained full use of all her armament, even in heavy seas.

NAME	BUILDER	LAID DOWN	LAUNCHED	COMPLETED	FATE
Rurik	Baltic Works	31 May 1890	Nov 1892	1895	Sunk at Battle of Ulsan by *Naniwa* and *Takachiho* 14 Aug 1904

The ship was refitted in 1900–1, and part of the rigging removed.

On the outbreak of the Russo-Japanese War *Rurik* was based at Vladivostock, and initially carried out a number of sorties aimed at interfering with the Japanese sea lines of communication. During one of these sorties *Rurik*, in company with *Gromoboi* and *Rossija*, sank the steamers *Idzumi Maru* and *Hitachi Maru* and damaged *Sado Maru*. The loss of these ships was a serious blow to Japanese plans, for *Hitachi Maru* had been carrying eighteen 11in siege guns which the Japanese Army required for its siege of Port Arthur.

Displacement: 10,940 tons
Dimensions: 435ft (oa) × 67ft × 27ft 3in (132.49m × 20.41m × 8.3m)
Machinery: reciprocating (VTE) four engines; 2 shafts; 8 cylindrical boilers; IHP 13,350; 18.7kts
Bunkers & Radius: 2,000 tons coal; 20,000nm at 12kts
Protection: main belt 5/10in closed by 10/12in bulkheads (127/254mm 254/305mm)
deck 2½/3½in (63/89mm)
battery 9/10in (228/254mm)
CT 12in (305mm)
Armament: four (4×1) 8in/35cal (203mm)
sixteen (16×1) 6in/45cal (152mm)
six 4.7in/45cal (120mm)
six 3pdr (47mm)
twelve 1pdr (37mm)
six (above water) 15in TT (381mm)
Complement: 824

Above: Rumours abounded concerning *Rurik*, but when completed it was found that she was outclassed by cruisers in other navies. The picture shows her as completed with a 3-mast full rig. (Author's collection)

ROSSIJA ARMOURED CRUISER

Rossia was much larger than *Rurik*, but was also considered to be an inferior design being under-armed and underpowered for her size. Also, the armament was poorly sited and the guns lacked virtually any protection. Despite these criticisms, she was an improvement on *Rurik*. Because she was underpowered only the two outer shafts could be used at full power, the centre shaft having to idle. The centre shaft was used for cruising, the two outer shafts being disconnected. As in *Rurik* the main armament was mounted behind shields on sponsons on the upper deck. She was severely damaged by Japanese cruisers at the Battle of Ulsan on 14 August 1904.

In 1906 she underwent a major refit when changes were made to the armament. Six extra 6in were added in sponsons on the upper deck, while the 6in originally mounted under the forecastle deck were resited on top of the deck. Light armament was also altered, three extra 3in being added, but the number of 3pdr was reduced to two, and three torpedo tubes were removed. She was frequently used on minelaying operations in the Baltic during the First World War, when she carried up to 100 mines. In 1916–17 armament was again altered, two 6in being removed and two extra 8in added forward and aft to give a much improved firepower over the ahead and astern arcs.

Above: *Rossija* as completed. (P. A. Vicary)

NAME	BUILDER	LAID DOWN	LAUNCHED	COMPLETED	FATE
Rossia	Baltic Works	1894	12 May 1896	1897	Scrapped 1922

Displacement: 13,676 tons
Dimensions: 480 ft 6 in (oa) × 68 ft 6 in × 26 ft (146.34 m × 20.86 m × 7.92 m)
Machinery: reciprocating (VTE); 3 shafts; 32 Belleville boilers; IHP 15,500; 20.2 kts
Bunkers & Radius: 2,500 tons coal; 19,000 nm at 10 kts
Protection: main belt 4/8 in closed by 5 in bulkheads (102/203 mm 127 mm)
deck 2/3.75 in (51/95 mm)
battery 5 in (127 mm)
CT 12 in (305 mm)
Armament: four (4×1) 8 in/45 cal (203 mm)
sixteen (16×1) 6 in/45 cal (152 mm)
twelve 3 in (75 mm)
twenty 3 pdr (47 mm)
sixteen 1 pdr (37 mm)
five (above water) 15 in TT (381 mm)
Complement: 842

Above: *Rossija* following the 1906 refit during which armament was modified and the mainmast removed, and four upright funnels replaced the raked funnels previously fitted. (Marius Bar)

Right: *Svietlana.* Note the accentuated ram bow. She was fitted out as an Imperial Yacht in peacetime. (Marius Bar)

SVIETLANA PROTECTED CRUISER

The protected cruiser *Svietlana*, built in France, was completed with a high freeboard and very pronounced French-style bow ram. She was used as an Imperial Yacht in peacetime, by the Commander-in-Chief of the Russian Navy and carried a considerable amount of embellishment with regard to interior fittings, etc.

Machinery spaces were protected by a 2 in cover and 5 in glacis over the hatches. The forward 6 in gun ammunition hoist was protected by 2 in steel and 2 in thick patches of steel protected the torpedo tubes. Two of the 6 in guns were sited forward and aft, commanding good arcs of fire, while the remaining four 6 in guns were carried on sponsons on the main deck abreast the fore and main masts.

The cruiser was sunk at the Battle of Tsushima by the Japanese cruisers *Niitaka* and *Otawa*.

NAME	BUILDER	LAID DOWN	LAUNCHED	COMPLETED	FATE
Svietlana	Le Havre	Dec 1895	Dec 1896	1897	Sunk at Tsushima 28 May 1905

Displacement:	3,862 tons
Dimensions:	331 ft 4 in (wl) × 42 ft 8 in × 18 ft 8 in (100.91 m × 12.99 m × 5.68 m)
Machinery:	reciprocating (VTE); 2 shafts; 18 Belleville boilers; IHP 8,500; 21.6 kts
Bunkers:	400 tons coal
Protection:	deck 1/2 in (25/51 mm) CT 4 in (102 mm)
Armament:	six (6×1) 6 in/45 cal (152 mm) ten 3 pdr (47 mm) two (above water) 15 in TT (381 mm) 20 mines
Complement:	401

PALLADA Class PROTECTED CRUISERS

This class was distinguished by a high forecastle deck which extended aft as far as the bridge. Apart from the forward and after 6 in guns, the remaining 6 in weapons were mounted on sponsons, two on each broadside abreast the bridge and first funnel, and one on each broadside abreast the mainmast. The 3 in were mounted on the main and upper decks.

Pallada was torpedoed during the Japanese night attack on Port Arthur, but not seriously damaged. She later succumbed to the Japanese guns which pounded the harbour during the long siege. When they captured Port Arthur the Japanese raised *Pallada*, and recommissioned her into their Navy as *Tsugaru*.

Various changes were made to the armament. During the First World War *Aurora* had an extra six 6 in added. *Diana* had her 6 in removed and ten 5.1 in/55 cal guns added instead.

NAME	BUILDER	LAID DOWN	LAUNCHED	COMPLETED	FATE
Aurora	New Admiralty	4 June 1897	24 May 1900	16 July 1903	Preserved
Diana	Galernii Island	Dec 1895	12 Oct 1899	1902	Scrapped 1922
Pallada	Galernii Island	Dec 1895	27 Aug 1899	1902	Sunk Port Arthur 8 Dec 1904

Aurora is preserved in Leningrad as a museum to the Revolution, in which she played an important role.

Displacement:	6,823 (*Diana* 6,657) tons
Dimensions:	415 ft 8 in (oa) × 55 ft × 21 ft 6 in (126.6 m × 16.75 m × 6.55 m)
Machinery:	reciprocating (VTE); 3 shafts; 24 Belleville boilers; IHP 11,600; 19 kts
Bunkers & Radius:	1,430 tons coal; 5,600 nm at 10 kts
Protection:	deck 2.5 in (63 mm) CT 6 in (152 mm)
Armament:	eight (8 × 1) 6 in/45 cal (152 mm) twenty-four 3 in (75 mm) eight 1 pdr (37 mm) three (submerged) 15 in TT (381 mm)
Complement:	571

Below: *Aurora*. Note the 6 in guns in sponsons forward. (Marius Bar)

Opposite page: *Gromoboi* as completed. (Marius Bar)

GROMOBOI ARMOURED CRUISER

The basic design of *Gromoboi* was the same as that of *Rossija*. Some major changes were incorporated however, principally concerning the machinery. The boiler arrangement was changed so that sufficient power was available to drive all three shafts. Armament disposition and protection was considerably improved, the two forward 8in guns being mounted in casemates sited above the two forward casemated 6in guns. The eight 6in guns mounted on the main deck were also sited in casemates. The after 8in were mounted behind shields on sponsons abreast the after mast. The protective deck was sloped to give extra reinforcement to the armour belt.

The cruiser was in action during the Russo-Japanese War, being severely damaged at the Battle of Ulsan in August 1904. She was later mined off Vladivostock on 23 May 1905. She was subsequently repaired and refitted in 1906 when an extra six 6in were added on the upper deck, while the forward casemated 6in were resited on the forecastle deck. At this stage light armament comprised nineteen 3in and six 3pdr.

Gromoboi served in the Baltic during the First World War and armament was again altered in 1916–17 when the forward and after 6in were removed and replaced by 8in/45cal guns, and four 3in AA guns were added.

NAME	BUILDER	LAID DOWN	LAUNCHED	COMPLETED	FATE
Gromoboi	Baltic Works	1897	20 May 1899	1900	Scrapped 1922

Displacement:	13,220 tons
Dimensions:	481ft (oa) × 68ft 6in × 27ft 10in (146.5m × 20.86m × 8.48m)
Machinery:	reciprocating (VTE); 3 shafts; 32 Belleville boilers; IHP 15,500; 20kts
Bunkers:	1,720 tons coal
Protection:	main belt 6in closed by 6in bulkheads (152mm 152mm) deck 2/3in (51/76mm) casemates 2/5in (51/127mm) CT 12in (305mm)
Armament:	four (4×1) 8in/45cal (203mm) sixteen (16×1) 6in/45cal (152mm) twenty-four 3in (75mm) four 3pdr (47mm) four 1pdr (37mm) four (submerged) 15in TT (381mm)
Complement:	877

Above: *Gromoboi* seen passing through the Suez Canal in 1903. (P. A. Vicary)

Left: *Gromoboi* seen during the early part of the First World War. Note that the stern has been cut down aft and the mainmast removed. (Author's collection)

Right: Protected cruiser *Variag c.*1903. (Author's collection)

VARIAG PROTECTED CRUISER

To build up the fleet in preparation for war with Japan, an order for a protected cruiser was placed in the USA. *Variag* was distinguished by her four tall, thin funnels and long forecastle deck extending far aft to between the first and second funnels.

She was in action with the Japanese battleship *Asama* at Chemulpo on 9 February 1904 and was scuttled by her crew. The Japanese raised the cruiser and commissioned her into their own navy as *Soya*. She was sold back to Russia in 1916, being renamed *Variag*. She served in the White Sea and in February 1917 was sent to England for a refit. Because of the Revolution the refit was never carried out and the hulk was eventually scrapped in Britain.

NAME	BUILDER	LAID DOWN	LAUNCHED	COMPLETED	FATE
Variag	Cramp	May 1898	31 Oct 1899	July 1900	Scrapped 1921

Displacement:	6,500 tons	Armament:	twelve (12×1) 6 in/45 cal (152 mm) twelve (12×1) 3 in/60 cal (75 mm) eight 3 pdr (47 mm) two 1 pdr (37 mm) six (above water) 15 in TT (381 mm) 22 mines
Dimensions:	425 ft (oa) × 52 ft × 20 ft 8 in (129.44 m × 15.84 m × 6.29 m)		
Machinery:	reciprocating (VTE); 2 shafts; 30 Niclausse boilers; IHP 21,000; 23.2 kts		
Bunkers & Radius:	1,300 tons coal; 4,500 nm at 10 kts		
Protection:	deck 1½/3 in (38/76 mm) CT 6 in (152 mm) hoists 1½ in (38 mm)	Complement:	580

ASKOLD PROTECTED CRUISER

Askold was immediately recognizable by her flush deck and five very tall and very thin funnels. The lower deck of the bridge extended forward and on this was mounted the forward 6in gun. The remaining 6in guns were all mounted on the upper deck, one aft and the five others on each broadside. The lighter guns were mounted on the main deck.

Askold was a fast cruiser and during the First World War was initially operational in the Mediterranean. She was later transferred to the White Sea and was seized there by the British during the Interventionist War. She was commissioned into the Royal Navy in August 1918 as *Glory IV*.

Displacement:	5,905 tons
Dimensions:	437ft (oa) × 49ft 2in × 20ft 4in (133.1m × 14.97m × 6.19m)
Machinery:	reciprocating (VTE); 3 shafts; 9 Schulz-Thornycroft boilers; IHP 20,420; 23.8kts
Bunkers:	1,100 tons coal
Protection:	deck 2/4in (51/102mm) CT 6in (152mm)
Armament:	twelve (12×1) 6in/45 cal (152mm) twelve 3in (75mm) eight 3pdr (47mm) two 1pdr (37mm) six (two submerged) 15in TT (381mm)
Complement:	576

NAME	BUILDER	LAID DOWN	LAUNCHED	COMPLETED	FATE
Askold	Krupp, Germania	Aug 1898	2 Mar 1900	1901	Scrapped 1921

Above: *Askold* seen at an Imperial Review during her first commission. (P. A. Vicary)

Left: *Askold* in the White Sea in 1918 before being seized by British forces. (P. A. Vicary)

Left: *Askold* interned in Shanghai, 10 August 1904. (Author's collection)

Below left: *Bogatyr* as completed. Note searchlights on outer bridge wings. (Marius Bar)

NAME	BUILDER	LAID DOWN	LAUNCHED	COMPLETED	FATE
Bogatyr	Vulkan, Stettin	May 1898	30 Jan 1901	1902	Scrapped 1922
Kagul	Nicolaiev	Sept 1901	2 June 1902	July 1905	Renamed *Pamiat Merkuria* 7 April 1907 Renamed *Komintern*. Sunk 17 July 1942
Oleg	New Admiralty	Nov 1901	27 Aug 1903	Aug 1904	Sunk by *CMB 4* 17 June 1919
Ochakov	Sevastopol	Mar 1901	1 Oct 1902	9 Nov 1905	Renamed *Kagul* 7 April 1907. Renamed *Ochakov* April 1917. To Bizerta 1920

BOGATYR Class PROTECTED CRUISERS

These ships were a considerable improvement on the previous protected cruisers, being much better armed and protected. For the first time the main armament of 6in guns was mounted in turrets, two twin mounts being sited forward and aft on the short forecastle and poop decks. The remaining 6in guns were sited in casemates on the upper deck abreast the fore and main masts, and the remaining four in sponsons on the upper deck amidships.

Bogatyr and *Oleg* were re-armed during the First World War, twelve 5.1in/55 cal guns replacing the 6in, and four 3in AA being added. Provision was also made for carrying 100 mines. *Kagul* also had her 6in removed, but only twelve 5.1in were added to this ship. Various sources credit *Pamiat Merkuria* with having an extra four 6in added.

Kagul was renamed *Ochakov* and finally *General Kornilov*, escaping to Bizerta in 1920. After the Revolution *Pamiat Merkuria* was renamed *Komintern* and with the third funnel removed was used as a training ship. She was later disarmed and used as a stores ship.

Displacement:	6,645 tons
Dimensions:	439ft 8in (oa) × 54ft 5½in × 20ft 7½in (133.91m × 16.59m × 6.28m)
Machinery:	reciprocating (VTE); 2 shafts; 16 Normand boilers; IHP 23,000; 23kts
Bunkers & Radius:	1,100 tons coal; 2,100nm at 12kts
Protection:	deck 1.3/3.3in (33/84mm) turrets 1/5in (25/127mm) casemates 0.75/3.25in (19/82mm) CT 5½in (140mm)
Armament:	twelve (2×2, 8×1) 6in/45cal (152mm) twelve 3in (75mm) eight 3pdr (47mm) two 1pdr (37mm) two (submerged) 15in TT (381mm)
Complement:	576

Above: *Oleg*. Note slightly different bridge structure and lack of searchlights compared to *Bogatyr*. See data on previous page. (Marius Bar)

NOVIK PROTECTED CRUISER

Novik was a very lightly protected cruiser and is generally considered to have been an enlarged destroyer with a turtle-back forecastle deck. She had a low freeboard which was augmented towards the bows by a low forecastle. With her very high speed she could have served as a destroyer flotilla leader, in much the same way as some of the lighter British cruisers. Although intended for use in a scouting role, her bunkers were really too small to allow her to undertake such a role effectively.

During the Russo-Japanese war she was in action with the cruiser *Tsushima* and was scuttled at Sakhalin following the action. She was raised and repaired by the Japanese and commissioned into their Navy as *Suzuya*.

Displacement:	3,080 tons
Dimensions:	360 ft 5 in (wl) × 40 ft × 16 ft 5 in (109.77 m × 12.18 m × 5 m)
Machinery:	reciprocating (VTE); 3 shafts; 12 Schulz-Thornycroft boilers; IHP 17,000; 25 kts
Bunkers & Radius:	500 tons coal; 5,000 nm at 10 kts
Protection:	deck 1.75/3 in (44/76 mm)

NAME	BUILDER	LAID DOWN	LAUNCHED	COMPLETED	FATE
Novik	Schichau	1899	15 Aug 1900	1901	Scuttled 28 Aug 1904

Armament:	six (6×1) 4.7 in/45 cal (120 mm) six 3 pdr (47 mm) five (above water) 15 in TT (381 mm)
Complement:	337

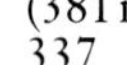

Below: *Novik* as completed. (P. A. Vicary)

BOYARIN PROTECTED CRUISER

NAME	BUILDER	LAID DOWN	LAUNCHED	COMPLETED	FATE
Boyarin	Burmeister & Wain	1899	8 June 1901	1902	Mined 12 Feb 1904

Boyarin was a smaller, lighter armed version of *Bogatyr*, lacking the turrets of the latter. The 4.7 in guns were mounted forward and aft on the short forecastle and poop decks, the remaining guns being sited in sponsons on the upper deck, abreast the fore and mainmasts.

Displacement: 3,200 tons
Dimensions: 345 ft (wl) × 41 ft × 16 ft (105.08 m × 12.49 m × 4.87 m)
Machinery: reciprocating (VTE); 2 shafts; 16 Belleville boilers; IHP 11,500; 22 kts
Bunkers: 600 tons coal
Protection: deck 1.25/2 in (32/51 mm) CT 3 in (76 mm)
Armament: six (6×1) 4.7 in/45 cal (120 mm) eight 3 pdr (47 mm) four 1 pdr (37 mm) five (above water) 15 in TT (381 mm)
Complement: 266

Above: *Boyarin c.*1903. (Author's collection)

BAYAN Class ARMOURED CRUISERS

NAME	BUILDER	LAID DOWN	LAUNCHED	COMPLETED	FATE
Admiral Makarov	La Seyne	April 1905	28 May 1906	April 1908	Scrapped 1922
Bayan (I)	La Seyne	Feb 1899	12 June 1900	Feb 1903	Sunk Port Arthur 8 Dec 1904
Bayan (II)	New Admiralty	Aug 1905	15 Aug 1907	Dec 1911	Scrapped 1922
Pallada	New Admiralty	Aug 1905	10 Nov 1906	Feb 1911	Sunk by *U 26* 11 Oct 1914

Below: The first *Bayan* (shown here as completed) was sunk at Port Arthur, captured and incorporated into the Imperial Japanese Navy. (P. A. Vicary)

Although much smaller than *Gromoboi* and *Rossija*, these ships were much better designed with armour protection improved. Main armament was mounted in turrets forward and aft, the 6 in being sited in casemates on the main deck while the 3 in guns were sited behind light shields on open mounts above the 6 in guns on the upper deck.

The first *Bayan* took an active part in the Russo-Japanese War, being mined on 27 July 1904. She was taken back to Port Arthur and sunk there during the siege. The wreck was captured by the Japanese and repaired and recommissioned as *Aso*. During the First World War the surviving ships received additional armament in the form of two 3 in or 3 pdr AA guns. They were used as minelayers on a number of occasions, carrying up to 150 mines. The second *Bayan* was set on fire and seriously damaged during the action off Moon Sound on 17 October 1917.

Displacement: 7,775 tons (*Bayan I* 7,725)
Dimensions: 449 ft 7 in (oa) × 57 ft 6 in × 22 ft (136.93 m × 17.51 m × 6.7 m)
Machinery: reciprocating (VTE); 2 shafts; 26 Belleville boilers; IHP 16,500; 21 kts
Bunkers: 1,100 tons coal
Protection: main belt 2½/7 in (*Bayan I* 2½/8 in) closed by 8 in bulkheads (63/178 mm (63/203 mm) 203 mm) deck 2 in (51 mm) turrets 5.25/6 in (*Bayan I* 6/

	6.75 in) (133/152 mm (152/171 mm))
	casemates 2½ in (63 mm)
	CT 5½ in (*Bayan I* 6.75 in) (140 mm)
Armament:	two (2×1) 8 in/45 cal (203 mm)
	eight (8×1) 6 in/45 cal (152 mm)
	twenty 3 in (*Bayan I* sixteen) (75 mm)
	four 6 pdr (*Bayan I* eight 3 pdr) (47 mm)
	two (submerged) 18 in (*Bayan I* 15 in) TT (457 (381) mm)
Complement:	568

IZUMRUD Class PROTECTED CRUISERS

The design of this class was a repeat of *Novik* with a marginal increase in displacement and dimensions. They were distinguishable from *Novik* by their three masts. *Jemtchug* was modernized in 1907–8 and two extra 4.7 in guns were added.

NAME	BUILDER	LAID DOWN	LAUNCHED	COMPLETED	FATE
Izumrud	Nevski	1902	Oct 1903	1904	Wrecked 29 May 1905
Jemtchug	Nevski	14 June 1902	27 Aug 1903	1904	Sunk by *Emden* 28 Oct 1914

Displacement:	3,103 tons
Dimensions:	364 ft (oa) × 40 ft × 16 ft 5 in (110.86 m × 12.18 m × 5 m)
Machinery:	reciprocating (VTE); 3 shafts; 16 Yarrow boilers; IHP 17,000; 24 kts
Bunkers & Radius:	510 tons coal; 4,000 nm at 10 kts
Armament:	six (6×1) 4.7 in/45 cal (120 mm)
	six 3 pdr (47 mm)
	two 1 pdr (37 mm)
	three (above water) 18 in TT (457 mm)
Complement:	350

Left: *Jemtchug* seen during the First World War. (Marius Bar)

Right: *Rurik* with single mast, as delivered by Vickers. (Vickers)

Left: *Bayan I.* (Author's collection)

Right: *Admiral Makarov* with single pole mainmast in 1914. See data on pages 99 and 100. (Author's collection)

RURIK ARMOURED CRUISER

Rurik was the largest and finest armoured cruiser laid down for the Russian Navy, and is generally considered to have been one of the finest armoured cruisers ever built. She was a typical Vickers design and some of the design features surpassed even features in Royal Navy armoured cruisers. She was armed with a new powerful 10in gun carried in a newly designed turret which allowed an elevation of 35 degrees. The magazines were equipped with flooding and spraying arrangements to counteract fire in the event of flashback from the turret. Armour protection was well designed and the ship was fitted with two armoured decks.

During the First World War *Rurik* was operational in the Baltic and on a number of occasions was involved in minelaying operations carrying up to 400 mines.

NAME	BUILDER	LAID DOWN	LAUNCHED	COMPLETED	FATE
Rurik	Vickers Sons & Maxim Ltd	Sept 1905	17 Nov 1906	Sept 1908	Scrapped 1923

Displacement: 15,190 tons
Dimensions: 529ft (oa) × 75ft × 26ft (161.12m × 22.84m × 7.91m)
Machinery: reciprocating (VTE); 2 shafts; 28 Belleville boilers; IHP 19,700; 21kts
Bunkers: 1,920 tons coal
Protection: main belt 4/6in closed by 3/4in bulkheads (102/152mm 76/102mm)
decks 1/1.5in (25/38mm)
turrets 7.25in/8in (184/203mm)
secondary turrets 6/7in (152/178mm)
battery 3in (76mm)
CT 8in (203mm)
Armament: four (2×2) 10in/50cal (254mm)
eight (4×2) 8in/50cal (203mm)
twenty (20×1) 4.7in/50cal (120mm)
four 3pdr (47mm)
two (submerged) 18in TT (457mm)
Complement: 899

Above: *Rurik.* (Marius Bar)

Left: Stern of *Rurik* seen in 1912. (Author's collection)

MURAVIEV AMURSKI Class CRUISERS

A somewhat smaller version of the *Svetlana* class (see below) designed for service in the Pacific. The general arrangement followed that of *Svetlana* and the 35 kt destroyers then under construction, the intention being that both the light protected cruisers and 35 kt destroyers would form homogeneous squadrons, along the lines of the British forces. On the outbreak of war the ships were seized by the Germans and they were completed for the German Navy.

Displacement: 4,500 tons (normal)
Dimensions: 443 ft 10 in (oa) × 44 ft 6 in × 18 ft 4 in (135.18 m × 13.55 m × 5.58 m)
Machinery: turbines; 2 shafts; 10 Yarrow boilers; SHP 30,000; 27.5 kts
Bunkers: 620 tons coal, 580 tons oil
Protection: deck 3 in (76 mm)
shields 2 in (51 mm)
CT 3 in (76 mm)
Armament: eight (8×1) 5.1 in/55 cal (130 mm)
four 63 mm/55 cal AA (63 mm)
five 18 in TT (457 mm)
150 mines
Complement: 359

NAME	BUILDER	LAID DOWN	LAUNCHED	COMPLETED	FATE
Admiral Nevelskoi	Schichau, Danzig	Feb 1913	21 Nov 1914	1 Sept 1915	Seized 5 Aug 1914 Renamed *Elbing*
Muraviev Amurski	Schichau, Danzig	Feb 1913	11 April 1914	14 Dec 1914	Seized 5 Aug 1914 Renamed *Pillau*

SVETLANA Class CRUISERS

This class went through various design changes before emerging as light cruisers, carrying guns in open shields. The initial specification provided for a single 8 in gun and three twin 4.7 in guns in turrets. This subsequently changed to four triple 6 in turrets and then twelve single 5.1 in guns in shields. Just before the design was finalized it was decided to incorporate facilities for handling a seaplane. Later it was decided to provide facilities for two seaplanes. Shortage of materials and labour problems seriously delayed completion and none of the ships were completed to serve in the Imperial Navy.

Displacement: 6,750 tons (normal)
Dimensions: 519 ft 8 in × 50 ft 2 in × 18 ft 3 in (158.27 m × 15.28 m × 5.56 m)
Machinery: Brown-Curtiss (*Admiral Butakov, Admiral Spiridov* Parsons) geared turbines; 4 shafts; 13 Yarrow boilers; SHP 50,000; 29.5 kts
Bunkers: 1,167 tons oil
Protection: main belt 3 in (76 mm)
deck 1½ in (38 mm)
shields 1 in (25 mm)
CT 3 in (76 mm)
Armament: fifteen (15×1) 5.1 in/55 cal (130 mm)
four 63 mm/55 cal AA (63 mm)
two (submerged) 18 in TT (457 mm)
one seaplane
100 mines
Complement: 630

NAME	BUILDER	LAID DOWN	LAUNCHED	COMPLETED	FATE
Admiral Butakov	Putilov	29 Nov 1913	5 Aug 1916	–	Renamed *Voroshilov* 1928
Admiral Greig	Russo-Baltic	7 Nov 1913	9 Dec 1916	24 Dec 1916	Completed as oil tanker *Azneft*
Admiral Spiridov	Putilov	29 Nov 1913	9 Sept 1916	24 Dec 1916	Completed as oil tanker *Groznyeft*
Svetlana	Russo-Baltic	7 Dec 1913	27 Nov 1915	1 July 1928	Renamed *Profintern* Dec 1922

ADMIRAL NAKHIMOV Class CRUISERS

The original design for these ships showed a repeat *Svetlana*, but following design review with assistance from the British yard of John Brown the design was modified to give a ship with higher speed and displacement increased by 1,000 tons.

Displacement: 7,600 tons (normal)
Dimensions: 535 ft 6 in (wl) × 51 ft 6 in × 18 ft 3 in (163.1 m × 15.68 m × 5.56 m)
Machinery: Brown-Curtiss geared turbines; 4 shafts; 14 Yarrow boilers; SHP 55,000; 29.5 kts
Bunkers & Radius: 1,230 tons oil; 1,200 nm at 14 kts
Protection: main belt 3 in (76 mm)
deck 1.5 in (38 mm)
shields 1 in (25 mm)
CT 3 in (76 mm)
Armament: fifteen 5.1 in/55 cal (130 mm)
four 63 mm/55 cal AA
two (submerged) 18 in TT (457 mm)
1 seaplane
100 mines
Complement: 630

NAME	BUILDER	LAID DOWN	LAUNCHED	COMPLETED	FATE
Admiral Istomin	Navy Yard Nicolaiev	July 1914	–	–	Broken up incomplete 1938
Amiral Kornilov	Russud	July 1914	1922	–	Broken up incomplete 1922
Admiral Lazarev	Navy Yard Nicolaiev	31 Oct 1913	21 June 1916	25 Jan 1932	Renamed *Krasni Kavkaz*
Admiral Nakhimov	Russud	31 Oct 1913	6 Nov 1915	27 Feb 1927	Renamed *Chervonaya Ukraina*

COAST DEFENCE SHIPS

***VARIAG* Class** WOODEN-SCREW CORVETTES

These wooden-screw corvettes were designed as unarmoured full-rig ships. Following the action between *Monitor* and *Merrimac* in the United States, doubts were voiced as to the wisdom of proceeding with the construction of the last unit, *Askold*. During their career armament was frequently changed, reflecting gunnery developments at that time. As completed the ships were armed with 17 smooth-bore guns. Later, as rifled armament developed, *Variag* was re-armed with one 6in/23cal and ten 4.1in/20cal, while *Vitiaz* carried eight 6in/23cal and four 4.2in/20cal guns.

NAME	BUILDER	LAID DOWN	LAUNCHED	COMPLETED	FATE
Askold	Crichton	1862	1863	1864	Stricken *c.*1890
Variag	Uleaborg	1861	1862	1863	Stricken *c.*1887
Vitiaz	Berneborg	1861	1862	1863	Stricken *c.*1894

Askold was armed in a similar way to *Vitiaz*, carrying in addition a 3.4in gun and spar torpedoes.

Displacement: 2,155 tons (*Vitiaz* 2,350 tons, *Askold* 2,200 tons)
Dimensions: 217ft 6in (wl) × 39ft 8in × 20ft 1in (66.2m × 12.08m × 6.12m)
Machinery: ?; 1 shaft; rectangular boilers; IHP 1,018; *c.*10kts
Armament: 17 smooth-bore
Complement: 324

Left: Broadside ironclad *Netron Menya.* (Author's collection)

Right: *Netron Menya* with reduced rig and cap to funnel. (Author's collection)

Far right: *Pervenetz.* (Author's collection)

PERVENETZ Class COAST DEFENCE IRONCLADS

These 3-masted schooner-rigged ships were completely armoured with a wrought iron belt extending for the entire length of the ship above the waterline. *Kreml* had a shortened armour belt which did not extend right to the bow or stern. All the 8in and 6in guns were mounted in the battery, except for three 6in in *Pervenetz* which were carried on the unarmoured upper deck, two 6in in *Kreml* and two 8in in *Netron Menya*. The engines for *Kreml* and *Netron Menya* were taken from wooden-screw ships that were to be scrapped.

NAME	BUILDER	LAID DOWN	LAUNCHED	COMPLETED	FATE
Kreml	Baltic Works	1864	1865	1866	Stricken 1905
Netron Menya	Mitchell	1863	1864	1865	Stricken 1905
Pervenetz	Thames Iron Works	1862	1863	1864	Stricken 1905

Displacement: 3,277 tons (*Kreml* 4,000 tons, *Netron Menya* 3,340 tons)
Dimensions: 221ft 9in/225ft 1in (wl) × 53ft 9in × 19ft 6in (67.53/68.55m × 16.37m × 5.94m)
Machinery: reciprocating (HDA); 1 shaft; rectangular boilers; IHP 1,067/1,630; 9/10kts
Bunkers: 250/500 tons coal
Protection: belt 4½in (114mm) battery 4½in (*Kreml* 5½in) (114mm (140mm) CT 4½in (114mm)
Armament: 34 smooth-bore *Kreml* – eight 8in/22 cal, six 6in/23 cal (203mm 152mm) *Netron Menya* – fourteen 8in/22 cal, four 3.4in, two 2½pdr (203mm 80mm)
Complement: 395

BRONENOSETZ Class COAST DEFENCE MONITORS

The basic hull design and general layout of this class, which featured a very low freeboard, appears to have followed that of the American single-turret monitors of the *Passaic* class. Two of the units, *Koldun* and *Vyeshtchun*, were built in sections and shipped to Russia where they were assembled.

Although the ships carried extensive wrought iron side armour, there was no protection against plunging shells (except in *Perun* which had a 1in armoured deck), or underneath as there was no double bottom. Considering the role for which these vessels were designed, this was a serious weakness. The smooth-bore 9in were later replaced by two 9in/20cal guns which in *Latnik* and *Lava* were further replaced by 22 cal weapons.

Displacement: *c.*2,000 tons (?)
Dimensions: 201ft (wl) × 46ft × 12ft 7in (61.22m × 14.01m × 3.83m)

NAME	BUILDER	LAID DOWN	LAUNCHED	COMPLETED	FATE
Bronenosetz	Carr & Macpherson	1863	1864	1865–6	Stricken *c.*1900
Edinorog	Galernii	1863	1864	1865–6	Stricken *c.*1900
Koldun	Cockerill	1863	1864	1865–6	Stricken *c.*1900
Latnik	Carr & Macpherson	1863	1864	1865–6	Stricken *c.*1900
Lava	Baltic Works	1863	1864	1865–6	Stricken *c.*1900
Perun	Baltic Works	1863	1864	1865–6	Stricken *c.*1900
Stryeletz	Galernii	1863	1864	1865–6	Stricken *c.*1900
Tifon	New Admiralty	1863	1864	1865–6	Stricken *c.*1900
Uragan	New Admiralty	1863	1864	1865–6	Stricken *c.*1900
Vyeshtchun	Cockerill	1863	1864	1865–6	Stricken *c.*1900

Machinery: reciprocating (HDA); 1 shaft; 2 rectangular boilers; IHP 340/530; 6.5/8kts
Bunkers: 100 tons coal
Protection: main belt 9in reducing to 3/5in at ends (228mm 76/127mm) turret 10in (254mm) CT 8in (203mm)
Armament: two 9in SB (228mm) four 2½pdr
Complement: 111

Left: Coast defence monitor *Vyeshtchun*. (Author's collection)

SMERCH COAST DEFENCE TURRET SHIP

Like the previous class this coast defence ship had a very low freeboard. Although smaller than the *Bronenosetz* class, wrought iron protection was much better, the ship having a partial double bottom, while above the water the hull was fully armoured and she had a 1in armoured deck. Three pole masts were fitted from which signals could be hoisted. Armament was altered at some later date to two single 9in/20cal guns, four 4pdr QF and four 1pdr (37mm) QF guns.

Displacement: 1,460 tons

NAME	BUILDER	LAID DOWN	LAUNCHED	COMPLETED	FATE
Smerch	Mitchell	Nov 1863	23 June 1864	1865	Scrapped 1904

Dimensions: 188ft 2in (wl) × 38ft 2in × 12ft (57.31m × 11.62m × 3.65m)
Machinery: reciprocating (HDA); 2 shafts; 3 rectangular boilers; IHP 700; 8kts
Bunkers: 250 tons coal
Protection: main belt 4.5in reducing to 4in at ends (114mm 102mm) deck 1in (25mm) turrets 4.5/6in (114/152mm) CT 4.5in (114mm)
Armament: two (2×1) 9in SB (228mm) one 4pdr QF
Complement: 155

CHARODEIKA Class COAST DEFENCE TURRET SHIPS

A larger wrought iron armoured version of the previous ship, with improved armament and only two pole masts. The main armament was mounted in turrets of the Coles type, the turrets being enlarged over the previous class to accommodate two guns. At a later date two of the 9in were replaced by 22 cal guns, and two 3 pdr (47 mm) and two 1 pdr (37 mm) QF guns were added.

NAME	BUILDER	LAID DOWN	LAUNCHED	COMPLETED	FATE
Petr Veliki	Mitchell	Mar 1866	12 Sept 1867	1869	Renamed *Charodeika* 1872. Scrapped 1907
Russalka	Mitchell	1866	12 Sept 1867	1869	Lost 19 Sept 1893

Displacement: 2,100 tons
Dimensions: 210 ft 1 in × 42 ft × 12 ft 7 in (64 m × 12.79 m × 3.83 m)
Machinery: reciprocating (HDA); 2 shafts; 2 rectangular boilers; IHP 875; 8.5 kts
Bunkers: 250 tons coal
Protection: main belt 4.5 in (114 mm) turrets 6 in (152 mm) CT 4.5 in (114 mm)
Armament: four (2×2) 9 in/20 cal (228 mm) one 4 pdr
Complement: 178

ADMIRAL LAZAREV Class COAST DEFENCE TURRET SHIPS

Like the previous ships these coast defence vessels were fitted with wrought iron armour protection, but lacked any armoured deck. They were completed with a fore and aft rig on three masts. They underwent two major refits during their long career, the machinery being completely overhauled and new boilers fitted. During the second refit in 1900–3, cylindrical boilers replaced the rectangular boilers. During these refits armament was considerably modified. During the first refit the 9 in guns were replaced by three single 11 in/20 cal weapons, and two to four 3.4 in were added. At the second refit the 20 cal 11 in guns were replaced by 22 cal weapons, and a single 3 pdr and two 1 pdr QF guns were added.

NAME	BUILDER	LAID DOWN	LAUNCHED	COMPLETED	FATE
Admiral Greig	Carr & Macpherson	28 April 1866	18 Oct 1867	1869	Scrapped 1910
Admiral Lazarev	Carr & Macpherson	1866	21 Sept 1867	1869	Stricken 1909

Displacement: 3,820 (*Admiral Greig* 3,768) tons
Dimensions: 254 ft 10 in (wl) × 43 ft × 20 ft 6 in (77.61 m × 13.1 m × 6.24 m)
Machinery: reciprocating (HDA); 1 shaft; 4 rectangular boilers; IHP 2,020; 10 kts
Bunkers: 300 tons coal
Protection: main belt 4.5 in reducing to 3 in at ends (114 mm 76 mm) turrets 6/6.5 in (152/162 mm) CT 5 in (127 mm)
Armament: six (3×2) 9 in/20 cal (228 mm)
Complement: 269

Right: *Admiral Greig.* (Author's collection)

ADMIRAL CHICHAGOV Class COAST DEFENCE TURRET SHIPS

The design of these two ships followed closely that of the previous class, but differed in having two instead of three turrets and much thicker wrought iron armour. Like the previous class the 9in guns were later replaced by two single 11in/20cal guns. Four 3.4in were added and later a single 3pdr and four 1pdr QF guns. *Chichagov* was further modified with two single 11in/22cal guns replacing the 20cal weapons. *Chichagov* was reboilered with cylindrical boilers in 1887; *Spiridov* was similarly reboilered in 1904.

NAME	BUILDER	LAID DOWN	LAUNCHED	COMPLETED	FATE
Admiral Chichagov	Baltic Works	1867	13 Oct 1868	1870	Stricken 1909
Admiral Spiridov	Baltic Works	1867	28 Aug 1868	1870	Stricken 1909

Displacement: 3,925 (*Spiridov* 3,851) tons
Dimensions: 254ft 5in (wl) × 43ft × 20ft 5in (77.49m × 13.1m × 6.22m)
Machinery: reciprocating (HDA); 1 shaft; 4 rectangular boilers; IHP 2,030; 10.5kts
Bunkers: 300 tons coal
Protection: main belt 6in (152mm) turrets 6in (*Spiridov* 7in) (152 (178)mm)
Armament: four (2×2) 9in/20cal (228mm)
Complement: 260

Left: *Admiral Lazarev*. See data on the previous page. (Author's collection)

Above: *Admiral Chichagov*. (P. A. Vicary)

Right: *Admiral Spiridov*. (Marius Bar)

NOVOGOROD COAST DEFENCE SHIP

NAME	BUILDER	LAID DOWN	LAUNCHED	COMPLETED	FATE
Novgorod	Nicolaiev	1872	1873	1874	Stricken *c.*1900

Novogorod was the first of two unique circular coast defence ships designed to defend the base of Nicolaiev and the Dneiper estuary. She was built in sections at St. Petersburg and transported to Nicolaiev where she was assembled. The hull was surrounded with wood/copper sheathing for extra protection. She was refitted at some point in her career when the two outer propellers and their engines were removed, reducing IHP to 2,000 and with a consequent reduction in speed to 5.5 kts.

Displacement:	2,491 tons
Dimensions:	101 ft diameter × 13 ft 6 in draft (30.76 m × 4.11 m)
Machinery:	reciprocating (HC); 6 shafts; 8 cylindrical boilers; IHP 3,000; 6/7 kts
Bunkers:	160 tons coal
Protection:	belt 7/9 in (178/228 mm) barbette 9 in (228 mm)
Armament:	two (1×2) 11 in/20 cal (280 mm) two 3.4 in (80 mm) two 2½ pdr spar torpedoes
Complement:	149

VICE-ADMIRAL POPOV COAST DEFENCE SHIP

NAME	BUILDER	LAID DOWN	LAUNCHED	COMPLETED	FATE
Vice-Admiral Popov (ex-*Kiev*)	Nicolaiev	1874	1875	1877	Stricken *c*.1900

Vice-Admiral Popov was a much larger version of the previous ship, with armour protection considerably increased in thickness. The main belt and armour around the barbette was as in *Novgorod*, but strengthened with the addition of a belt of wood 4in thick and a further outer belt of 7in-thick wrought iron plates. The main armament was carried on a hydraulically powered disappearing mounting. As with *Novgorod*, the two outer propellers and associated engines were removed reducing IHP to 3,066 and speed to 6kts. Two of the 3.4in were also removed.

Displacement:	3,550 tons
Dimensions:	120ft diameter × 13ft 6in draft (36.55m × 4.11m)
Machinery:	reciprocating (HC); 6 shafts; 8 cylindrical boilers; IHP *c*.4,500; 8kts
Bunkers:	170 tons coal
Armament:	two (1×2) 12in/20cal (305mm) eight 3.4in (80mm) two 1pdr QF (37mm) spar torpedoes
Complement:	203

Left: *Novgorod* as completed. (P. A. Vicary)

Above: *Vice-Admiral Popov*. Note small torpedo-boats in foreground. (Marius Bar)

Below: *Vice-Admiral Popov* under construction. (P. A. Vicary)

GUNBOATS

ALMAZ Class GUNBOATS

These wooden-hulled barque-rigged vessels were specifically designed for long-range operations showing the flag overseas where Russia lacked a presence. They were later re-armed with three 6in/23cal and four 4.2in/20cal guns.

NAME	BUILDER	LAID DOWN	LAUNCHED	COMPLETED	FATE
Almaz	?Mitchell	1860	1861	Nov 1862	Stricken 1884
Izumrud	?New Admiralty	1861	Sept 1862	1863	Stricken *c.*1887
Jemtchug	?Mitchell	1860	Oct 1861	Nov 1862	Stricken *c.*1887
Yakhont	?Galernii Island	1861	Oct 1862	1863	Stricken *c.*1880

Displacement: 1,530 tons
Dimensions: 240ft (wl) × 30ft 9in × 17ft 2in (73.1m × 9.36m × 5.23m)
Machinery: reciprocating (HDA?); 1 shaft; ? rectangular boilers; IHP 1,250/1,450; 11kts
Bunkers: ?
Armament: seven guns
Complement: 169

OPYT GUNBOAT

The small iron-hulled *Opyt* was re-armed with a single 11in/20cal gun and two 3.4in/20cal guns. The 3.4in guns were themselves later replaced by 2½pdrs and the 11in was removed. She ended her career as a torpedo school tender.

NAME	BUILDER	LAID DOWN	LAUNCHED	COMPLETED	FATE
Opyt	Carr & Macpherson	1861	Oct 1861	1862	Stricken 1906

Displacement: 270 tons
Dimensions: 123ft 7in × 22ft 3in × 6ft (37.64m × 6.78m × 1.83m)
Machinery: reciprocating (HP); 2 shafts; 1 boiler; 9kts
Bunkers: ?
Armament: three smooth-bore guns
Complement: 43

SOBOL Class GUNBOATS

These were wooden-hulled barque-rigged ships which resembled gunboats built before 1860. They were re-armed with two 6in/23cal guns which replaced the 64pdr guns in positions forward and aft on swivel mountings. Four 3.4in/20cal guns replaced the 9pdr weapons.

NAME	BUILDER	LAID DOWN	LAUNCHED	COMPLETED	FATE
Gornostai	Berneborg	Sept 1862	May 1863	1864	Harbour service 1888
Sobol	Berneborg	Sept 1862	May 1863	1867	Harbour service 1888

Displacement: 455 tons
Dimensions: 148ft 9in × 22ft 11in × 8ft 4in (45.3m × 6.98m × 2.54m)
Machinery: NHP 80
Bunkers: ?
Armament: two 64pdr SB, four 9pdr SB
Complement: 90

PISHTCHAL Class GUNBOATS

These two iron-hulled ships were built for service in the Caspian Sea. Being near to sources of oil, this was burnt in a residual form in the engines. They were re-engined in 1872.

NAME	BUILDER	LAID DOWN	LAUNCHED	COMPLETED	FATE
Pishtchal	Watkins	?	1866	?	Stricken *c.*1898
Syekira	Watkins	?	1866	?	Stricken *c.*1898

Displacement: 328 tons
Dimensions: 121ft 3in × 25ft 2in × 7ft 2in (36.93m × 7.65m × 2.18m)
Machinery: IHP 120/170
Bunkers: ?
Armament: one 6in/23cal (152mm), two 3.4in/20cal (85mm)
Complement: ?

ERSH GUNBOAT

The composite-hulled *Ersh* carried a single heavy 11 in gun mounted on a pivot on a downward sloping platform. The gun had a very limited arc of fire and was trained using a steam capstan. It proved so cumbersome to handle and inefficient that it was eventually removed. At some later date the ship received four 4 pdr QF guns.

NAME	BUILDER	LAID DOWN	LAUNCHED	COMPLETED	FATE
Ersh	New Admiralty	20 Oct 1873	17 Aug 1874	1875	Stricken 1906

Displacement: 321 tons
Dimensions: 91 ft (wl) × 28 ft 6 in × 6 ft 8 in (29.54 m × 8.53 m × 2.23 m)
Machinery: reciprocating (HDA); 2 shafts; 1 cylindrical boiler; IHP 240; 8 kts
Bunkers: ?
Armament: one 11 in/20 cal (279 mm)
Complement: 44

KREISER Class GUNBOATS

These barque-rigged ships were constructed using a variety of materials. The major part of the hull was of iron sheathed in wood. However, *Nayezdnik*, *Opritchnik* and *Plastun* had composite hulls, while *Vyestnik* incorporated a limited amount of steel in her construction. Apart from these differences, there were many other relatively minor differences, largely incorporated at the shipyards' instigation during construction.

The armament was sited on the upper deck where it could be trained on either broadside. Later *Djigit* and *Kreiser* had their old 6 in/23 cal replaced by more modern 6 in/28 cal weapons. *Nayezdnik* and *Stryelok* received one of the new 6 in guns in place of an older one, while *Razboinik* had all her old 6 in removed and just two of the new model 6 in fitted.

Displacement: 1,653 tons
Dimensions: 207 ft 6 in (wl) × 33 ft × 16 ft 8 in (63.2 m × 10.05 m × 5.08 m)
Machinery: reciprocating (HC); 1 shaft; cylindrical boilers; IHP 1,200/1,780; 11.4/13.5 kts
Bunkers: ?
Armament: three 6 in/23 cal (152mm)
four 4.2 in/20 cal (105 mm)
four to six 1 pdr QF (37 mm)
one (*Djigit* none, *Nayezdnik* two) (above water) 15 in TT
Complement: 185

Above: *Razboinik*. (Author's collection)

NAME	BUILDER	LAID DOWN	LAUNCHED	COMPLETED	FATE
Djigit	Galernii Island	1874	1876	1877	Scuttled Port Arthur 2 Jan 1905
Kreiser	Galernii Island	1873	1875	1876	Stricken 1908
Nayezdnik	Galernii Island	1876	1878	1879	Stricken 1902
Opritchnik	Baltic Works	1879	1880	1881	Hulked 1898
Plastun	Baltic Works	1877	1879	1880	Stricken 1906
Razboinik	Nevski	1877	1878	1880	Scuttled Port Arthur 2 Jan 1905
Stryelok	Baltic Works	1878	1879	1880	Stricken 1906
Vyestnik	Nevski	1878	1880	1881	Stricken 1905

Left: Gunboat *Vyestnik* differed from her sister ships in being built partly of steel. (Author's collection)

NERPA GUNBOAT

The wooden-hulled *Nerpa* was transferred to the Far East on completion.

NAME	BUILDER	LAID DOWN	LAUNCHED	COMPLETED	FATE
Nerpa	Nicolaiev	1876	1877	1877–8	Harbour service 1888

Displacement: 380 tons
Dimensions: 124 ft 8 in × 24 ft 6 in × 8 ft (37.97 m × 7.46 m × 2.44 m)
Machinery: NHP 60
Armament: one 6 in/23 cal (152 mm), two 4.2 in/20 cal (105 mm), two 3.4 in/20 cal (85 mm)
Complement: 90

BURUN Class GUNBOATS

Similar to *Ersh*, but with increased length and greater displacement. Later the 3.4in were replaced by 2½pdr guns and *Burun*, *Dojd* and *Tutcha* had a single 3pdr and two 1pdr QF added. Light armament varied between individual ships.

Displacement:	383/400 tons
Dimensions:	119ft 4in (wl) × 29ft × 8ft (*Burun, Burya, Groza, Tutcha*) (36.35m × 8.83m × 2.44m) 110ft (wl) × 35ft 5in × 8ft 6in (*Dojd, Grad, Snyeg*) (33.5m × 10.79m × 2.59m) 110ft (wl) × 38ft × 7ft (*Vikhr*) (33.5m × 11.57m × 2.13m)

NAME	BUILDER	LAID DOWN	LAUNCHED	COMPLETED	FATE
Burya	New Admiralty	4 Feb 1879	17 July 1880	1881	Stricken 1906
Burun	New Admiralty	28 June 1878	24 Sept 1879	1880	Stricken 1907
Dojd	Galernii Island	30 Sept 1878	21 Oct 1879	1880	Stricken 1907
Grad	Crichton	1879	1881	1881	Stricken 1904
Groza	New Admiralty	4 Feb 1879	17 July 1880	1881	Stricken 1907
Snyeg	Crichton	1879	1881	1881	Stricken 1902
Tutcha	New Admiralty	28 June 1878	24 Sept 1879	1880	Stricken 1906
Vikhr	New Admiralty	9 Oct 1878	6 Nov 1879	1880	Stricken 1907

Machinery:	reciprocating (IDA/HDA); 2 shafts; 1/2 boilers; IHP 250 (*Dojd, Grad, Snyeg, Vikhr* 440); 8/9kts
Bunkers:	?
Armament:	one 11in/20cal (*Burya* two 11in/22cal) (279mm) two 3.4in/20cal (85mm)
Complement:	18

SIVUTCH Class GUNBOATS

These ships were designed for operations in shallow water areas, having a flat bottom and shallow draught. The 9in gun was mounted right forward with a limited training arc of only 36 degrees. The 6in was sited right aft with a training arc of 270 degrees. The ships were originally completed with a brig-rig, but this was later altered and three masts were fitted.

Displacement:	1,134 (*Bobr* 1,187) tons
Dimensions:	187ft 6in (wl) × 35ft × 9ft 6in (57.11m × 10.66m × 2.89m)
Machinery:	reciprocating (HC); 2 shafts; 6 cylindrical boilers; IHP 1,130; 11.5kts
Bunkers:	180 (*Bobr* 200) tons coal
Armament:	one 9in/30cal (228mm) one 6in/28cal (152mm) six 4.2in/20cal (105mm) four 1pdr QF (37mm)
Complement:	170

NAME	BUILDER	LAID DOWN	LAUNCHED	COMPLETED	FATE
Bobr	Crichton	1883	1885	1885	Sunk Port Arthur 26 Dec 1904
Sivutch	Bergsund	1883	1884	1885	Scuttled River Liao 3 July 1904

Right: *Bobr* with brig rig. (Author's collection)

KORIETZ Class GUNBOATS

These barquentine-rigged ships of relatively shallow draught were considered poor sailers, possibly because they carried too great a weight of canvas for their size. The ram bow was much more pronounced in *Korietz* than in her sister ship. The two 8in guns were mounted behind 0.75in-thick shields on sponsons abreast the foremast; the 6in were mounted aft. The 4.2in were carried on broadside mountings amidships, those in *Korietz* being in sponsons.

Displacement:	1,270 (*Mandjur* 1,437) tons
Dimensions:	206ft (wl) × 35ft × 12ft 4in (62.74m × 10.66m × 3.76m)
Machinery:	reciprocating (HC); 2 shafts; 6 cylindrical boilers; IHP 1,560/1,960; 13.3kts
Bunkers:	?
Armament:	two 8in/35cal (203mm) one 6in/35cal (152mm) four 4.2in/20cal (105mm) two 3pdr QF (47mm) four 1pdr QF (37mm) one 15in TT (381mm)
Complement:	179

NAME	BUILDER	LAID DOWN	LAUNCHED	COMPLETED	FATE
Korietz	Bergsund	1885	Aug 1886	1887	Scuttled Chemulpo 9 Feb 1904
Mandjur	Burmeister & Wain	1886	Dec 1886	1888	Scrapped 1923

Right: *Korietz* 1901. (P. A. Vicary)

Below: *Mandjur* following refit and reduction of sailing rig. Note that the ram bow is not so pronounced as in *Korietz*. (P. A. Vicary)

LEITENANT ILIN TORPEDO GUNBOAT

NAME	BUILDER	LAID DOWN	LAUNCHED	COMPLETED	FATE
Leitenant Ilin	Baltic Works	Dec 1885	24 July 1886	1887	Scrapped *c.*1910

This was a powerful-looking, two-funnelled ship with a very pronounced bow ram, and two masts, the foremast being sited well forward. Five of the torpedo tubes were in fixed positions: two facing ahead, one on each bow, and one in the stern. The remaining two tubes were on swivel mounts on each broadside. Spare torpedoes were carried in racks on the lower deck and moved to the torpedo tubes on railways tracks running the whole length of the ship to loading positions at the rear of the tubes. Armament was later changed; two of the 3 pdr and all the 3 pdr QF guns being removed, four 1 pdr guns being added, and the two trainable torpedo tubes removed.

Displacement: 714 tons
Dimensions: 237 ft 3 in (oa) × 24 ft 4 in × 10 ft 7 in (72.26 m × 7.41 m × 3.22 m)
Machinery: reciprocating (VTE); 2 shafts; 4 locomotive boilers; IHP 3,500; 20.8 kts
Bunkers: 97 tons coal
Protection: deck 0.5/0.75 in (13/19 mm)
Armament: seven 3 pdr (47 mm)
six 3 pdr QF (47 mm)
six 1 pdr QF (37 mm)
seven 15 in TT (16 torpedoes) (381 mm)
Complement: 132

Right: *Leitenant Ilin* as originally armed. (P. A. Vicary)

KAPITAN SAKEN TORPEDO GUNBOAT

NAME	BUILDER	LAID DOWN	LAUNCHED	COMPLETED	FATE
Kapitan Saken	Nicolaiev	1886	12 May 1889	1890	Stricken 1909

This design was almost identical with that of the previous torpedo gunboat, but carrying fewer guns. Torpedo tubes were disposed as in the previous ship. She was reboilered in 1898 with six Belleville boilers. Later four of the torpedo tubes were removed.

Displacement: 742 tons
Dimensions: 235 ft (oa) × 24 ft 4 in × 10 ft 3 in (71.57 m × 7.41 m × 3.12 m)
Machinery: reciprocating (VTE); 2 shafts; 6 locomotive boilers; IHP 3,000; 18.3 kts
Bunkers: 97 tons coal
Armament: six 3 pdr (47 mm)
four 1 pdr QF (37 mm)
seven 15 in TT (19 torpedoes) (381 mm)
Complement: 125

KUBANETZ Class GUNBOATS

Built for operations in the Black Sea, these ships were considered to have been poorly designed and those ships built at Nicolaiev are said to have suffered from poor workmanship. The design was very similar to that of *Korietz*, with identical siting of armament. However, only the guns of the ships built at Nicolaiev were carried behind shields. By the start of the First World War surviving units had been re-armed with two 6in/45cal, a single 4.7in/45cal and two 3in guns. Machinery had also been updated, the cylindrical boilers having been replaced by four Belleville boilers.

On 29 October 1914 *Donetz* was torpedoed in Odessa harbour by the Turkish destroyer *Gairet*. She was subsequently salvaged and repaired and put back into service. After the Revolution *Teretz* (renamed *Znamya Sozialisma*) was used as a school ship. *Kubanetz* was converted to an oiler for service during the Second World War and renamed *Krasni Kuban*.

NAME	BUILDER	LAID DOWN	LAUNCHED	COMPLETED	FATE
Chernomoretz	Nicolaiev	1886	29 Aug 1887	1890	Stricken 1911
Donetz	Nicolaiev	1886	30 Nov 1887	1890	Sunk May 1919
Kubanetz	Russian Steam Navigation Co	1886	9 April 1887	1888	Sunk 1941–5
Teretz	Russian Steam Navigation Co	1886	29 Aug 1887	1889	Scrapped *c.*1941
Uraletz	Russian Steam Navigation Co	1886	8 Dec 1887	1889	Lost 1 Dec 1913
Zaporozhetz	Nicolaiev	1886	4 June 1887	1890	Stricken 1911

Displacement:	1,224/1,393 tons
Dimensions:	220ft 6in (oa) × 35ft × 12ft 8in (67.16m × 10.66m × 3.86m)
Machinery:	reciprocating (HC); 2 shafts; 6 cylindrical boilers; IHP 1,500; 12/14kts
Bunkers:	250 tons coal
Armament:	two 8in/35cal (203mm) one 6in/35cal (152mm) six 3pdr QF (47mm) two 15in TT (381mm)
Complement:	180

GROZYASHCHI Class GUNBOATS

Small armoured gunboats in which the single 9 in was sited forward in a protected mounting beneath the bridge, allowing for a training arc of 100 degrees. The 6 in gun was mounted aft in a shield. The ships were fitted with a steel armoured belt which extended from the stern to within about 30 ft of the bow. The belt extended above the waterline for 2 ft and below for 3 ft. In the area of the 9 in gun the armoured deck increased in thickness to 1½ in. *Grozyashchi* was re-armed during the First World War, the 9 in gun being removed and a 6 in/45 cal gun being sited forward. Three other 6 in/45 cal guns were sited on the centreline aft and two 3 in AA added.

NAME	BUILDER	LAID DOWN	LAUNCHED	COMPLETED	FATE
Gremyashchi	New Admiralty	1890	May 1892	1893	Mined Port Arthur 18 Aug 1904
Grozyashchi	New Admiralty	1889	31 May 1890	1891	Scrapped 1922
Otvajni	Baltic Works	1890	May 1892	1894	Scuttled Port Arthur 2 Jan 1905

Displacement: 1,627 (*Gremyashchi* 1,700, *Otvajni* 1,854) tons

Dimensions: 237 ft 1 in (oa) × 41 ft 7 in × 12 ft 2 in (72.21 m × 12.66 m × 3.71 m)

Machinery: reciprocating (VTE); 2 shafts; 6 Belleville boilers; IHP 2,050/2,500; 13/14 kts

Bunkers: 200 tons coal

Protection: main belt 2½/5 in closed in by 3½ in bulkheads (63/127 mm 89 mm) deck 1/1½ in (25/38 mm) CT 1 in (25 mm)

Armament: one 9 in/35 cal (228 mm) one 6 in/35 cal (152 mm) four to six 3 pdr (47 mm) four 1 pdr QF (37 mm) two 15 in TT (381 mm) 20 mines

Complement: 178/188

Right: *Grozyashchi* as completed. (Author's collection)

Right: The gunboat *Gremyashchi* seen at Algiers shortly after completion. (US Naval Historical Center)

Left: Gunboat *Teretz* with 8 in gun in sponson abreast the bridge. (Marius Bar)

KAZARSKI Class TORPEDO GUNBOATS

Designed by Schichau, these ships were completed with merchant lines carrying a single funnel and two masts. One torpedo tube was mounted in a fixed position in the bows and one in a trainable launcher on the deck.

Griden and *Kazarski* both served in the Black Sea. *Gaidamak* and *Vsadnik* both served with the First Pacific Squadron and were captured by the Japanese when they overran Port Arthur. They were recommissioned into the Japanese Navy as *Shikinami* and *Makikumo* respectively. The three German-built boats were used as dispatch vessels during the First World War and armed with two or three 3 in guns, the bow torpedo tube being removed. *Posadnik* and *Voevoda* were taken over by Finland at the end of the war in 1918 and renamed *Matti Kurki* and *Klas Horn*. *Kazarski* was disarmed after the Revolution.

NAME	BUILDER	LAID DOWN	LAUNCHED	COMPLETED	FATE
Gaidamak	Crichton	1892	Sept 1893	1894	Scrapped 1914
Griden	Nicolaiev	1892	12 Nov 1893	1895	Stricken 1907
Kazarski	Schichau	1889	1889	1890	Scrapped 1927
Posadnik	Schichau	1891	13 April 1892	1892	Scrapped 1938
Voevoda	Schichau	1891	8 Dec 1892	1892	Scrapped 1938
Vsadnik	Crichton	1892	July 1883	1894	Scrapped 1914

Displacement:	394/432 tons
Dimensions:	197 ft 6 in (oa) × 24 ft 4 in × 11 ft 6 in (60.15 m × 7.41 m × 3.5 m)
Machinery:	reciprocating (VTE); 2 shafts; 2 locomotive boilers; IHP 3,500; 22.5 kts
Bunkers & Radius:	90 tons coal; 4,000 nm at 10 kts
Armament:	six 3 pdr QF (47 mm) three 1 pdr (37 mm) two 15 in TT (381 mm)
Complement:	65

Right: *Khrabri* as completed. (P. A. Vicary)

Left: Torpedo gunboat *Gaidamak.* (Marius Bar)

Right: Gunboat *Khrabri.* (US Naval Historical Center)

KHRABRI GUNBOAT

When completed *Khrabri* was considerably overweight in comparison with her designed displacement of 1,492 tons. To remedy this, and to reduce her draught, some of the armour backing was removed in 1899–1900 when she underwent a refit at Toulon. The Harvey armour protection followed the same general arrangement as that in the *Grozyashchi* class. The 8in guns were carried in sponsons abreast the foremast, while the 6in guns were all mounted behind thin shields aft. During the First World War the 8in and 6in guns were replaced by five 5.1in/55cal weapons. Apart from the 5.1in guns sited in the sponsons, another 5.1in gun was mounted on the forecastle and two on the centreline aft. For AA defence she carried two 3pdr and one 2pdr guns.

NAME	BUILDER	LAID DOWN	LAUNCHED	COMPLETED	FATE
Khrabri	New Admiralty	1894	21 Nov 1895	1896	Scrapped *c.*1962

After the Revolution she was renamed *Krasnoye Znamya* and served as a gunnery tender, being torpedoed by a Finnish MTB in the autumn of 1942. She was salvaged and repaired and finally scrapped in the early 1960s.

Displacement:	1,735 tons
Dimensions:	237ft 1in (oa) × 41ft 7in × 12ft 6in (72.21m × 12.66m × 3.81m)
Machinery:	reciprocating (VTE); 2 shafts; 8 Niclausse boilers; IHP 2,100; 14kts
Bunkers & Radius:	130 tons coal; 1,370nm at 10kts
Protection:	main belt 3½/5in closed by 3½in bulkheads (89/127mm 89mm) deck 1/1½in (25/38mm) CT 1in (25mm)
Armament:	two (2×1) 8in/45cal (203mm) one 6in/45cal (152mm) five 3pdr (47mm) four 1pdr (37mm) two 15in TT (381mm) 20 mines
Complement:	135

ABREK TORPEDO GUNBOAT

Abrek was designed as an improved *Leitenant Ilin* and proved to be a much better seaboat. Armament was improved, the 3 in guns being protected behind shields of 1 in steel. The torpedo tubes were sited one in a fixed position in the bow and one on a trainable mount aft. During the First World War she served as dispatch vessel.

Displacement: 675 tons
Dimensions: 215 ft (oa) × 25 ft 5 in × 10 ft 6 in (65.48 m × 7.74 m × 3.2 m)
Machinery: reciprocating (VTE); 2 shafts; 4 Normand/Du Temple boilers; IHP 4,500; 21.2 kts
Bunkers: 120 tons coal
Armament: two 3 in (75 mm)
four 3 pdr (47 mm)
two 15 in TT (381 mm)
Complement: 88

NAME	BUILDER	LAID DOWN	LAUNCHED	COMPLETED	FATE
Abrek	Crichton	June 1895	23 May 1896	Sept 1887	Scrapped *c.*1946

KHIVINETZ GUNBOAT

Khivinetz was distinguished by a high freeboard and silhouette, resembling an unprotected cruiser. The main armament was mounted on the forecastle and aft on the centreline, with the 3 in guns in unprotected casemates on the main deck. During the First World War she was re-armed, two extra 4.7 in being added together with two 3 pdr guns for AA defence. She was renamed *Krasnaya Zviezda* after the Revolution and relegated to the role of gunnery tender.

Displacement: 1,340 tons
Dimensions: 231 ft 2 in (oa) × 37 ft × 11 ft 4 in (70.41 m × 11.27 m × 3.45 m)
Machinery: reciprocating (VTE); 2 shafts; 8 Belleville boilers; IHP 1,400; 13.5 kts
Bunkers: 250 tons coal
Armament: two 4.7 in/45 cal (120 mm)
eight 3 in (75 mm)
Complement: 161

NAME	BUILDER	LAID DOWN	LAUNCHED	COMPLETED	FATE
Khivinetz	New Admiralty	1904	11 May 1905	1906	Scrapped *c.*1946

Left: Torpedo gunboat *Abrek.* The torpedo tubes have been removed and the vessel is operating on the Revenue Service. (Marius Bar)

Above: Gunboat *Khivinetz* as originally completed, with just a pole foremast. (Author's collection)

GILYAK Class GUNBOATS

These were a smaller version of *Khivinetz*, but with the stern cut down one deck and with military foremast and pole mainmast. They carried a reduced secondary armament, of which only the two forward 3 in guns were sited in casemates. During the First World War *Korietz* was equipped with four additional 3 in guns.

In August 1915 *Korietz* and *Sivutch* were intercepted by German forces in the Gulf of Riga. *Sivutch* was sunk by the dreadnought *Posen*, but *Korietz* managed to escape, only to run aground where she was destroyed by her crew. When Russia signed the Armistice in April 1918, *Bobr* was taken over by the Germans who renamed her *Bieber*. She was then handed over to Estonia in 1919 and renamed *Lembit*. At the Russian Armistice *Gilyak* was taken over by Finland.

NAME	BUILDER	LAID DOWN	LAUNCHED	COMPLETED	FATE
Bobr	Nevski	1905	Aug 1907	1908	German *Bieber* April 1918, Estonaian *Lembit* 1919
Gilyak	New Admiralty	1905	27 Oct 1906	1908	To Finland 1918
Korietz	Putilov	1905	May 1907	1908	Scuttled 20 Aug 1915
Sivutch	Nevski	1905	1 Aug 1907	1908	Sunk by *Posen* 19 Aug 1915

Displacement:	875 tons
Dimensions:	218 ft 2 in (oa) × 36 ft × 7 ft 11 in (66.45 m × 10.96 m × 2.41 m)
Machinery:	reciprocating (VTE); 2 shafts; 4 Belleville boilers; IHP 900; 12 kts
Bunkers:	130 tons coal
Armament:	two 4.7 in/45 cal (120 mm) four 3 in (75 mm) 40 mines
Complement:	140

Right: *Bobr* taken as prize at Hango, Finland, 3 April 1918. (Author's collection)

ARDAGAN Class GUNBOATS

These vessels were the first diesel-engined units to enter service with the Imperial Navy. The 3 in guns were later replaced by two 4 in.

Both vessels served with the Caspian Sea Flotilla where they were captured by British forces during the Revolution. They were subsequently taken over by the new Soviet Navy and served until the 1950s when they were scrapped.

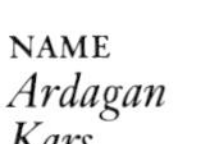

NAME	BUILDER	LAID DOWN	LAUNCHED	COMPLETED	FATE
Ardagan	Admiralty Yard	–	25 September 1909	–	Renamed *Trotski* May 1920
Kars	Admiralty Yard	–	1909	–	Renamed *Lenin* May 1920

Displacement:	623 tons
Dimensions:	200 ft × 20 ft × 8 ft (61 m × 8.5 m × 2.4 m)
Machinery:	2 diesels; 2 shafts; BHP 1,000; 14 kts
Bunkers:	30 tons oil
Armament:	two 4.7 in (120 mm) four 3 in (75 mm) four MG
Complement:	128

Right: *Kars* on the slip ready for launching. (Author's collection)

DESTROYERS

SOKOL DESTROYER

The first destroyer to be completed for the Imperial Russian Navy was the Yarrow-designed *Sokol* ordered in 1894. When completed, she was one of the fastest destroyers in the world, exceeding 30 kts on trials. The design followed the general lines of contemporary destroyers with four funnels and a single mast. To conserve weight the superstructure incorporated a certain amount of aluminium. The single 3 in gun was mounted on top of the bridge. Two of the 3 pdr guns were mounted one on each side aft of the first funnel and the third was mounted on the centreline just forward of the fourth funnel. The two single torpedo tubes were mounted on the centreline aft.

NAME	BUILDER	LAID DOWN	LAUNCHED	COMPLETED	FATE
Sokol	Yarrow	1894	22 Aug 1895	1895	Renamed *Prytki* Mar 1902. Scrapped 1922

The ship subsequently received a second 3 in gun which was mounted towards the stern and aft of the torpedo tubes. She was also equipped to carry up to ten mines on rails. She was later renamed *Prytki*, and served as a minesweeper during the First World War.

Displacement:	220 tons
Dimensions:	190 ft (oa) × 18 ft 6 in × 7 ft 6 in (57.87 m × 5.63 m × 2.28 m)
Machinery:	reciprocating (VTE); 2 shafts; 8 Yarrow boilers; IHP 3,800; 29 kts
Bunkers:	60 tons coal
Armament:	one 3 in (75 mm) three 3 pdr (47 mm) two 15 in TT (6 torpedoes) (381 mm)
Complement:	54

Right: *Sokol* just after arriving in Russia from Yarrow. (Marius Bar)

PUILKI Class DESTROYERS

Although the design of this class was almost identical with that of *Sokol*, they were not so fast, although some units have been credited with speeds approaching that of *Sokol*. Displacement in some units was slightly greater. On completion the four boats built by Crichton at Okhta (*Fazan*, *Lebed*, *Pavlin* and *Pelikan*) were sent to the Black Sea. The two units which survived in the Black Sea, *Strogi* and *Sviryepi*, were renamed *Badina* and *Leitenant Schmidt* after the Revolution. The ships were later re-armed, carrying two 3in (one atop the bridge and one aft) as well as the torpedo tubes, and in some units provision was made to carry from 10 to 12 mines.

In 1907 *Pronzitelni* and *Puilki* were transferred to the Caspian Sea. *Baklan*, *Bekas*, *Drozd*, *Dyatel*, *Gorlitza*, *Gratch*, *Kondor*, *Kulik*, *Perepel*, *Shtchegol*, *Skvoretz* and *Strij* were all sent to the Pacific in sections via the trans-Siberian railway, and assembled at Port Arthur. They all took part in the Russo-Japanese war, *Silni* being scuttled there on 2 January 1905. She was subsequently raised by the Japanese and renamed *Fumizuki*. The Japanese also captured *Ryeshitelni*, at Chefoo on 12 August 1904, and renamed her *Yamabiko*. The remaining units were all based at Vladivostock during the First World War.

NAME	BUILDER	LAID DOWN	LAUNCHED	COMPLETED	FATE
Albatros	Izhora	1898	3 June 1901	1901	Renamed *Podvizhni* 1902 To Finland 1918
Baklan	Nevski	1899	–	Assembled 1902	Renamed *Silni* 1902 Scuttled Port Arthur 2 Jan 1905
Bekas	Nevski	1899	3 Nov 1901	Assembled 1902	Renamed *Serditi* 1902 Scrapped 1922
Berkut	Izhora	1897	26 Sept 1899	1900	Renamed *Pronzitelni* 1902 Scrapped 1911
Drozd	Izhora	1899	–	Assembled 1902	Renamed *Razyashchi* 1902 Scuttled Port Arthur 2 Jan 1905
Dyatel	Izhora	1899	–	Assembled 1902	Renamed *Rastoropni* 1902 Scuttled 16 Nov 1904
Fazan	Crichton	1899	1 Oct 1901	1902	Renamed *Stremitelni* 1902 Scuttled 18 June 1918
Filin	Nevski	1898	23 June 1900	1901	Renamed *Retivi* 1902 Scrapped 1922
Gagara	Nevski	1898	3 July 1899	1901	Renamed *Prozorlivi* 1902 To Finland 1918
Gorlitza	Nevski	1899	10 Feb 1903	Assembled 1902	Renamed *Smyeli* 1902 Scrapped 1922
Gratch	Nevski	1899	–	Assembled 1902	Renamed *Torozhevoi* 1902 Scuttled Port Arthur 2 Jan 1905
Kondor	Izhora	1897	–	Assembled 1902	Renamed *Ryeshitelni* 1902 Captured Chefoo 12 Aug 1904
Korshun	Crichton	1896	May 1898	1898	Renamed *Poslushni* 1902 To Finland 1918

Left: *Stroini*. Note cowl on fore funnel, and bridge aft. (Author's collection)

Right: *Ryeshitelni*. Note plain fore funnel and no bridge aft. (Author's collection)

On completion *Albatros*, *Filin*, *Gagara*, *Korshun*, *Nyrok*, *Sova*, *Voron* and *Yastreb* were all assigned to the Baltic and served as minesweepers there during the First World War. As renamed, *Podvizhni*, *Poslushni*, *Prozorlivi*, *Ryani* and *Ryezvi* were all taken over by Finland in 1918 and renamed *S1–S5*.

Displacement:	220–240 tons
Dimensions:	190 ft (oa) × 18 ft 6 in × 7 ft 6 in (57.87 m × 5.63 m × 2.28 m)
Machinery:	reciprocating (VTE); 2 shafts; 4 Yarrow boilers (*Berkut*, *Kondor*, *Korshun*, *Kretchet*, *Nyrok*, *Yastreb* and possibly *Albatros* 8 smaller boilers); IHP 3,800; 27.5 kts
Bunkers:	60 tons coal
Armament:	One 3 in (75 mm) three 3 pdr (47 mm) two 15 in TT (381 mm)
Complement:	51–58

NAME	BUILDER	LAID DOWN	LAUNCHED	COMPLETED	FATE
Kretchet	Crichton	1896	28 May 1898	1898	Renamed *Puilki* 1902 Scrapped 1911
Kulik	Nevski	1900	–	Assembled 1903	Renamed *Steregushchi* 1902 Sunk 10 Mar 1904
Lebed	Crichton	1899	2 Aug 1901	1902	Renamed *Strogi* 1902 Stricken 1929
Nyrok	Izhora	1897	12 Dec 1898	1900	Renamed *Porazhayushchi* 1902 Scrapped 1922
Pavlin	Crichton	1899	7 Sept 1901	1902	Renamed *Sviryepi* 1902 Stricken 1927
Pelikan	Crichton	1899	2 Aug 1901	1902	Renamed *Smyetlivi* 1902 Scuttled 18 June 1918
Perepel	Nevski	1900	17 May 1903	Assembled 1903	Renamed *Skori* 1902 Scrapped 1922
Shtchegol	Nevski	1900	21 Nov 1903	Assembled 1903	Renamed *Statni* 1902 Scrapped 1922
Skvoretz	Nevski	1900	–	Assembled 1903	Renamed *Strashni* 1902 Sunk 13 April 1904
Sova	Nevski	1898	6 July 1900	1901	Renamed *Ryani* 1902 To Finland 1918
Strij	Nevski	1900	–	Assembled 1903	Renamed *Stroini* 1902 Sunk 13 Nov 1904
Voron	Nevski	1898	31 Aug 1899	1901	Renamed *Ryezvi* 1902 To Finland 1918
Yastreb	Izhora	1897	1 Oct 1898	1900	Renamed *Prochni* 1902 Scrapped 1922

Left: *Serditi* lying disarmed at Vladivostock in 1916. See data on previous page. (Author's collection)

SOM DESTROYER

Typical Laird four-funnelled destroyer design with main gun mounted as in previous classes, i.e., on top of the bridge. The two single torpedo tubes were mounted aft of the second and fourth funnel.

She was torpedoed by a Japanese torpedo-boat on 24 July 1904 and severely damaged, but managed to reach the safety of Port Arthur where she was subsequently scuttled at the end of the siege.

Displacement: 350 tons

NAME	BUILDER	LAID DOWN	LAUNCHED	COMPLETED	FATE
Som	Laird	1898	1899	1900	Renamed *Boevoi* 1902 Scuttled Port Arthur 2 Jan 1905

Dimensions: 213 ft (wl) × 21 ft 6 in × 9 ft 7 in (64.87 m × 6.55 m × 2.92 m)
Machinery: reciprocating (VTE); 2 shafts; 4 Laird boilers; IHP 6,000; 27.5 kts
Bunkers: 80 tons coal
Armament: one 3 in (75 mm) five 3 pdr (47 mm) two 15 in TT (381 mm)
Complement: 62

BEZSTRASHNI Class DESTROYERS

These four destroyers differed from the earlier designs in having only two, widely spaced funnels. The torpedo tubes were mounted on the centreline and sited one aft of the second funnel and two between the funnels. The 3 pdr guns were removed in 1912 and a second 3 in added aft. *Bezstrashni*, *Bezposhtchadni* and *Bezshumni* were all interned at Kiao Chau after the abortive sortie of 10 August 1904. They were handed back to Russia at the end of the Russo-Japanese War and based at Vladivostock until 1917 when they made the long journey back to join the embryo White Sea Fleet.

NAME	BUILDER	LAID DOWN	LAUNCHED	COMPLETED	FATE
Delfin	Schichau	1898	12 Aug 1899	1900	Renamed *Bezstrashni* 1902. Scrapped 1922
Kasatka	Schichau	1898	17 Mar 1900	1900	Renamed *Bezshumni* 1902. Scrapped 1922
Kit	Schichau	1898	1900	1900	Renamed *Bditelni* 1902. Scuttled Port Arthur 2 Jan 1905
Skat	Schichau	1898	25 Oct 1899	1900	Renamed *Bezposhtchadni* 1902. Scrapped 1923

Displacement: 346 tons
Dimensions: 202 ft 7 in (oa) × 22 ft × 9 ft 6 in (61.7 m × 6.7 m × 2.89 m)
Machinery: reciprocating (VTE); 2 shafts; 4 Schichau boilers; IHP 6,900; 27 kts
Bunkers: 80 tons coal
Armament: one 3 in (75 mm) five 3 pdr (47 mm) three 15 in TT (6 torpedoes) (381 mm)
Complement: 64

LEITENANT BURAKOV DESTROYER

This destroyer was originally built for the Chinese Navy as *Hai Hoha*. She was captured during the Boxer Rebellion by the British destroyers *Fame* and *Whiting* in the attack on the Taku Forts. She was handed over to Russia and renamed. Although smaller than other Russian destroyers, she was easily the most powerful and certainly the fastest unit in the Russian fleet during the Russo-Japanese War. She was sunk to the east of Port Arthur by two small launches from the battleships *Mikasa* and *Fuji*.

NAME	BUILDER	LAID DOWN	LAUNCHED	COMPLETED	FATE
Leitenant Burakov (ex-*Hai Hoha*)	Schichau	1898	–	–	Sunk 24 July 1904

Displacement: 280 tons
Dimensions: 193 ft 7 in (oa) × 21 ft × 8 ft 6 in (58.96 m × 6.39 m × 2.59 m)
Machinery: reciprocating (VTE); 2 shafts; 4 Thornycroft boilers; IHP 6,000; 33.6 kts
Bunkers: 67 tons coal
Armament: six 3 pdr (47 mm) two 14 in TT (355 mm)
Complement: 56

VNIMATELNI Class DESTROYERS

For her next class of destroyers Russia turned to France. These units resembled the French *Durandal* class, being distinguished by four funnels mounted in groups of two. The siting of the main gun remained as in previous designs, and the torpedo tubes were mounted one each on the centreline behind each group of funnels. As in previous ships gun armament was subsequently modified to just two 3 in guns.

Following the abortive sortie of 10 August 1904 during the Russo-Japanese War, *Grozovoi* escaped to Shanghai where she was interned. Likewise *Vlastni* fled from Port Arthur just before the siege ended and was interned at Chefoo. Both vessels were handed back to Russia and were based at Vladivostock during the First World War before being transferred to the embryo White Sea Fleet.

NAME	BUILDER	LAID DOWN	LAUNCHED	COMPLETED	FATE
Forel	Normand	1898	1900	1901	Renamed *Vnimatelni* 1902. Wrecked 26 May 1904
Kefal	F & C	1899	28 Nov 1901	1902	Renamed *Vlastni* 1902. Scrapped 1921
Losos	F & C	1899	11 Mar 1902	1902	Renamed *Grozovoi* 1902. Scrapped 1921
Osetr	F & C	1898	1900	1902	Renamed *Vnushitelni* 1902. Sunk 25 Feb 1904
Sterlyad	Normand	1898	1901	1902	Renamed *Vuinoslivi* 1902. Mined 24 Aug 1904

They were subsequently captured by Britain in 1918.

Displacement:	312 tons
Dimensions:	185 ft 8 in (oa) × 19 ft 4 in × 9 ft 11 in (56.55 m × 5.89 m × 3.02 m)
Machinery:	reciprocating (VTE); 2 shafts; 4 Normand boilers; IHP 5,200; 26.4 kts
Bunkers:	60–70 tons coal
Armament:	one 3 in (75 mm) five 3 pdr (47 mm) two 15 in TT (381 mm)
Complement:	57/59

Below: *Vnushitelni.* She is seen carrying her original name *Osetr.* Note the torpedo tubes amidships. (Musée de la Marine)

BOIKI Class DESTROYERS

These four-funnelled destroyers were an enlarged version of *Sokol*. The torpedo tubes were mounted two on the centreline just abaft the fourth funnel, and the third right aft at the stern. As with other destroyers, the 3pdr guns were later removed before the First World War and a second 3in added. In addition the stern torpedo tube was removed and some sources have credited a number of units as having been re-armed with 18in torpedo tubes.

Byedovoi, with the severely injured Admiral Rozhdestvensky on board, was captured by the Japanese at Tsushima. She was recommissioned into the Japanese Navy as *Satsuki*. During the First World War *Gromyaschi* and *Vidni* served with the Baltic Fleet, while *Zhivoi* was operational in the Black Sea, subsequently being lost in the Sea of Azov when operating with the Wrangel Fleet.

NAME	BUILDER	LAID DOWN	LAUNCHED	COMPLETED	FATE
Akula	Nevski	1900	24 Aug 1901	1902	Renamed *Boiki* 1902 Stricken 1923
Beluga	Belgian Works	1902	1903	1903	Renamed *Zaveytni* 1902 Scuttled 1 May 1918
Bychok	Nevski	1900	1901	1902	Renamed *Buini* 1902 Scuttled 28 May 1905
Gromki	Nevski	1903	1904	1904	Sunk 28 May 1905
Gromyaschi	Nevski	1903	1904	1905	Scrapped 1922
Grozny	Nevski	1903	19 July 1904	1904	Scrapped 1923
Karp	Belgian Works	1902	1903	1903	Renamed *Zavidni* 1902 Scrapped 1923
Keta	Nevski	1900	1902	1903	Renamed *Byedovoi* 1902. Captured by Japanese 28 May 1905
Makrel	Nevski	1900	1901	1902	Renamed *Burni* 1902 Driven ashore 11 Aug 1904
Nalim	Nevski	1900	12 Oct 1901	1902	Renamed *Bravi* 1902 Stricken 1931?

Bravi, *Zavidni* and *Grozni* were renamed after the Revolution, becoming *Anisimov*, *Balybank* and *Marti* respectively.

Displacement:	350 tons
Dimensions:	210 ft (oa) × 21 ft × 8 ft 6 in (63.96 m × 6.39 m × 2.59 m)
Machinery:	reciprocating (VTE); 2 shafts; 4 Yarrow boilers (*Beluga*, *Karp*, *Zadorni*, *Zorki*, *Zvonki* – Normand); IHP 5,700; 26 kts
Bunkers:	80 tons
Armament:	one 3 in (75 mm) five 3 pdr (47 mm) three 15 in TT (6 torpedoes) (381 mm) 12/18 mines
Complement:	62/69

NAME	BUILDER	LAID DOWN	LAUNCHED	COMPLETED	FATE
Okun	Nevski	1900	1901	1902	Renamed *Blestyashtchi* 1902 Scuttled 28 May 1905
Paltus	Nevski	1900	1902	1903	Renamed *Bezuprechni* 1902 Sunk 28 May 1905
Peksar	Nevski	1900	17 May 1902	1902	Renamed *Bodri* 1902 Scrapped 1922
Plotva	Nevski	1900	1901	1902	Renamed *Buistri* 1902 Driven ashore 28 May 1905
Sig	Nevski	1900	1905	1905	Renamed *Vidni* 1902 Scrapped 1922
Zadorni	Belgian Works	1903	Nov 1904	1905	Renamed *Leitenant Pushkin* 8 April 1907. Sunk 9 Mar 1916
Zharki	Nicolaiev	1902	1904	1906	To Bizerta 1920
Zhivoi	Nicolaiev	1902	10 April 1904	1905	Sunk 16 Nov 1920
Zhivuchi	Nicolaiev	1902	1904	1906	Sunk 25 April 1916
Zhutki	Nicolaiev	1902	1904	1906	Scrapped 1922
Zorki	Belgian Works	1903	Oct 1904	1905	To Bizerta 1920
Zvonki	Belgian Works	1903	Nov 1905	1905	To Bizerta 1920

Left: *Biedovy.* This destroyer rescued Admiral Rozhestvenski at the Battle of Tsushima. She was captured by the Japanese. (Author's collection)

Right: *Zaveytni.* (Author's collection)

TVERDI Class DESTROYERS

This class was an almost identical repeat of the *Puilki* class, with 18 in torpedo tubes replacing the 15 in tubes of the previous designs. The ships were sent to Vladivostock in sections where they were assembled. They were modernized in 1910–11 when the 3 pdr guns were removed and replaced by an extra 3 in gun. After the Revolution *Tochni* and *Tverdi* were renamed *Potapenko* and *Lazo* respectively.

NAME	BUILDER	LAID DOWN	LAUNCHED	COMPLETED	FATE
Ing. Mech. Anastasov	Crichton	1905	19 Aug 1907	Assembled 1908	Scrapped 1922
Leitenant Malyeev	Crichton	1905	18 Sept 1907	Assembled 1908	Scrapped 1922
Tochni	Nevski	1904	10 Dec 1906	Assembled 1906	Renamed *Potapenko* Stricken 1927
Trevozhni	Nevski	1904	June 1906	Assembled 1906	Scrapped 1923
Tverdi	Nevski	1904	2 Oct 1906	Assembled 1906	Renamed *Lazo* 1922 Stricken 1927

Displacement: 240 tons
Dimensions: 190 ft (oa) × 18 ft 6 in × 7 ft 6 in (57.87 m × 5.63 m × 2.28 m)
Machinery: reciprocating (VTE); 2 shafts; 4 Yarrow boilers; IHP 3,800; 26 kts
Bunkers: 60 tons coal
Armament: one 3 in (75 mm); three 3 pdr (47 mm); two 18 in TT (457 mm)
Complement: 60

LOVKI Class DESTROYERS

These destroyers were built to a French design by Normand, and were similar in design to the previous French-built ships of the *Vnimatelni* class, but with slightly increased displacement. They carried a more powerful armament than the previous ships, the 3 pdr guns having been dispsensed with in favour of 3 in guns, and 18 in torpedo tubes being the standard fit. The two 3 in guns were mounted one each on top of the bridge and after superstructure; the two single torpedo tubes were mounted one each abaft each of the funnels. Provision was also made later for the carriage of ten mines. The destroyers were operational with the Baltic Fleet during the First World War, *Ispolnitelni* being sunk after one of her own mines exploded.

Displacement:	335 tons
Dimensions:	185 ft 8 in (oa) × 21 ft × 11 ft 2 in (56.55 m × 6.39 m × 3.4 m)
Machinery:	reciprocating (VTE); 2 shafts; 4 Normand boilers; IHP 5,700; 27 kts
Bunkers:	100/110 tons coal
Armament:	two 3 in (75 mm) two 18 in TT (457 mm)
Complement:	67

Top left: *Tverdi* lying disarmed at Vladivostock in 1916. (Author's collection)

Right: *Kryepki.* (Author's collection)

Left: *Kryepki* formed part of the 4th T-Boat Division at the start of the First World War. (Author's collection)

NAME	BUILDER	LAID DOWN	LAUNCHED	COMPLETED	FATE
Iskusni	La Seyne	1904	11 July 1905	1906	Scrapped 1922
Ispolnitelni	La Seyne	1904	30 July 1905	1906	Mined 12 Dec 1914
Kryepki	La Seyne	1904	24 Aug 1905	1906	Scrapped 1925
Legki	La Seyne	1904	27 Sept 1905	1906	Scrapped 1922
Leitenant Burakov	F & C	1904	19 June 1905	1906	Mined 12 Aug 1917
Letuchi	Normand	1904	16 Nov 1905	1906	Capsized 12 Dec 1914
Likhoi	Normand	1904	13 Dec 1905	1906	Scrapped 1922
Lovki	Normand	1904	15 Oct 1905	1906	Scrapped 1922
Molodetzki	F & C	1904	15 Sept 1905	1906	Scrapped 1922
Moshchni	F & C	1904	3 Oct 1905	1906	Scrapped 1923
Myetki	F & C	1904	24 June 1905	1906	Scrapped 1922

BDITELNI Class DESTROYERS

These German-built destroyers followed the standard destroyer design then emerging, of two widely spaced funnels and short forecastle deck. The main guns were mounted forward and aft, with the torpedo tubes in single mounts on the centreline amidships. Later the ships were equipped to carry sixteen mines.

Sergyeev and *Yurasovski* were initially operational in the Pacific Fleet during the First World War, and later transferred to the White Sea. The remainder of the class were all operational in the Baltic. Following the Revolution *Dmitriev*, *Vnushitelni*, *Vuinoslivi* and *Zvyerev* were renamed *Roshal II*, *Martinov*, *Artemev* and *Zhemchuzny* respectively.

NAME	BUILDER	LAID DOWN	LAUNCHED	COMPLETED	FATE
Bditelni	Schichau	1904	17 Mar 1906	1906	Mined 27 Nov 1917
Boevoi	Schichau	1904	9 Jan 1906	1906	Scrapped 1922
Burni	Schichau	1904	7 Feb 1906	1906	Scrapped 1922
Ing. Mech. Dmitriev	Schichau	1904	4 Nov 1905	1906	Scrapped 1920
Ing. Mech. Zvyerev	Schichau	1904	7 Oct 1905	1906	Scrapped 1930
Kapitan Yurasovski	Schichau	1904	1905	1906	Scrapped 1923
Leitenant Sergyeev	Schichau	1904	1905	1906	Scrapped 1923
Vnimatelni	Schichau	1904	20 Feb 1906	1906	Scrapped 1922?
Vnushitelni	Schichau	1904	5 April 1906	1906	Stricken 1948?
Vuinoslivi	Schichau	1904	31 Mar 1906	1906	Stricken 1948?

Displacement: 380 tons
Dimensions: 208 ft 6 in (oa) × 23 ft × 8 ft 6 in (63.5 m × 7 m × 2.59 m)
Machinery: reciprocating (VTE); 2 shafts; 4 Schulz/Thornycroft boilers; IHP 6,000; 27 kts
Bunkers: 125 tons coal
Armament: two 3 in (75 mm) three 18 in TT (457 mm)
Complement: 65

STOROZHEVOI Class DESTROYERS

These destroyers were built to a Yarrow design similar to the *Boiki* class. The two 3 in guns (no 3 pdr guns were mounted) were sited as in the previous class. Only two 18 in torpedo tubes were carried and these were mounted forward and aft of the after superstructure. Later, facilities were provided for the carriage of twelve mines.

The class served with the Baltic Fleet. During the First World War *Stroini* grounded in the Gulf of Riga where she was attacked by German aircraft and so severely damaged that she was abandoned.

Displacement: 350 tons
Dimensions: 210 ft (oa) × 21 ft × 8 ft 6 in (63.96 m × 6.39 m × 2.59 m)

NAME	BUILDER	LAID DOWN	LAUNCHED	COMPLETED	FATE
Dostoini	Nevski	1905	20 July 1907	1907	Scrapped 1922
Dyelni	Nevski	1905	21 May 1907	1907	Scrapped 1922
Dyeyatelni	Nevski	1905	20 July 1907	1907	Scrapped 1923
Rastoropni	Nevski	1905	21 May 1906	1907	Scrapped 1922
Razyashchi	Nevski	1904	17 Sept 1906	1907	Scrapped 1922
Silni	Nevski	1904	5 Sept 1906	1906	Scrapped 1922
Storozhevoi	Nevski	1904	24 Aug 1906	1906	Scrapped 1925
Stroini	Nevski	1904	2 Jan 1907	1907	Constructive total loss 21 Aug 1917

Machinery: reciprocating (VTE); 2 shafts; 4 Normand boilers; IHP 5,800; 27 kts
Bunkers: 100 tons coal
Armament: two 3 in (75 mm) two 18 in TT (457 mm)
Complement: 67

UKRAINA Class DESTROYERS

These were the first large destroyers to be built for the Russian Navy and followed the general concept of destroyer design then emerging, of high forecastle deck with bridge at rear, three widely spaced large funnels, and ventilator cowls. They adopted the standard disposition for armament used in most contemporary destroyer designs with torpedo tubes amidships (and in this design including a new twin mount), main guns forward and aft and lighter guns on each beam amidships. Initially top-heavy, stability was restored by the addition of 35 tons of ballast. In 1910 they were re-armed with two 4 in/60 cal guns in place of the 3 in guns, and the twin torpedo tube mount was removed and two single tubes were fitted forward and aft of third funnel.

All ships served in the Baltic and during the First World War the armament was again modified, three 4 in/60 cal guns being carried aft and a single 40 mm for AA being mounted on the forecastle. After the Revolution *Turkhmenetz*, *Ukraina* and *Voiskovoi* were renamed *Altvater*, *Bakinski Rabochi* and *Markin* respectively, the ships being transferred to the Caspian Sea where they served as gunboats.

NAME	BUILDER	LAID DOWN	LAUNCHED	COMPLETED	FATE
Donskoi-Kazak	Lange & Sohn	1905	10 Mar 1906	1906	Scrapped 1922
Kazanetz	Lange & Sohn	1904	11 May 1905	1905	Mined 28 Oct 1916
Steregushchi	Lange & Sohn	1904	1905	1906	Scrapped 1922
Strashni	Lange & Sohn	1905	1905	1906	Scrapped 1922
Turkhmenetz Stavropolski	Lange & Sohn	1904	18 Feb 1905	1905	Stricken 1958?
Ukraina	Lange & Sohn	1904	3 Oct 1904	1905	Stricken 1958?
Voiskovoi	Lange & Sohn	1904	26 Nov 1904	1905	Stricken 1958?
Zaibaikaletz	Lange & Sohn	1904	27 April 1906	1906	Scrapped 1922

Displacement: 580 tons
Dimensions: 240 ft (oa) × 23 ft 6 in × 7 ft 6 in (74 m × 7.16 m × 2.28 m)
Machinery: reciprocating (VTE); 2 shafts; 4 Normand boilers; IHP 7,000; 26 kts
Bunkers: 134 tons coal
Armament: two 3 in (75 mm) four 6 pdr (57 mm) three 18 in TT (457 mm)
Complement: 90

Top: *Bditelni.* (Author's collection)

Above: *Dyelni.* (Marius Bar)

Right: *Voiskovoi* c.1913. (Author's collection)

EMIR BUKHARSKI Class DESTROYERS

Ordered in 1905, these destroyers were built to a Schichau design and generally resembled the *Bditelni* design, reverting to two funnels, but they were much larger and carried a heavier armament. Machinery was also supplied by Schichau. Just before the start of the First World War the 3in guns were replaced by 4in/60cal weapons. During the war the increasing danger of air attack resulted in a single 37mm gun being added to provide AA protection. Facilities were also provided for the carriage of twenty mines.

Moskvityanin was sunk by British forces in the Caspian at Alexandrovsk. After the Revolution *Bukharski* and *Finn* were renamed *Yacob Sverdlov* and *Karl Liebknecht* respectively, and served in the Caspian Sea.

NAME	BUILDER	LAID DOWN	LAUNCHED	COMPLETED	FATE
Dobrovoletz	Putilov	1904	12 June 1905	1906	Mined 21 Aug 1916
Emir Bukharski	Skeppsdocka	1904	12 Jan 1905	1905	Scrapped 1925
Finn	Skeppsdocka	1904	1905	1905	Scrapped 1925
Moskvityanin	Putilov	1904	1905	1905	Sunk 21 May 1919

Displacement: 570 tons
Dimensions: 235ft 9in (oa) × 23ft 6in × 7ft 10in (71.8m × 7.16m × 2.38m)
Machinery: reciprocating (VTE); 2 shafts; 4 Schulz/Thornycroft boilers; IHP 6,500; 25kts
Bunkers: 150 tons coal
Armament: two 3in (75mm)
one 1pdr (37mm)
three 19.7in TT (500mm)
20 mines
Complement: 99

Above: Destroyer *Finn* as re-armed with 4in guns just before the First World War. (Author's collection)

Above: *Moskvityanin* in 1913 re-armed with 4 in guns. (Author's collection)

GAIDAMAK Class DESTROYERS

These German-designed two-funnelled destroyers were distinguished by a high forecastle and straight stem. They carried a very heavy secondary armament of six 6pdr guns which were sited on each beam abreast the second funnel and mainmast, and on sponsons recessed into each side of the forecastle deck beneath the bridge. The torpedo tubes and 3 in guns were sited as in earlier destroyers, i.e., forward and aft and torpedo tubes on the centreline amidships, and abaft the mainmast. The ships were re-armed just before the First World War, 4 in/60 cal guns replacing the 3 in and the forward 6 pdr guns in the sponsons being removed and the forecastle recess plated over. The need for AA protection led to the fitting of a single 37 mm AA gun and provision was made for carrying 25 mines.

Amuretz, *Ussurietz* and *Vsadnik* were renamed *Sladkov*, *Roshal* and *Zhelesniakov* after the Revolution and relegated to the role of training ships or gunboats.

Displacement:	570 tons
Dimensions:	235 ft 9 in (oa) × 23 ft 6 in × 7 ft 10 in (71.8 m × 7.16 m × 2.38 m)
Machinery:	reciprocating (VTE); 2 shafts; 4 Schulz/Thornycroft boilers; IHP 6,500; 25 kts
Bunkers:	205 tons coal
Armament:	two 3 in (75 mm) six 6 pdr (57 mm) three 18 in TT (457 mm) 25 mines
Complement:	99

NAME	BUILDER	LAID DOWN	LAUNCHED	COMPLETED	FATE
Amuretz	Broberg	1905	1905	1906	Renamed *Zelezhniakov*
Gaidamak	Krupp, Germania	1904	July 1905	1906	Scrapped 1926
Ussurietz	Broberg	1905	1907	1907	Renamed *Rosal*
Vsadnik	Krupp, Germania	1904	July 1905	1906	Renamed *Sladkov*

OKHOTNIK Class DESTROYERS

This was a slightly enlarged, two-funnelled version of the *Ukraina* class with a ram bow and turtleback forecastle. Armament was disposed as in the previous class, except that the forward 6pdr guns were not mounted in recessed sponsons beneath the bridge, but sited in an open position abreast the forward funnel. The remaining 6pdr guns were mounted abreast the second funnel and mainmast. Just before the First World War, 4in/60cal guns replaced the 3in, as in other destroyers, and during the War another 4in/60cal gun was added on top of the after superstructure. In addition, two 3pdr AA guns were fitted and forty mines were carried, the ships being used as minelayers.

NAME	BUILDER	LAID DOWN	LAUNCHED	COMPLETED	FATE
General Kondratenko	Skeppsdocka	1905	1906	1906	Scrapped 1922
Okhotnik	Crichton	1905	1906	1906	Mined 26 Sept 1917
Pogranichnik	Crichton	1905	1906	1906	Scrapped 1925
Sibirski Stryelok	Skeppsdocka	1905	1906	1906	Scrapped 1930s

After the Revolution *Sibirski Stryelok* was renamed *Konstruktor*.

Displacement:	615 tons
Dimensions:	246ft 8in (oa) × 26ft 10in × 8ft (75.13m × 8.17m × 2.44m)
Machinery:	reciprocating (VTE); 2 shafts; 4 Normand boilers; IHP 7,300; 25.5kts
Bunkers:	215 tons coal
Armament:	two 4.7in (120mm) six 6pdr (57mm) three 18in TT (457mm)
Complement:	102

Left: *Pogranichnik.* (Author's collection)

Right: *Novik* as completed. (Author's collection)

LEITENANT SHESHTAKOV Class DESTROYERS

These ships resembled the *Gaidamak* class in general appearance, but differed in armament. In place of the 3 in on the forecastle, a 4.7 in/30 cal gun was sited, while 3 in guns replaced some of the 6 pdr guns of the *Gaidamak* class. These were sited one on each beam in recessed sponsons beneath the bridge, one on each beam abreast the forward funnel, and one aft. Although heavily armed, the design was not a success, the ships being too slow to be of any value in the Black Sea where they were stationed. They were later re-armed, an extra 4.7 in/30 cal gun replacing the after 3 in weapon and two 3 pdr AA being added. They were also equipped to carry up to forty mines.

NAME	BUILDER	LAID DOWN	LAUNCHED	COMPLETED	FATE
Kapitan Saken (ex-*Leitenant Pushchin*)	Belgian Works	1905	14 Sept 1907	1908	To Bizerta 1920
Kapt Leitenant Baranov	Belgian Works	1905	5 Nov 1907	1908	Scuttled 18 June 1918
Leitenant Shestakov	Belgian Works	1905	28 July 1907	1908	Scuttled 18 June 1918
Leitenant Zatzarenni	Belgian Works	1905	22 Oct 1907	1908	Mined 30 June 1917

Displacement: 640 tons
Dimensions: 243 ft 3 in (oa) × 27 ft 2 in × 9 ft (74.09 m × 8.27 m × 2.74 m)
Machinery: reciprocating (VTE); 2 shafts; 4 Normand boilers; IHP 6,500; 25 kts
Bunkers: 200 tons coal
Armament: one 4.7 in/30 cal (120 mm)
five 3 in (75 mm)
three 18 in TT (457 mm)
Complement: 91

NOVIK DESTROYER

Compared to previous destroyers the experimental *Novik* was considerably larger, much better armed and achieved a much higher speed. From the outset the specification called for a high speed, turbine-powered destroyer. In designing the destroyer the Russians received considerable assistance from the German Vulkan shipyard, who also supplied much of the machinery. The original specification called for an armament of only two 4 in guns, but this was subsequently increased to four. Following modifications to the boilers she carried out a second set of trials on which she achieved a maximum speed of 37.2 kts to make her the fastest ship in the world at the time.

NAME	BUILDER	LAID DOWN	LAUNCHED	COMPLETED	FATE
Novik	Putilov	1 Aug 1910	7 July 1911	4 Sept 1913	Renamed *Yakov Sverdlov* 1918 Mined 28 Aug 1941

Following the Revolution she was laid up and converted to a Flotilla Leader and renamed *Yakov Sverdlov.*

Displacement: 1,280 tons
Dimensions: 336 ft 3 in × 31 ft 3 in × 9 ft 10 in (102.4 m × 9.52 m × 2.99 m)
Machinery: AEG geared turbines; 3 shafts; 6 Vulkan boilers; SHP 40,000; 36 kts
Bunkers: 450 tons oil
Armament: four 4 in/60 cal (102 mm)
eight (4×2) 18 in TT (457 mm)
60 mines
Complement: 130

Left: *Novik* seen on trials in 1913. See data on previous page. (Author's collection)

Left: *Bespokoiny* at Sevastopol in 1919. (Author's collection)

Right: Destroyer *Gromki* seen in the Black Sea *c.*1916. Note the camouflage paint scheme. The destroyer was scuttled at Sevastopol on 18 June 1918. (Boris Drashpil/US Naval Historical Center)

BESPOKOINY Class DESTROYERS

The design for this class was heavily influenced by the successful *Novik* design. The original specification called for a 35 kt destroyer armed with two 4 in guns and four 18 in torpedo tubes and a displacement of 1,025 tons. This was subsequently altered before the ships were ordered, and additional armament of a single 4 in and six extra torpedo tubes increased the displacement by 50 tons. The design proved somewhat disappointing, however, for none of the boats reached the designed speed, the best being 32.7 kts achieved by *Bespokoiny*.

Following the Revolution, the Germans seized the surviving boats and recommissioned *Schastlivy* into the German Navy as *R0 1*. Two other destroyers, *Bystry* and *Gnevny*, were also renumbered *R0 2* and *R0 3* respectively, but were not commissioned. All the vessels were taken over by the British at the Armistice and subsequently transferred to the Wrangel Squadron in September 1919. The scuttled *Bystry* was later raised by the Soviets and renamed *Frunze*.

NAME	BUILDER	LAID DOWN	LAUNCHED	COMPLETED	FATE
Bespokoiny	Navy Yard Nicolaiev	–	31 Oct 1913	Oct 1914	Sold 1924
Bystry	Metal Works	–	7 June 1914	1915	Scuttled 6 April 1919
Derzki	Navy Yard Nicolaiev	–	15 Mar 1914	Oct 1914	Sold 1924
Gnevny	Navy Yard Nicolaeiv	–	31 Oct 1913	Oct 1914	Sold 1924
Gromki	Nevski	–	18 Dec 1913	1916	Scuttled Novorossisk 18 June 1918
Pospeshny	Nevski	–	4 April 1914	1916	Sold 1924
Pronzitelni	Navy Yard Nicolaiev	–	15 Mar 1914	Oct 1914	Scuttled Novorossisk 18 June 1918
Puilki	Metal Works	–	28 July 1914	–	Sold 1924
Schastlivy	Putilov	–	29 Mar 1914	–	Stranded 24 Oct 1919

Displacement: 1,320 (Nevski-built boats, 1,460) tons
Dimensions: 321 ft 6 in × 30 ft 6 in × 10 ft 6 in (97.92 m × 9.29 m × 3.2 m)
Machinery: Brown Boveri (Nevski and Putilov-built boats AEG) geared turbines; 2 shafts; 5 Thornycroft (Nevski and Putilov-built boats Vulkan) boilers; SHP 25,500; 34 kts
Bunkers: 350 tons oil
Armament: three 4 in/60 cal (102 mm)
two 47 mm AA
ten (5×2) 18 in TT (457 mm)
80 mines
Complement: 160

*LEITENANT ILIN, AZARD† AND GAVRIIL** Classes DESTROYERS

These destroyers were ordered under the 1912 Programme to replace losses suffered in the Russo-Japanese War. Designed for service in the Baltic and Black Seas, they were planned as an improved *Bespokoiny* with a very heavy torpedo armament of twelve torpedo tubes carried in six twin mounts. This was later modified to four triple mounts, as it was felt that the after mounts would suffer from the blast of the after 4in gun. During construction armament was again altered, the after torpedo tube mount being replaced by a single 4in gun, which was later increased to two 4in mounts, it being considered that the destroyers were undergunned for use in the Baltic, particularly as there were no suitable light cruisers available to act as escorts to destroyer flotillas. The machinery for *Gavriil, Ilin, Mikhail* and *Zotov* was to have been delivered by German manufacturers, but was seized in Germany in August 1914 and used in the German *B 97*-class destroyers.

After the Revolution a number of the destroyers served the Soviet forces with distinction. *Kapitan I Ranga Miklucha-Maklai* ran aground while trying to escape from a superior British force and was captured, subsequently being handed over to Estonia. *Azard* and *Gavriil* were responsible for sinking the British submarine *L 55*, while *Gavriil* went on to sink *CMB 24* and *CMB 62*.

Displacement:	1,260 (*1,350) tons
Dimensions:	321ft 6in (*351ft) × 30ft 6in × 9ft 10in (*12ft 9in) (97.92(107)m × 9.29m × 2.99 (3.9)m)
Machinery:	AEG (†Parsons) geared turbines; 2 shafts; 4 French (†Thornycroft, *Vulkan) boilers; SHP 31,500 (†30,000, *32,700); 35kts
Bunkers:	400 tons oil
Armament:	four (*five) 4in/60cal (102mm) one 40mm AA nine (3×3) 18in TT (457mm) 50 mines
Complement:	168 (†150)

NAME	BUILDER	LAID DOWN	LAUNCHED	COMPLETED	FATE
Azard†	Metal Works	July 1915	4 June 1916	23 Oct 1916	Renamed *Zinoviev* Dec 1922
Desna†	Metal Works	Nov 1914	4 Nov 1915	25 Aug 1916	Renamed *Engels* Dec 1922
*Gavriil**	Russo-Baltic	7 Dec 1913	5 Jan 1915	7 Oct 1916	Mined 21 Oct 1919
Grom†	Metal Works	1914	May 1915	3 Jan 1916	Sunk by German battleship *Kaiser* 14 Oct 1917
Kapitan Belli	Putilov	29 Oct 1913	23 Oct 1915	Oct 1927	Renamed *Karl Liebknecht* 1928
Kapitan Izylmetev	Putilov	29 Oct 1913	4 Nov 1914	24 July 1916	Renamed *Lenin* Dec 1922
Kapitan Kern	Putilov	4 Dec 1913	27 Aug 1915	Oct 1927	Renamed *Rykov* 1927
Kapitan Miklucha-Maklai (ex-*Kapitan Kinsbergen*	Putilov	5 Nov 1914	27 Aug 1915	Dec 1917	Renamed *Spartak* 18 Dec 1918 To Estonia 1919
Kapitan Konon-Zotov	Putilov	4 Dec 1913	23 Oct 1915	–	Scrapped incomplete 1923
Kapitan Kroun	Putilov	26 Nov 1914	4 Aug 1916	–	Scrapped incomplete 1923
*Konstantin**	Russo-Baltic	7 Dec 1913	12 June 1915	19 May 1917	Mined 21 Oct 1919
Leitenant Dubasov	Putilov	29 Oct 1913	9 Sept 1916	–	Scrapped incomplete 1923
Leitenant Ilin	Putilov	29 Nov 1913	28 Nov 1914	12 Dec 1916	Renamed *Garibaldi* July 1919
Letun†	Metal Works	Nov 1914	4 Nov 1915	24 July 1916	Scrapped 1925
Mechislav (ex-*Leitenant Lombard**	Russo-Baltic	20 Jan 1915	1917	–	Scrapped incomplete 1923
*Mikhail**	Russo-Baltic	7 Dec 1913	1916	–	Scrapped incomplete 1923
Orfei†	Metal Works	Nov 1914	5 Nov 1915	1 April 1916	Scrapped 1929
Pobeditel†	Metal Works	1914	5 Nov 1914	5 Nov 1915	Renamed *Volodarski* Dec 1922
Samson†	Metal Works	1914	5 June 1915	4 Dec 1916	Renamed *Stalin* Dec 1922
*Sokol**	Russo-Baltic	20 Jan 1915	1917	–	Scrapped incomplete 1923
*Vladimir**	Russo-Baltic	7 Dec 1913	18 Aug 1915	1917	Renamed *Svoboda* 12 Sept 1917
Zabijaka†	Metal Works	1914	5 Nov 1914	24 Nov 1915	Renamed *Uritski* Dec 1922

Top right: *Samson.* (Author's collection)

Right: *Kapitan Izylmetev* under construction. (Author's collection)

IZYASLAV Class DESTROYERS

These destroyers were designed with the help of the French Normand yard, who also supplied much of their equipment. Frequent alterations were made to the armament and its disposition during construction, mainly concerning the number of triple torpedo tube mounts and the gun armament, it being considered in the light of war experience that the ships were undergunned. They were eventually completed with a mix of machinery because on the outbreak of the First World War the neutral Swiss prohibited delivery of the Brown Boveri turbines originally specified.

NAME	BUILDER	LAID DOWN	LAUNCHED	COMPLETED	FATE
Avtroil	Russian SB Co	9 Nov 1913	13 Jan 1915	12 Aug 1917	Captured by British 27 Dec 1919 handed over to Estonia Jan 1920
Bryachislav	Russian SB Co	9 Nov 1913	9 Aug 1915	–	Scrapped incomplete 1923
Fedor Stratilat	Russian SB Co	6 Dec 1913	–	–	Scrapped on slip Feb 1918
Izyaslav	Russian SB Co	9 Nov 1913	22 Nov 1914	1916	Renamed *Gromonosets* 27 June 19 and *Karl Marx* Dec 1922
Pryamyslav	Russian SB Co	9 Nov 1913	9 Aug 1914	1927	Renamed *Kalinin* 1927

Displacement: 1,350 (normal) tons
Dimensions: 351 ft 6 in × 31 ft 3 in × 9 ft 10 in (107.05 m × 9.52 m × 2.99 m)
Machinery: Parsons geared turbines; 2 shafts; 5 Normand boilers; SHP 32,700; 35 kts
Bunkers: ?
Armament: five 4 in/60 cal (102 mm)
one 40 mm AA
nine (3×3) 18 in TT (457 mm)
50 mines
Complement: 168

GOGLAND Class DESTROYERS

Designed and ordered in December 1913 from Schichau, these destroyers were to be assembled under Schichau supervision at the Ziese Muhlgraben Works at Riga. Like the previous class the designed armament underwent changes reflecting the concern that current designs were undergunned for service in the Baltic. With the outbreak of war, construction ceased until June 1915. In 1916 the Metal Works yard at Petrograd was ordered to complete *Gogland*, *Grengamn*, *Patras* and *Strisuden* as minesweepers armed with five 4 in, one 40 mm AA and six 18 in TT. The remaining units were reordered as repeats of the *Azard* class. Work on just the minesweepers had started when the Revolution began, and the whole class was cancelled.

NAME	BUILDER	LAID DOWN	LAUNCHED	COMPLETED	FATE
Gogland	Ziese	Dec 1913	–	–	Cancelled 14 Oct 1917. Scrapped 1920s
Grengamn	Ziese	Dec 1913	–	–	Cancelled 14 Oct 1917. Scrapped 1920s
Khios	Ziese	1913	–	–	Cancelled 14 Oct 1917 Scrapped on slip Sept 1917
Kulm	Ziese	–	–	–	Cancelled 14 Oct 1917
Patras	Ziese	Dec 1913	–	–	Cancelled 14 Oct 1917. Scrapped 1920s
Rymnik	Ziese	1913	–	–	Cancelled 14 Oct 1917 Scrapped on slip Sept 1917
Smolensk	Ziese	1913	–	–	Cancelled 14 Oct 1917 Scrapped on slip Sept 1917
Strisuden	Ziese	Dec 1913	–	–	Cancelled 14 Oct 1917 Scrapped on slip Sept 1917
Tenedos	Ziese	1913	–	–	Cancelled 14 Oct 1917 Scrapped on slip Sept 1917

Displacement: 1,350 tons
Dimensions: 325 ft × 30 ft 10 in × 8 ft 10 in (98.98 m × 9.39 m × 2.69 m)
Machinery: Schichau geared turbines; 2 shafts; 5 Schichau boilers; SHP 32,000; 35 kts
Bunkers: 400 tons oil
Armament: four 4 in/60 cal (102 mm)
nine (3×3) 18 in TT (457 mm)
80 mines
Complement: 150

***KERCH* Class** DESTROYERS

Ordered in 1915, this class was planned as an enlarged standard 35 kt-design for service in the Black Sea. The final design depicted an improved *Bespokoiny* design, with an extra 4 in gun. A further twelve destroyers of this class were ordered in 1916 from the Russud yard. An unknown number had been laid down by the outbreak of the Revolution, but work then ceased and the order was cancelled.

NAME	BUILDER	LAID DOWN	LAUNCHED	COMPLETED	FATE
Fidonisi	Nicolaiev	–	31 May 1916	1917	Torpedoed by *Kerch* 18 June 1918
Gadzhibei	Nicolaiev	–	27 Aug 1916	1917	Scuttled Novorossisk 18 June 1918
Kaliakriya	Nicolaiev	–	27 Aug 1916	1918	Scuttled Novorossisk 18 June 1918
Kerch	Nicolaiev	–	31 May 1916	1917	Scuttled 19 June 1918
Korfu	Nicolaiev	–	1924	10 May 1925	Renamed *Petrovski* 1923
Levkas	Nicolaiev	–	1924?	12 Dec 1926	Renamed *Shaumyan* 1925
Tserigo	Nicolaiev	–	1917	–	Sold 1924
Zante	Nicolaiev	–	1917	1923	Renamed *Nezamozhnyi* Nov 1923

Displacement: 1,570 tons
Dimensions: 334 ft 9 in × 31 ft 3 in × 9 ft 9 in (102 m × 9.5 m × 3 m)
Machinery: Parsons geared turbines; SHP 32,500; 34 kts
Bunkers: ?
Armament: four 4 in/60 cal (102 mm)
one 47 mm
two 40 mm AA
nine (3×3) 18 in TT (457 mm)
60 mines
Complement: ?

Left: *Avtroil* under Estonian colours. (P. A. Vicary)

Right: *Petrovski*, ex-*Korfu*. (Author's collection)

TORPEDO-BOATS

VZRUIV TORPEDO-BOAT

Vzruiv was the first large torpedo-boat to enter service with the Russian Navy, all previous boats having been no more than small launches armed with spar torpedoes, of which large numbers were built. In addition a large number of craft were built to a Yarrow design, but full details are not available. The torpedo tubes in *Vzruiv* were carried on each beam in about the amidships position.

Displacement: 160 tons

NAME	BUILDER	LAID DOWN	LAUNCHED	COMPLETED	FATE
Vzruiv	Baltic Works	–	1 Aug 1877	–	Scrapped 1908

Dimensions: 119 ft 8 in (oa) × 16 ft 2 in × 11 ft 1 in (36.45 m × 4.92 m × 3.37 m)
Machinery: reciprocating (VC); 1 shaft; 2 locomotive boilers; IHP 800; 12 kts
Bunkers: 25 tons coal
Armament: two 1 pdr QF (37 mm); one 15 in TT (381 mm)
Complement: 33

BATUM TORPEDO-BOAT

By 1879 the Navy had accepted the value of the torpedo-boat and put forward a requirement for a sea-going boat with a range of 500 nautical miles and adequate crew accommodation. Built by Yarrow, *Batum* is generally regarded as the world's first sea-going torpedo-boat. She followed the general design features of torpedo-boats at that time: a ram bow and turtle foredeck. The two funnels were mounted side by side. The torpedo tubes were mounted in the bow beneath the turtle deck. Armament was later amended to one 1 pdr QF.

NAME	BUILDER	LAID DOWN	LAUNCHED	COMPLETED	FATE
Batum	Yarrow	–	12 June 1880	–	Renumbered *No 251*. Stricken 1908

Displacement: 43 tons
Dimensions: 96 ft 6 in (oa) × 11 ft 1.5 in × 6 ft 3 in (29.39 m × 3.39 m × 1.9 m)
Machinery: reciprocating (VC); 1 shaft; 1 locomotive boiler; IHP 500; 22.5 kts
Bunkers: 10 tons coal
Armament: two 1 pdr QF (37 mm); two 15 in TT (4 torpedoes) (381 mm)
Complement: 15

SUKHUM TORPEDO-BOAT

Sukhum was built by Thornycroft, the other British builder of torpedo-boats. Like *Batum* she featured a ram bow and turtle foredeck with torpedo tubes in the bow and two funnels mounted side by side. She was also fitted with three masts which could carry sails in the event of machinery breakdown.

Displacement: 64 tons

NAME	BUILDER	LAID DOWN	LAUNCHED	COMPLETED	FATE
Sukhum	Thornycroft	–	1883	–	Renumbered *No 256*. Stricken 1908

Dimensions: 112 ft 11 in (oa) × 12 ft 6 in × 6 ft 6 in (34.39 m × 3.8 m × 1.98 m)
Machinery: reciprocating (VC); 1 shaft; 1 locomotive boiler; IHP 704; 17.9 kts
Bunkers: 10 tons coal
Armament: two 1 pdr (37 mm); two 15 in TT (381 mm)
Complement: 18

POTI TORPEDO-BOAT

The third large torpedo-boat built for the Russians was ordered from the Normand yard in France. She underwent a major refit in the early 1900s when oil-burning machinery was installed in place of the original reciprocating machinery. From 1910 to 1913 the ship was used as a minesweeper, but was disarmed in 1915 and re-rated as a dispatch vessel.

NAME	BUILDER	LAID DOWN	LAUNCHED	COMPLETED	FATE
Poti	Normand	–	1883?	–	Renumbered *No 258*. Dispatch vessel 1916

Displacement: 63 tons
Dimensions: 124 ft 7 in (oa) × 10 ft × 6 ft 8 in (37.94 m × 3.04 m × 2.03 m)
Machinery: reciprocating (VC); 1 shaft; 1 locomotive boiler; IHP 575; 18.5 kts
Bunkers: 11 tons coal
Armament: two 1 pdr (37 mm); two 15 in TT (381 mm)
Complement: 18

GHELENDJIK TORPEDO-BOAT

Like the previous torpedo-boat, *Ghelendjik* was built in France and was very similar in appearance to the previous torpedo-boats. Like *No 258*, she was used as a minesweeper from 1910 to 1913, and as a dispatch vessel in 1916.

NAME	BUILDER	LAID DOWN	LAUNCHED	COMPLETED	FATE
Ghelendjik	La Seyne	–	1884	–	Renumbered *No 255*

Displacement: 70.5 tons
Dimensions: 122 ft 8 in (oa) × 12 ft 5 in × 7 ft (37.36 m × 3.78 m × 2.13 m)
Machinery: reciprocating (VC); 1 shaft; 1 locomotive boiler; IHP 520; 18 kts
Bunkers: 11 tons coal
Armament: one 1 pdr (37 mm)
one 1 pdr QF (37 mm)
two 15 in TT (381 mm)
Complement: 18

Right: *Ghelendjik*. The bow door has been lifted to expose the two torpedo tubes mounted in the bows. (L. Accorsi)

Right: Normand-type torpedo-boat *Poti* with two funnels abreast. (Author's collection)

GAGRI TORPEDO-BOAT

Also built in France, *Gagri*, like *Poti*, was refitted to burn oil during the early 1900s.

NAME	BUILDER	LAID DOWN	LAUNCHED	COMPLETED	FATE
Gagri	Claparede	–	1884	–	Renumbered *No 254*. Stricken 1907

Displacement: 80 tons
Dimensions: 120 ft 7 in (oa) × 13 ft 4 in × 6 ft 6 in (36.73 m × 4.06 m × 1.98 m)
Machinery: reciprocating (VC); 1 shaft; 1 locomotive boiler; IHP 574; 17.8 kts
Bunkers: 12 tons coal
Armament: one 1 pdr (37 mm) one 1 pdr QF (37 mm) two 15 in TT (381 mm)
Complement: 18

KOTLIN TORPEDO-BOAT

First torpedo-boat to be built in Russia after *Vzruiv*. The design was developed following experience with the previous foreign designs and showed a number of differences from these. The turtle back foredeck was modified to a rounded bow with spur on top and the deck curved with a cover over it to house the two fixed torpedo tubes. The arrangement did not prove a success as it was difficult to reload the torpedo tubes. In service the boats were found to be underpowered and were unable to make their designed speed of 18 kts.

NAME	BUILDER	LAID DOWN	LAUNCHED	COMPLETED	FATE
Kotlin	Baltic Works	–	1885	–	Renumbered *No 101*. Stricken 1906

Displacement: 67 tons
Dimensions: 124 ft 6 in (oa) × 12 ft 11 in × 4 ft 6 in (37.92 m × 3.93 m × 1.37 m)
Machinery: reciprocating (VC); 1 shaft; 1 locomotive boiler; IHP 472; 16.5 kts
Bunkers: 14 tons coal
Armament: two 1 pdr QF (37 mm) two 15 in TT (381 mm)
Complement: 21

VIBORG TORPEDO-BOAT

For their next torpedo-boat the Russians again turned to Britain, who led the world in torpedo-boat design. *Viborg*, like *Kotlin*, had a rounded bow ram and followed the accepted practice of the time with a turtle deck. In addition to the two fixed torpedo tubes in the bow, *Viborg* carried a third torpedo tube on a trainable mount abaft the twin funnels which were mounted side by side. She was converted to burn oil fuel during the early 1890s.

NAME	BUILDER	LAID DOWN	LAUNCHED	COMPLETED	FATE
Viborg	Clydebank	–	6 July 1886	–	Renumbered *No 102*. Stricken 1910

Displacement: 106 tons
Dimensions: 142 ft 6 in (oa) × 17 ft × 7 ft (43.4 m × 5.18 m × 2.13 m)
Machinery: reciprocating (VC); 2 shafts; 2 locomotive boilers; IHP 1,300; 20 kts
Bunkers: 40 tons coal
Armament: two 1 pdr QF (37 mm) three 15 in TT (6 torpedoes) (381 mm)
Complement: 24

ABO Class TORPEDO-BOATS

The next class of torpedo-boats was ordered from the German yard of Schichau. They differed from previous boats in having a straight stem with rounded stern and a single funnel instead of the two small funnels mounted side by side. They were fitted with two conning positions, one forward and one aft.

NAME	BUILDER	LAID DOWN	LAUNCHED	COMPLETED	FATE
Abo	Schichau	–	1886	–	Renumbered *No 108*. Stricken 1910
Libava	Schichau	–	1886	–	Renumbered *No 110*. Stricken 1910
Vindava	Schichau	–	1886	–	Renumbered *No 109*. Stricken 1910

Displacement: 76 (86 full load) tons
Dimensions: 126 ft 4 in (oa) × 14 ft 10 in × 6 ft 3 in (38.48 m × 4.52 m × 1.9 m)
Machinery: reciprocating (VC); 1 shaft; 1 locomotive boiler; IHP 640; 20 kts
Bunkers: ?
Armament: four 1 pdr QF (37 mm) two 15 mm TT (6 torpedoes) (381 mm)
Complement: 21

YALTA Class TORPEDO-BOATS

The six boats of this class were an improved *Abo* design. The main difference related to the machinery, which in these boats was of the triple expansion type, rather than the horizontal compound type of the previous boats. All the units except *Novorossisk* were converted to oil burning in 1899–1900.

NAME	BUILDER	LAID DOWN	LAUNCHED	COMPLETED	FATE
Kilia	Schichau	–	1886	–	Renumbered *No 262*. Stricken 1911
Kodor	Schichau	–	1886	–	Renumbered *No 261*. Stricken 1911
Novorossisk	Schichau	–	1886	–	Renumbered *No 263*. Stricken 1913
Reni	Schichau	–	1886	–	Renumbered *No 264*. Stricken 1911
Tchardak	Schichau	–	1886	–	Renumbered *No 265*. Stricken 1911
Yalta	Schichau	–	1886	–	Renumbered *No 266*. Stricken 1911

Displacement: 85/90 tons
Dimensions: 126 ft 6 in (*Reni* 128 ft 6 in) (oa) × 15 ft × 6 ft 2 in (38.53 (39.14) m × 4.57 m × 1.88 m)
Machinery: reciprocating (VTE); 1 shaft; 1 locomotive boiler; IHP 900; 20 kts
Bunkers: 21 tons coal
Armament: two 1 pdr QF (37 mm) two 15 in TT (381 mm)
Complement: 18

IZMAIL Class TORPEDO-BOATS

These boats were a Russian-built repeat of the Normand-designed *Poti*. As with many Russian-built copies of foreign designs, they were not particularly successful. They were slightly larger than *Poti*, and could develop only about half her power with a consequent reduction in speed from the 18.5 kts of *Poti* to 15.8 kts – although it was claimed that the lead ship *Izmail* developed 520 IHP on trials to give her a speed of 17.5 kts. In 1889 *Lakhta*, *Luga* and *Narva* were reboilered with Yarrow oil-burning boilers, *Izmail* being similarly reboilered in 1902. *Izmail* was re-rated minesweeper *No 9* in 1908.

NAME	BUILDER	LAID DOWN	LAUNCHED	COMPLETED	FATE
Izmail	Nicolaiev	–	1886	–	Renumbered *No 267*. Stricken 1913
Lakhta	New Admiralty	–	1886	–	Renumbered *No 105*. Stricken 1906
Luga	New Admiralty	–	1887	–	Renumbered *No 106*. Stricken 1910
Narva	New Admiralty	–	1888	–	Renumbered *No 107*. Stricken 1910

Displacement: 73/76 tons
Dimensions: 127 ft 7 in (oa) × 11 ft 7 in × 7 ft 6 in (38.86 m × 3.53 m × 2.28 m)
Machinery: reciprocating (VC); 1 shaft; 1 locomotive boiler; IHP 296 (*Izmail* 520); 15.8 (*Izmail* 17.5) kts
Bunkers: 17 tons coal
Armament: four (*Izmail* two) 1 pdr QF (37 mm)
two 15 in TT (381 mm)
Complement: 21

SVEABORG Class TORPEDO-BOATS

These Normand-built boats were a considerable advance on the previous *Poti* which they had built. Displacement was increased by some 36 tons and length increased by just over 25 ft. Indicated horse-power was increased by about 160 to give an increase in speed of just over 1 kt. All in all these boats proved very satisfactory in service. Torpedo tubes were sited two in fixed positions in the bow and one on a trainable mount abaft the funnel. They were shipped to Vladivostock in sections and assembled there. They were re-rated as dispatch vessels in 1911.

Displacement: 96 (*Revel* 107.5) tons
Dimensions: 153 ft 6 in (oa) × 11 ft 3 in (*Revel* 12 ft 3 in) × 8 ft 8 in (*Revel* 8 ft 3 in) (46.75 m × 3.43 (3.73) m × 2.64 (2.51) m)
Machinery: reciprocating (VTE); 1 shaft; 1 Normand boiler; IHP 737 (*Revel* 837); 19.2 (*Revel* 19.7) kts
Bunkers: 29 tons coal
Armament: two 1 pdr QF (37 mm)
three 15 in TT (381 mm)
Complement: 21

NAME	BUILDER	LAID DOWN	LAUNCHED	COMPLETED	FATE
Revel	Normand	–	1886	–	Renumbered *No 206*. Stricken 1913
Sveaborg	Normand	–	1886	–	Renumbered *No 205*. Stricken 1913

Above: *Revel*. (Author's collection)

Below: No. *265* (ex-*Tchardak*, ex-No. *13*). (P. A. Vicary)

Below: No. *265* (ex-*Tchardak*, ex-No. *13*). (P. A. Vicary)

SUTCHENA Class TORPEDO-BOATS

Built in Russia, these torpedo-boats were a copy of the German-built *Abo* class. Improved machinery was installed leading to an increase in indicated horsepower of 330. Despite the increased power, however, overall speed was reduced compared to the *Abo* class, being some 2.5 kts less. Like the previous class they were taken to Vladivostock in sections and assembled there.

NAME	BUILDER	LAID DOWN	LAUNCHED	COMPLETED	FATE
Sutchena	Nevski	–	1887	–	Renumbered *No 202*. Stricken 1911
Yantchikhe	Nevski	–	1887	–	Renumbered *No 201*. Wrecked 21 Aug 1904

Displacement: 76 tons
Dimensions: 127 ft 11 in (oa) × 14 ft 10 in × 6 ft 1 in (38.96 m × 4.52 m × 1.85 m)
Machinery: reciprocating (VC); 1 shaft; 1 locomotive boiler; IHP 970; 17.2 kts
Bunkers: 29 tons coal
Armament: two 1 pdr QF (37 mm)
two 15 in (381 mm)
Complement: 21

ANAKRIA TORPEDO-BOAT

Typical Schichau-built torpedo-boat, with one torpedo in a fixed position in the bows and one on a trainable mounting amidships. She was converted to oil burning at the turn of the century.

NAME	BUILDER	LAID DOWN	LAUNCHED	COMPLETED	FATE
Anakria	Schichau	–	1889	–	Renumbered No 260. Re-rated dispatch vessel *Miner* 1915

Displacement: 100 tons
Dimensions: 126 ft 6 in (oa) × 15 ft 8 in × 6 ft 10 in (38.53 m × 4.77 m × 2.08 m)
Machinery: reciprocating (VTE); 1 shaft; 1 locomotive boiler; IHP 1,100; 21 kts
Bunkers: 18 tons coal
Armament: two 1 pdr QF (37 mm)
two 15 in TT (381 mm)
Complement: 16

SUNGARI Class TORPEDO-BOATS

These torpedo-boats were assembled at Vladivostock, having been transhipped there in sections.

NAME	BUILDER	LAID DOWN	LAUNCHED	COMPLETED	FATE
Sungari	Crichton	–	1889	–	Renumbered *No 203*. Stricken 1911
Ussuri	Crichton	–	1889	–	Renumbered *No 204*. Scuttled 30 June 1904

Displacement: 175 tons
Dimensions: 135 ft 2 in (oa) × 16 ft 5 in × 8 ft 8 in (41.17 m × 5 m × 2.64 m)
Machinery: reciprocating (VTE); 2 shafts; 2? locomotive boilers; IHP 1,956 (*Ussuri* 2,039); 20.3 (*Ussuri* 19.5) kts
Bunkers: 30 tons coal
Armament: three 1 pdr QF (37 mm)
three 15 in TT (381 mm)
Complement: 21

ADLER TORPEDO-BOAT

Also built by Schichau, this torpedo-boat was much larger than the previous boats they had built for the Russians. The increased size allowed much more powerful machinery to be installed, enabling the boat to reach a maximum speed in excess of 26 kts. Apart from the single fixed torpedo tube carried in the bows, the other two tubes were each carried on a trainable mounting amidships. Like many of the other torpedo-boats, this vessel was converted to oil burning at the turn of the century. Just before the start of the First World War two 3 pdr guns were added and the ship was re-rated as a dispatch vessel.

NAME	BUILDER	LAID DOWN	LAUNCHED	COMPLETED	FATE
Adler	Schichau	–	4 Sept 1890	–	Renumbered *No 259*. Renamed *Letuchi* 1914 Stricken 1917

Displacement: 164 tons
Dimensions: 153 ft 10 in (oa) × 16 ft 7 in × 6 in 8 in (46.85 m × 5.05 m × 2.03 m)
Machinery: reciprocating (VTE); 1 shaft; 1 locomotive boiler; IHP 2,000; 26.7 kts
Bunkers: 20 tons coal
Armament: two 1 pdr QF (37 mm)
three 15 in TT (381 mm)
Complement: 22

EKENES Class TORPEDO-BOATS

Borgo was shipped to Vladivostock in sections for assembly there.

NAME	BUILDER	LAID DOWN	LAUNCHED	COMPLETED	FATE
Borgo	Crichton	–	1890	–	Renumbered *No 207*. Lost 1900
Ekenes	Crichton	–	1890	–	Renumbered *No 117*. Stricken 1910

Displacement: 106 tons
Dimensions: 136 ft 8 in (oa) × 14 ft 8 in × 8 ft 5 in (41.62 m × 4.47 m × 2.56 m)
Machinery: reciprocating (VTE); 1 shaft; 1 locomotive boiler; IHP 1,245; 20 kts
Bunkers: ?
Armament: two 1 pdr QF (37 mm)
two 15 mm TT (381 mm)
Complement: 21

Right: No. *207* (ex-*Borgo*). (Author's collection)

Far right: The *Dago* class torpedo-boat No. *256* (ex-*Kotka*). (Marius Bar)

BIERKE Class TORPEDO-BOATS

These single-funnelled torpedo-boats carried two masts to which sails could be bent if required. The two single torpedo tubes were mounted abreast the bridge on each side and angled outwards. *Rotchensalm* and *Moonzund* were later fitted with oil-burning boilers, *Rotchensalm* having a Yarrow boiler.

Displacement:	81 tons
Dimensions:	126 ft (oa) × 14 ft 8 in × 8 ft 5 in (38.38 m × 4.47 m × 2.56 m)
Machinery:	reciprocating (VTE); 1 shaft; 1 locomotive boiler; IHP 1,000/1,100; 17.8/19 kts
Bunkers:	17 tons coal
Armament:	two 1 pdr QF (37 mm) two 15 in TT (381 mm)
Complement:	21

NAME	BUILDER	LAID DOWN	LAUNCHED	COMPLETED	FATE
Bierke	Putilov	–	1890	–	Renumbered *No 111*. Stricken 1910
Gapsal	Putilov	–	1891	–	Renumbered *No 113*. Stricken 1910
Moonzund	Putilov	–	1891	–	Renumbered *No 114*. Stricken 1910
Rotchensalm	Putilov	–	1890	–	Renumbered *No 112*. Stricken 1910

Right: *Rotchensalm.* (Author's collection).

DAGO Class TORPEDO-BOATS

The torpedo tubes in this class were mounted one in a fixed position in the bow, and the other aft on a trainable mounting. *No 256* was reboilered in 1908.

Displacement:	100/104 tons
Dimensions:	152 ft 6 in/153 ft 6 in (oa) × 12 ft 10 in × 8 ft (46.45/46.75 m × 3.91 m × 2.44 m)
Machinery:	reciprocating (VTE); 1 shaft; 1 locomotive boiler; IHP 1,000/1,030; 16.2/19 kts

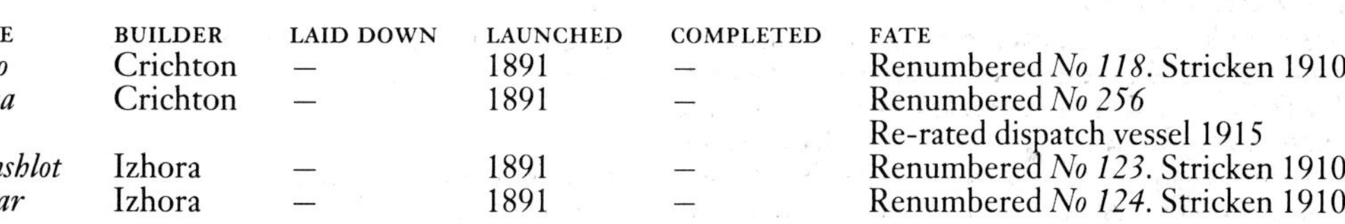

NAME	BUILDER	LAID DOWN	LAUNCHED	COMPLETED	FATE
Dago	Crichton	–	1891	–	Renumbered *No 118*. Stricken 1910
Kotka	Crichton	–	1891	–	Renumbered *No 256* Re-rated dispatch vessel 1915
Kronshlot	Izhora	–	1891	–	Renumbered *No 123*. Stricken 1910
Seskar	Izhora	–	1891	–	Renumbered *No 124*. Stricken 1910

Bunkers:	15 tons coal
Armament:	two 1 pdr QF (*Dago* two 3 pdr QF) (37 (47) mm) two 15 in TT (381 mm)
Complement:	21

ANAPA Class TORPEDO-BOATS

These boats were built to the same design as the *Bierke* class, but with increased displacement. They were re-rated as dispatch vessels in 1915.

NAME	BUILDER	LAID DOWN	LAUNCHED	COMPLETED	FATE
Aitodor	Bellino-Fendrich	–	1892	–	Renumbered *No 253*. Stricken 1917?
Anapa	Bellino-Fendrich	–	1891	–	Renumbered *No 252*. Stricken 1917?

Displacement: 91.5/96 tons
Dimensions: 126ft (oa) × 14ft 8in × 5ft (38.38m × 4.47m × 1.52m)
Machinery: reciprocating (VTE); 1 shaft; 1 locomotive boiler; IHP 1,000/1,100; 17.2/19kts
Bunkers: ?
Armament: two 1pdr (37mm) two 15in TT (381mm)
Complement: 18

PERNOV TORPEDO-BOAT

Pernov was built by Normand for the Baltic Fleet and was a two-funnelled design based on the French *Dragon* class. The three torpedo tubes were disposed one in a fixed position in the bows, and the other two each on a trainable mounting between the two funnels and aft of the second funnel. *Pernov* was refitted in 1899 with Yarrow oil-burning boilers. She was re-rated as a dispatch vessel in 1912.

NAME	BUILDER	LAID DOWN	LAUNCHED	COMPLETED	FATE
Pernov	Normand	–	1892	–	Renumbered *No 103*. Stricken 1910

Displacement: 120 tons
Dimensions: 137ft 10in (oa) × 14ft 9in × 6ft 9in (41.98m × 4.49m × 2.05m)
Machinery: reciprocating (VTE); 2 shafts; 2 Du Temple boilers; IHP 2,000; 26kts
Bunkers: 16 tons coal
Armament: two 1pdr QF (37mm) three 15in TT (381mm)
Complement: 21

SESTRORETSK TORPEDO-BOAT

This boat, also built by Normand, was a smaller version of *Pernov*, with only a single shaft instead of the two fitted in *Pernov*. She was re-armed in 1912 with a single 30mm and re-rated as a dispatch vessel.

NAME	BUILDER	LAID DOWN	LAUNCHED	COMPLETED	FATE
Sestroretsk	Normand	–	Mar 1894	–	Renumbered *No 104*. Stricken 1910

Displacement: 80 tons
Dimensions: 118ft (oa) × 13ft × 8ft (35.94m × 3.96m × 2.44m)
Machinery: reciprocating (VTE); 1 shaft; 1 Du Temple boiler; IHP 1,300; 23kts
Bunkers: 17 tons coal
Armament: two 1pdr QF (37mm) two 15in TT (381mm)
Complement: 21

TOSNA Class TORPEDO-BOATS

These boats were built to a Russian design developed from the Schichau-designed *Anakria*. There were minor variations in displacement, dimensions and machinery and five extra crew were carried. In 1899 the four Putilov-built boats were reboilered with Yarrow oil-burning boilers.

NAME	BUILDER	LAID DOWN	LAUNCHED	COMPLETED	FATE
Aspe	Putilov	–	1893	–	Renumbered *No 125*. Stricken 1910
Domesnes	Putilov	–	1893	–	Renumbered *No 116*. Stricken 1910
Gogland	Izhora	–	1894	–	Renumbered *No 122*. Stricken 1910
Nargen	Izhora	–	1894	–	Renumbered *No 121*. Stricken 1910
Tosna	Putilov	–	1893	–	Renumbered *No 115*. Stricken 1910
Tranzund	Putilov	–	1893	–	Renumbered *No 126*. Stricken 1910

Displacement: 85/99 tons
Dimensions: 127ft 5in/128ft 2in (oa) × 15ft 3in/15ft 6in × 6ft 10in (38.8/39.03m × 4.64/4.72m × 2.08m)
Machinery: reciprocating (VTE); 1 shaft; 1 Du Temple boiler; IHP 1,000; 20kts
Bunkers: 17 tons coal
Armament: two 1pdr QF (*Tosna* & *Domesnes* two 3pdr) (37 (47)mm) two 15in TT (381mm)
Complement: 21

POLANGEN Class TORPEDO-BOATS

These boats were a Russian copy of *Pernov*. The boats built at Nicolaiev differed from the rest of the class in that they were completed with three masts instead of two. In 1899 *Polangen*, *Pakerort*, *Nos 127–130* and *Nos 138–139* were reboilered with oil-burning boilers, *Polangen* and *Pakerort* having Yarrow boilers. In 1912 *Nos 119*, *120*, *128*, *129* and *142* were re-rated as dispatch vessels, while in 1915 *Nos 270*, *271* and *273* were re-rated as minesweepers.

Displacement: 120 tons
Dimensions: 137ft 10in × 14ft 9in × 6ft 9in (41.98m × 4.49m × 2.05m)
Machinery: reciprocating (VTE); 2 shafts; 2 Du Temple boilers; IHP 2,000; 23.2kts
Bunkers: 20 tons coal
Armament: two 1pdr QF (37mm) three 15in TT (381mm)
Complement: 21

NAME	BUILDER	LAID DOWN	LAUNCHED	COMPLETED	FATE
Pakerort	Crichton	–	1894	–	Renumbered *No 119*. Renamed *Periskop* 1912 Stricken 1913
Polangen	Crichton	–	1894	–	Renumbered *No 120*. Stricken 1913
127	Izhora	–	1896	–	Stricken 1911
128	Izhora	–	1896	–	Stricken 1921
129	Izhora	–	1897	–	Stricken 1921
130	Izhora	–	1897	–	Stricken 1911
133	Nevski	–	1896	–	Stricken 1911
134	Nevski	–	1896	–	Stricken 1914
135	Nevski	–	1896	–	Stricken 1911
136	Nevski	–	1896	–	Stricken 1913
137	Izhora	–	1897	–	Stricken 1911
138	Izhora	–	1897	–	Stricken 1911
139	Izhora	–	1897	–	Stricken 1911
140	Izhora	–	1897	–	Stricken 1914
141	Nevski	–	1897	–	Stricken 1914
142	Nevski	–	1897	–	Stricken 1921
270	Nicolaiev	–	1895	–	Stricken 1917
271	Nicolaiev	–	1895	–	Stricken 1917
272	Nicolaiev	–	1896	–	Sunk in collision 28 Aug 1914
273	Nicolaiev	–	1896	–	Stricken 1924

NUMBERS *131, 132, 268, 269* TORPEDO-BOATS

This design was a smaller version of the previous class, with length reduced by some 10ft and indicated horsepower reduced by 1,000. Only two torpedo tubes were carried, one in a fixed position in the bows and one on a trainable mount amidships.

NAME	BUILDER	LAID DOWN	LAUNCHED	COMPLETED	FATE
131	Izhora	–	1895	–	Stricken 1910
132	Izhora	–	1895	–	Stricken 1910. Re-rated minesweeper *Cheka*
268	Nicolaiev	–	1895	–	Stricken 1911
269	Nicolaiev	–	1895	–	Sunk in collision 1896

Displacement: 100 tons
Dimensions: 126ft 6in (oa) × 15ft 8in × 6ft 10in (38.53 × 4.77m × 2.08m)
Machinery: reciprocating (VTE); 2 shafts; 2 Du Temple boilers; IHP 1,000; 21kts
Bunkers: 20 tons coal
Armament: two 1pdr QF (37mm) two 15in TT (381mm)
Complement: 18

NUMBERS *208–211* TORPEDO-BOATS

This design, too, was almost identical with the *Polangen* class, but with reduced power and consequent reduction in speed (the maximum speed was only 18.5kts compared to the 23.2kts of the *Polangen* class). However, bunkerage was double giving a much improved radius of action. The units were all taken to Vladivostock in sections where they were assembled.

NAME	BUILDER	LAID DOWN	LAUNCHED	COMPLETED	FATE
208	New Admiralty	–	–	1899	Mined 17 July 1904
209	New Admiralty	–	–	1899	Stricken 1911
210	New Admiralty	–	–	1899	Stricken 1911
211	New Admiralty	–	–	1899	Stricken 1915

Displacement: 120 tons
Dimensions: 137ft 10in (oa) × 14ft 9in × 6ft 9in (41.98m × 4.49m × 2.05m)
Machinery: reciprocating (VTE); 2 shafts; ?2 Du Temple boilers; IHP 1,460; 18.5kts
Bunkers: 40 tons coal
Armament: two 1pdr (37mm) three 15in TT (381mm)
Complement: 21

Left: No. *213*. (Author's collection)

Left: No. *220*. (Author's collection)

NUMBERS *212–213* TORPEDO-BOATS

These were the largest torpedo-boats built for the Russian Navy. Designed by Yarrow, they featured three funnels and a bridge structure forward and small superstructure aft. They were re-armed in 1914 and re-rated as minesweepers.

NAME	BUILDER	LAID DOWN	LAUNCHED	COMPLETED	FATE
212	Crichton	–	1901	–	Scrapped 1922
213	Crichton	–	1901	–	Scrapped 1926

Displacement: 186 tons
Dimensions: 171 ft 9 in (oa) × 17 ft 3 in × 4 ft 10 in (52.31 m × 5.25 m × 1.47 m)
Machinery: reciprocating (VTE); 2 shafts; ?4 Yarrow boilers; IHP 3,800; 24 kts
Bunkers: 60 tons coal
Armament: three 1 pdr (37 mm)
three 15 in TT (381 mm)
Complement: 26

NUMBERS *214–223* TORPEDO-BOATS

These were the first Russian torpedo-boats to dispense with the fixed bow torpedo tube, the tubes being carried on a single trainable deck mounting. The design was based on the French *Cyclone*-class design. They were converted to a minesweeping role in 1914.

Displacement: 150 tons
Dimensions: 147 ft 8 in (oa) × 15 ft 3 in × 8 ft 9 in (44.97 m × 4.64 m × 2.66 m)
Machinery: reciprocating (VTE); 2 shafts; 2 Normand/Yarrow boilers; IHP 3,700; 29 kts
Bunkers: 30 tons coal

NAME	BUILDER	LAID DOWN	LAUNCHED	COMPLETED	FATE
214	Nevski	–	1902	–	Scrapped 1922
215	Nevski	–	1902	–	Scrapped 1922
216	Nevski	–	1902	–	Scrapped 1922
217	Nevski	–	1902	–	Scrapped 1922
218	Nevski	–	1902	–	Scrapped 1922
219	Crichton	–	1903	–	Scrapped 1922
220	Crichton	–	1902	–	Scrapped 1922
221	Crichton	–	1902	–	Foundered 1904
222	Crichton	–	1902	–	Scrapped 1922
223	Crichton	–	1902	–	Stricken 1921

Armament: two 3 pdr (47 mm)
two 15 in TT (381 mm)
Complement: 28

LASTOCHKA TORPEDO-BOAT

This Yarrow-built torpedo-boat was acquired in 1905 and was the first turbine-powered vessel to serve in the Russian Navy. She was an experimental design with a novel machinery arrangement in which the port shaft was powered by a high-pressure turbine and the starboard shaft by a low-pressure turbine. The centre shaft was driven by the reciprocating machinery. Two torpedo tubes were sited in fixed mountings abreast the bridge and angled outwards, and the third aft on the centreline.

NAME	BUILDER	LAID DOWN	LAUNCHED	COMPLETED	FATE
Lastochka (ex-*Caroline*)	Yarrow	–	1903	–	Stricken 1914

Displacement: 140 tons
Dimensions: 152 ft 6 in (oa) × 15 ft 3 in × 5 ft (46.45 m × 4.64 m × 1.52 m)
Machinery: reciprocating (VTE); 3 shafts; 2 Yarrow boilers; 2 Rateau turbines; SHP 2,000 plus IHP 250; 26.39 kts
Bunkers: ?
Armament: two 3 pdr (47 mm)
three 15 in TT (381 mm)
Complement: 23

MISCELLANEOUS SMALL TORPEDO-BOATS

Following the success of the torpedo during the Russo-Turkish War of 1877–8, it was decided to build a large number of small torpedo craft under the 1877 Programme. These vessels, some 60 to 60 ft in length, displaced about 25 tons, were powered with a small steam engine and one boiler driving a single shaft, and manned by a crew of about ten. They were usually armed with a single torpedo, the early vessels carrying a spar torpedo while later units were equipped with a single tube for a Whitehead torpedo. Some boats armed with spar torpedoes were later fitted with Drzewiecki drop collar torpedoes. Some boats were also later fitted with a small 37 mm gun. Many of these small torpedo-craft were carried by the larger cruisers and battleships. All units were subsequently numbered, in 1885, 1886 and again in 1895, the majority then being stricken during the early 1900s. These small craft have been listed in numerical/alphabetical order using the number/name first assigned.

NAME	BUILDER	DISPLACEMENT (tons)	DIMENSIONS (m)	MACHINERY IHP/Kts	FATE
1	Thornycroft	24.5	23 × 2.8 × 1	114/14	Lost 1877
2	Thornycroft	24.5	23 × 2.8 × 1	114/14	Stricken 1904
46	Thornycroft	17	18.4 × 2.6 × 1	220/?	Stricken 1900
Aist	New Admiralty	25	21.8 × 2.7 × 2	220/13	Stricken 1908
Akula	New Admiralty	25	21.8 × 2.7 × 2	220/13	Stricken 1908
Albatros	Baltic Yard	25	21.8 × 2.7 × 2	220/13	Stricken 1908
Bekas	Baltic Yard	25	21.8 × 2.7 × 2	220/13	Stricken 1906
Beluga	Izhora	23	21.8 × 2.7 × 2	220/14	Stricken 1908

NAME	BUILDER	DISPLACEMENT (tons)	DIMENSIONS (m)	MACHINERY IHP/Kts	FATE
Bomba	Schichau	23	20 × 2.5 × 1.2	220/16	Stricken 1900
Bulava	Schichau	23	20 × 2.5 × 1.2	220/16	?
Bychok	Baird	16	18.3 × 2.3 × 1	220/11.5	Sold to Bulgaria 1884
Chajka	Baltic Yard	23	21.8 × 2.7 × 2	220/14	Stricken 1907
Cherepakha	Baird	16	18.3 × 2.3 × 1	220/11.5	Sold to Bulgaria 1884
Chizhik	Baltic Yard	23	21.8 × 2.7 × 2	220/14	Stricken 1907
Delfin	Baltic Yard	23	21.8 × 2.7 × 2	220/14	Stricken 1908
Drakon	Baltic Yard	23	21.8 × 2.7 × 2	220/14	Stricken 1908
Drokhva	Nevski	23	21.8 × 2.7 × 2	220/14	Stricken 1895
Drozd	Baird	23	21.8 × 2.7 × 2	220/14	Stricken 1895
Dyatel	Baird	23	21.8 × 2.7 × 2	220/14	Stricken 1908
Fazan	Baltic Yard	23	21.8 × 2.7 × 2	220/14	Stricken 1908
Filin	Baltic Yard	23	21.8 × 2.7 × 2	220/14	Stricken 1908
Forel	Baltic Yard	23	21.8 × 2.7 × 2	220/14	Stricken 1907
Galka	Baltic Works	33.5	22.7 × 3.4 × 1	220/13	Stricken 1908
Glukhar	Baltic Yard	25	21.8 × 2.7 × 2	220/13	Stricken 1907
Golub	Nevski	23	21.8 × 2.7 × 2	220/14	Stricken 1902
Gorlitza	Nevski	23	21.8 × 2.7 × 2	220/14	Stricken 1908
Gratch	Nevski	23	21.8 × 2.7 × 2	220/14	Stricken 1908
Gus	Nevski	23	21.8 × 2.7 × 2	220/14	Stricken 1908
Indyuk	Baird	23	21.8 × 2.7 × 2	220/14	Stricken 1908
Ivolga	Baird	23	21.8 × 2.7 × 2	220/14	Stricken 1908
Kakadu	Baird	23	21.8 × 2.7 × 2	220/14	Stricken 1908
Kambala	Baird	23	21.8 × 2.7 × 2	220/14	Stricken 1908
Kanarejka	Baird	23	21.8 × 2.7 × 2	220/14	Stricken 1895
Karabin	Schichau	11.3	20 × 2.6 × 0.6	120/13	?
Karas	Baird	23	21.8 × 2.7 × 2	220/14	Stricken 1908
Kasatka	Baltic Yard	24	22 × 3 × 2	220/13	Stricken 1908
Kefal	Thornycroft	12.5	19 × 2.3 × 1	112/12	?
Khameleon	Baltic Yard	23	21.8 × 2.7 × 2	220/14	Stricken 1908
Kolibri	Baird	23	21.8 × 2.7 × 2	220/14	Stricken 1908
Konoplyanka	Baird	23	21.8 × 2.7 × 2	220/14	Stricken 1907
Kopchik	Baird	23	21.8 × 2.7 × 2	220/14	Stricken 1908
Kope	Schichau	23	20 × 2.5 × 1.2	220/16	?
Koryushka	Baird	23	21.8 × 2.7 × 2	220/14	Stricken 1908
Kretchet	Baird	23	21.8 × 2.7 × 2	220/14	Stricken 1907
Krokodil	Baird	23	21.8 × 2.7 × 2	220/14	Stricken 1907
Kukushka	Baird	23	21.8 × 2.7 × 2	220/14	Stricken 1908
Kuritsa	Baird	23	21.8 × 2.7 × 2	220/14	Stricken 1908
Kuropatka	Izhora	23	21.8 × 2.7 × 2	220/14	Stricken 1908
Lastochka	Izhora	23	21.8 × 2.7 × 2	220/14	Stricken 1908
Lebed	Izhora	23	21.8 × 2.7 × 2	220/14	Stricken 1908
Leshch	Izhora	23	21.8 × 2.7 × 2	220/14	Used as target 1885
Losos	Izhora	23	21.8 × 2.7 × 2	220/14	Stricken 1908
Luk	Schichau	23	20 × 2.5 × 1.2	220/16	?
Malinovka	Izhora	23	21.8 × 2.7 × 2	220/14	Stricken 1908
Mech	Schichau	23	20 × 2.5 × 1.2	220/16	?
Nalim	Harbour Workshops	23	21.8 × 2.7 × 2	220/14	Stricken 1908
Nyrok	Harbour Workshops	23	21.8 × 2.7 × 2	220/14	Stricken 1907
Orel	Baltic Yard	23	21.8 × 2.7 × 2	220/14	Stricken 1908
Osetr	Harbour Workshops	23	21.8 × 2.7 × 2	220/14	Stricken 1908
Palitsa	Schichau	23	20 × 2.5 × 1.2	220/16	?
Pavlin	Harbour Workshops	23	21.8 × 2.7 × 2	220/14	Stricken 1908
Pelikan	Harbour Workshops	23	21.8 × 2.7 × 2	220/14	Stricken 1908
Perepel	Harbour Workshops	23	21.8 × 2.7 × 2	220/14	Stricken 1908
Peskar	Harbour Workshops	23	21.8 × 2.7 × 2	220/14	Stricken 1907
Petukh	Crichton	23	21.8 × 2.7 × 2	220/14	Stricken 1908
Plotva	Harbour Workshops	23	21.8 × 2.7 × 2	220/14	Stricken 1908
Podorozhnik	Baltic Yard	23	21.8 × 2.7 × 2	220/14	Stricken 1908

NAME	BUILDER	DISPLACEMENT (tons)	DIMENSIONS (m)	MACHINERY IHP/Kts	FATE
Popugaj	Harbour Workshops	23	21.8 × 2.7 × 2	220/14	Stricken 1908
Prashch	Schichau	23	20 × 2.5 × 1.2	220/16	Stricken 1897
Raketa	Vulkan	33	24 × 3.3 × 1.7	250/13	?
Ryabchik	Crichton	23	21.8 × 2.7 × 2	220/14	Stricken 1908
Salamandra	Crichton	23	21.8 × 2.7 × 2	220/14	Stricken 1908
Samopal	Vulkan	33	24 × 3.3 × 1.7	250/13	Stricken 1908
Sardinka	Crichton	23	21.8 × 2.7 × 2	220/14	Stricken 1908
Seld	Crichton	23	21.8 × 2.7 × 2	220/14	Stricken 1908
Selezen	Baltic Works	33.5	22.7 × 3.4 × 1	220/13	Stricken 1902
Shchuka	Ropit	24.4	21.8 × 2.7 × 2	200/12.5	Stricken 1902
Shsheglenok	Ropit	24.4	21.8 × 2.7 × 2	200/12.5	Stricken 1905
Shtyk	Schichau	23	20 × 2.5 × 1.2	220/16	?
Sig	Crichton	23	21.8 × 2.7 × 2	220/14	Stricken 1908
Sirena	Baltic Works	29	27.4 × 2.7 × 2	220/13	Stricken 1908
Skorpion	Bellino-Fenderich	25.4	18.7 × 3 × 1.5	220/12	Used as target 1896
Skumbriya	Bellino-Fenderich	25.4	18.7 × 3 × 1.5	220/12	Stricken 1906
Skvorets	Britnev	23	21.8 × 2.7 × 2	220/14	Stricken 1908
Snigir	Britnev	23	21.8 × 2.7 × 2	220/14	Lost 1900
Sokol	Britnev	23	21.8 × 2.7 × 2	220/14	Stricken 1908
Solovej	Britnev	23	21.8 × 2.7 × 2	220/14	Stricken 1908

Below: Torpedo-boat seen on the cruiser *Makarov*. (Marius Bar)

NAME	BUILDER	DISPLACEMENT (tons)	DIMENSIONS (m)	MACHINERY IHP/Kts	FATE
Som	Britnev	23	21.8 × 2.7 × 2	220/14	Stricken 1908
Soroka	Baltic Works	24.3	23 × 3 × 1	220/13	Stricken 1904
Sova	Britnev	23	21.8 × 2.7 × 2	220/14	Stricken 1908
Sterlyad	Baltic Works	24.3	23 × 3 × 1	220/13	Stricken 1907
Straus	Baltic Works	24.3	23 × 3 × 1	220/13	Stricken 1907
Strela	Schichau	23	20 × 2.5 × 1.2	220/16	?
Sudak	Baltic Yard	23	21.8 × 2.7 × 2	220/14	Stricken 1908
Sultanka	Bellino-Fenderich	25.4	18.7 × 3 × 1.5	220/12	Stricken 1904
Sviristel	Baltic Yard	23	21.8 × 2.7 × 2	220/14	Stricken 1908
Teterev	Baltic Yard	23	21.8 × 2.7 × 2	220/14	Stricken 1907
Treska	Baltic Yard	23	21.8 × 2.7 × 2	220/14	Stricken 1908
Tsaplya	Baltic Yard	23	21.8 × 2.7 × 2	220/14	Used as target 1885
Udav	Baltic Yard	23	21.8 × 2.7 × 2	220/14	Lost 1886
Ugor	Baltic Yard	23	21.8 × 2.7 × 2	220/14	Stricken 1908
Utka	Baltic Yard	23	21.8 × 2.7 × 2	220/14	Stricken 1907
Uzh	Baltic Yard	23	21.8 × 2.7 × 2	220/14	Stricken 1908
Vorobey	Baird	25	21.8 × 2.7 × 2	220/13	Stricken 1889
Vorona	Baird	25	21.8 × 2.7 × 2	220/13	Used as target 1892
Voron	Baltic Yard	25	21.8 × 2.7 × 2	220/13	Stricken 1908
Yadro	Schichau	23	20 × 2.5 × 1.2	220/16	?
Yashcheritsa	Ropit	24.4	21.8 × 2.7 × 2	200/12	Stricken 1902
Yastreb	Baltic Yard	23	21.8 × 2.7 × 2	220/14	Stricken 1908
Zhavoronok	Baird	23	21.8 × 2.7 × 2	220/14	Stricken 1908
Zhuravl	Baird	23	21.8 × 2.7 × 2	220/14	Stricken 1908
Zmeya	Baird	23	21.8 × 2.7 × 2	220/14	Stricken 1895
Zyablik	Baird	23	21.8 × 2.7 × 2	220/14	Stricken 1907

Left: Torpedo-boat No. *158* (ex-*Som*). She was subsequently renumbered *100* (in 1886) and then *32* (in 1895). Note the single Whitehead torpedo tube in the bows. (Author's collection)

SUBMARINES

ALEKSANDROVSKI Type SUBMARINE

Russia was one of the first nations to realize the potential of the submarine and to seek ways and means of exploiting this novel ship for naval warfare. The first submarine to be built for the Navy was designed by a man called Aleksandrovski and was remarkable in a number of ways. Many of the design features were far ahead of their time. The triangular-shaped iron hull featured an enlarged bow section through which divers could be disembarked while the boat was submerged. Various trials were conducted on the hull, including depth diving trials. Initial trials showedd that the maximum diving depth that could be attained with safety was 60 ft. In 1871 trials were carried out to investigate the crushing depth, which was found to be 100 ft. After these trials the wreck was raised and scrapped.

NAME	BUILDER	LAID DOWN	LAUNCHED	COMPLETED	FATE
?	Baltic Yard	—	1865	May 1866	Scrapped 1873

Displacement: 355 tons

Dimensions: 110 ft × 13 ft × 12 ft (33.5 m × 3.96 m × 3.65 m)
Machinery: compressed air engines; 2 shafts; 1.5 kts
Range: 2.5 nm
Armament: 2 mines
Complement: 22

DRZEWIECKI Type SUBMARINE

Having made such a fine start with the Aleksandrovski-type submarine, the next submersibles built for the Russian Navy were a midget type developed for incursion duties during the Russo-Turkish War of 1877–8. Designed by the Polish engineer Drzewiecki, these midget submarines were built to three basic designs. The first Type 1 was a twin-hulled prototype boat in which the operator sat in the upper part on top of the ballest tank in the lower part. Following successful trials with the boat carrying two mines which were fixed to the target by suction devices, the Navy declined to proceed further with the project as the war had ended. The Army, however, which had responsibility for the defence of the coastal fortresses, took up the idea and ordered a second prototype. After successful trials a total of 50 were ordered. Two of these were later used in trials with an electric motor driving in one case a water jet and in the other a conventional screw. A third boat was renamed *Keta* and converted to carry two

Right: The experimental coastal submarine *Keta* designed by Lt Janovich. The 3-ton boat was built at St Petersburg and transported to the Pacific where she was assembled. (US Naval Historical Center)

Drzewiecki drop-collar torpedoes, and sent to the Far East during the Russo-Japanese War.

Type 1 Prototype

Displacement:	?
Dimensions:	15 ft × 5 ft × 5 ft (4.57 m × 1.52 m × 1.52 m)
Machinery:	treadle-driven; 1 shaft; 1.5 kts
Armament:	2 mines
Complement:	1

Built 1877

Type 2 Prototype

Displacement:	2.5 tons
Dimensions:	20 ft × 5 ft × 3 ft 6 in (6.09 m × 1.52 m × 1.06 m)
Machinery:	treadle-driven; 2 shafts (1 bow, 1 stern); 2 kts
Armament:	2 mines
Complement:	1

Built 1879

Type 3 Prototype

Displacement:	2.5 tons
Dimensions:	20 ft × 5 ft × 3 ft 6 in (6.09 m × 1.52 m × 1.06 m)
Machinery:	treadle-driven; 1 shaft; 2/3 kts
Armament:	2 mines
Complement:	4

Built 1878–81

NORDENFELT Type SUBMARINE

In 1887 a Nordenfelt submarine was sold to Russia. The boat was equipped with a conning tower at each end topped by a glass dome from which the captain and look-out navigated the boat when it was awash. The two Whitehead torpedoes were carried in internal discharge tubes.

Displacement:	?
Dimensions:	?
Machinery:	HP 1,300; 14 kts surfaced
Range:	20 nm at 5 kts submerged
Armament:	2 Whitehead torpedoes

DELFIN SUBMARINE

This single-hull type submarine was designed by engineer Bubnov. The design was not a success, and the boat suffered a number of mishaps. On 29 June 1904 she accidentally sank in the River Neva during a practice dive with the loss of 21 crew (11 were saved). She was raised and transferred to the Pacific in October 1904 for use against the Japanese. She was commissioned in February 1905, but was again sunk in May 1905, this time due to the ignition of petrol vapour, a problem from which a number of early petrol-engined submarines suffered. She was recommissioned again after the end of the Russo-Japanese War and was transferred to the Arctic in October 1916. She was finally removed from the active list in August 1917, the hulk being sunk.

Displacement:	113/124 tons
Dimensions:	64 ft 3 in × 10 ft × 9 ft 6 in (19.57 m × 3.04 m 2.89 m)
Machinery:	petrol/electric motor; 1 shaft; BHP 300 HP 120; 9/4.5 kts
Range:	243 nm surfaced, 35 nm at 2.5 kts submerged
Armament:	2 Drzewiecki drop-collar torpedoes
Complement:	22

NAME	BUILDER	LAID DOWN	LAUNCHED	COMPLETED	FATE
No 113	Baltic Works	—	1903	—	Renumbered *No 150*, renamed *Delfin* Sunk 5 Sept 1917

Left: The wreck of the submarine *Delfin* seen at Murmansk in 1919. (Imperial War Museum)

KASATKA Class SUBMARINES

NAME	BUILDER	LAID DOWN	LAUNCHED	COMPLETED	FATE
Feldmarshal Graf Sheremetev	Baltic Works	—	1904	May 1905	Renamed *Keta* Aug 1917 Scrapped 1922
Kasatka	Baltic Works	—	1904	Mar 1905	Scrapped 1922
Makrel	Baltic Works	—	1907	—	Scrapped 1922
Nalim	Baltic Works	—	8 Sept 1904	May 1905	Scuttled 26 April 1919
Okun	Baltic Works	—	1904	—	Scrapped 1922
Skat	Baltic Works	—	1904	Mar 1905	Scuttled 26 April 1919

The design for this class was developed by Bubnov, following his experience with *Delfin*. *Kasatka* was ordered under the 1903 Programme and the remaining boats under the 1904 Emergency Programme. The original design provided for a unique arrangement of three shafts, but because of the urgency with which the boats were required to meet a possible war with Japan, this was reduced to a single shaft. As completed the design was not altogether successful. Following the conclusion of the Russo-Japanese War the units were re-engined with diesel-electric machinery, and were fitted with a large conning tower. With the modifications surfaced displacement increased to 153 tons and submerged to 186 tons.

Sheremetev, *Kasatka*, *Nalin* and *Skat* were transported by rail to the Pacific in November/December 1904, becoming operational the following spring. During the First World War *Nalim* and *Skat* were transferred to the Black Sea and equipped with a 47 mm gun. They were both removed from active service in March 1917, but were re-activated in April 1918 for service against the Soviets. They were seized by the Germans when the Armistice was signed, taken over by the British in November 1918 when Germany surrendered, but were later sunk to avoid capture by the Soviets.

Displacement:	140/177 tons
Dimensions:	65 ft × 11 ft 6 in × 11 ft 3 in (33.5 m × 3.5 m × 3.43 m)
Machinery:	petrol/electric motor; 1 shaft; BHP 180, HP 60; 8.5/5.5 kts
Range:	700 nm at 8 kts surfaced, 50 nm at 3 kts submerged
Armament:	4 Drzewiecki torpedoes in drop-collars
Complement:	24

HOLLAND Type SUBMARINES

Like the previous class these boats were ordered under the 1904 Emergency Programme to strengthen the fleet for the likely event of war with Japan. To enable construction in Russia to proceed smoothly and speedily *Fulton* was purchased from the USA and delivered in sections for completion in Russia so that the builders could see how the boats were built. In the end only *Shchuka* and *Som* could be delivered in sections and assembled in Vladivostock in time for the war. The problems experienced with petrol engines and the development of the diesel led to a decision to re-engine the boats with diesels before the First World War. The boats served in various fleets during the war, but most of them ended their life in the Baltic

Right: The American-built submarine *Fulton* seen in Long Island Bay *c*.1902. The boat was not accepted by the American Navy and was sold to the Russian Navy, being renamed *Som*. (Floyd Houston/US Naval Historical Center)

where they were armed with a 47 mm gun, only *Losos* and *Sudak* ending their service in the Black Sea Fleet. For a while they operated against the Soviets before being seized by the Germans, and eventually taken over by the British when Germany surrendered.

Displacement:	105/122 tons
Dimensions:	65 ft 6 in × 11 ft 6 in × 9 ft 6 in (19.95 m × 3.5 m × 2.89 m)
Machinery:	petrol/electric motor; 1 shaft; BHP 160, HP 70; 8.5/6 kts
Range:	585 nm surfaced, 42 nm submerged

NAME	BUILDER	LAID DOWN	LAUNCHED	COMPLETED	FATE
Beluga	Nevski	–	1905	1905	Scuttled 25 Feb 1918
Losos	Nevski	–	1907	–	Scuttled Sevastopol 26 April 1919
Peskar	Nevski	–	1905	1905	Scuttled 25 Feb 1918
Shchuka	Nevski	–	April 1905	Nov 1905	Scuttled 25 Feb 1918
Som (ex-*Fulton*)	Nevski	–	1904	April 1905	Sunk in collision with Swedish merchant ship *Angermanland* 23 May 1916
Sterlyad	Nevski	–	1905	1906	Scuttled 25 Feb 1918
Sudak	Nevski	–	1907	–	Scuttled Sevastopol 26 April 1919

Armament:	one 15 in TT (381 mm)
Complement:	22

Left: The Fulton seen hauled out on the slip at Brigham's Yard USA. During the haul-out her deck was extended and life-lines installed. (Floyd Houston/US Naval Historical Center)

LAKE Type SUBMARINES

These boats were ordered from the USA under the 1904 Emergency Programme for assembly in Russia. *Osetr* featured retractable hydraulically operated wheels for travelling along the seabed – a feature revived in recent years by Soviet mini-submarines in the Baltic. She also featured a diving chamber for use when submerged. All except *Sig* were sent to the Pacific, arriving in the spring of 1905, becoming operational in the autumn.

Displacement:	153/187 tons
Dimensions:	72 ft × 12 ft × 12 ft 3 in (21.93 m × 3.65 m × 3.73 m)

NAME	BUILDER	LAID DOWN	LAUNCHED	COMPLETED	FATE
Bychek	Arsenal, Libau	–	1905	1906	Stricken 1913
Kefal	Arsenal, Libau	–	1905	Oct 1905	Stricken 1915
Osetr (ex-*Protector*)	Arsenal, Libau	15 June 1904	1905	Sept 1905	Stricken 1913
Paltus	Arsenal, Libau	–	1905	1906	Stricken 1913
Plotva	Arsenal, Libau	–	1905	1906	Stricken 1913
Sig	Arsenal, Libau	–	1905	1906	Stricken July 1914

Machinery:	2 petrol/electric motors; 2 shafts; BHP 240, HP 120; 8.5/4.5 kts
Range:	385 nm surfaced, 35 nm submerged
Armament:	three (2 bow, 1 stern) 15 in TT (381 mm)
Complement:	24

FOREL SUBMARINE

This small experimental submarine was designed by a French engineer at the Krupp Germania yard in Germany. Ordered in July 1902, the design was not a significant advance on French submarines of the period. The boat was purchased by Russia to build up her submarine strength in the Pacific in readiness for a possible conflict with Japan. She was commissioned into the Imperial Navy as *Forel* on 6 May 1904.

NAME	BUILDER	LAID DOWN	LAUNCHED	COMPLETED	FATE
Forel	Krupp	Feb 1903	8 June 1903	–	Stricken 1911

Displacement: 16.17 tons
Dimensions: 49.2 ft × 14 ft × 7 ft (15 m × 4.26 m × 2.13 m)
Machinery: 1 electric motor; 1 shaft; HP 65; 5.5 kts
Radius: 20 nm
Armament: 2 torpedoes
Complement: 5

KARP Class SUBMARINES

Thes twin-hull boats were also ordered under the 1904 Emergency Programme to a German design. In contrast to previous boats, they used kerosene to fuel their engines, the kerosene being far less prone to accidental ignition than the normal petrol. *Karp* and *Karas* were removed from active service in March 1917 and were reactivated for use against the Soviets in April 1918. They were seized by the Germans and then the British, who scuttled them to avoid their capture by the Soviets.

Displacement: 207/235 tons

NAME	BUILDER	LAID DOWN	LAUNCHED	COMPLETED	FATE
Kambala	Germaniawerft	–	1907	–	Sunk in collision with battleship *Rostislav* at Sevastopol 11 June 1909
Karas	Germaniawerft	–	1907	–	Scuttled 26 April 1919
Karp	Germaniawerft	–	1907	–	Scuttled 26 April 1919

Dimensions: 130 ft (oa) × 9 ft × 8 ft (39.59 m × 2.74 m × 2.94 m)
Machinery: 2 kerosene/electric motors; 2 shafts; BHP 400, HP 200; 10/8.5 kts
Range: 1,250 nm surfaced, 50 nm submerged
Armament: one 18 in TT, 2 Drzewiecki drop-collar torpedoes (457 mm)
Complement: 28

KAIMAN Class SUBMARINES

These boats were built to a Lake design based on *Protector*. They were considerably larger (length increased by 60 ft and an increase in displacement of 356 tons) to allow for a much heavier armament (four 18 in as opposed to three 15 in torpedo tubes) and to provide increased bunkerage to extend the radius so that the boats could operate in Japanese waters. Although the boats were completed in 1910, the Russian Navy refused to accept them because of various faults which became manifest during trials. Following various modifications, which included adding two Drezwiecki drop-collar torepdoes, the boats were finally commissioned towards the end of 1911. Although they handled well on the surface they proved rather unreliable in service.

NAME	BUILDER	LAID DOWN	LAUNCHED	COMPLETED	FATE
Alligator	Crichton	–	1908	Dec 1910	Scuttled Reval 25 Feb 1918
Drakon	Crichton	–	1908	Dec 1910	Scuttled Reval 25 Feb 1918
Kaiman	Crichton	–	Nov 1907	Dec 1910	Scuttled Reval 25 Feb 1918
Krokodil	Crichton	–	1908	Dec 1910	Scuttled Reval 25 Feb 1918

During the First World War the boats were armed with a 47 mm gun, *Drakon* having a 37 mm as well. They carried out a number of successful patrols during the war, but were removed from active service in November 1916 as their crews were required to man the new *AG*-class boats then commissioning.

Displacement: 409/482 tons
Dimensions: 134 ft 5 in × 15 ft × 13 ft (40.9 m × 4.57 m × 3.96 m)
Machinery: 2 petrol/electric motors; 2 shafts; BHP 1,200; HP 400; 10.5/7 kts
Range: 1,050 nm at 8 kts surfaced, 40 nm at 5 kts submerged
Armament: four (2 bow, twin rotating deck) 18 in TT (457 mm) 2 Drzwiecki drop-collar torpedoes
Complement: 20

MINOGA SUBMARINE

The design of this submarine owed much to the experience of the boats which operated in the Pacific during the Russo-Japanese War. Prepared by Bubnov, the boat was a single-hull design with saddle-tanks. The major design feature, however, was the change to diesel propulsion which paved the way for considerable improvement in future Russian submarine designs. However, the diesels fitted in this boat were not completely successful and suffered from various shortcomings which were remedied in future designs.

Displacement:	123/155 tons
Dimensions:	107 ft × 8 ft 10 in × 8 ft 10 (32.59 m × 2.7 m × 2.7 m)
Machinery:	2 diesels/1 electric motor; 1 shaft; BHP 240, HP 70; 11/5 kts
Bunkers & Radius:	11 tons oil; 600 nm at 10 kts surfaced, 50 nm at 3.5 kts submerged
Armament:	one 37 mm two (bow) 18 in TT (457 mm)
Complement:	22

NAME	BUILDER	LAID DOWN	LAUNCHED	COMPLETED	FATE
Minoga	Baltic Works	–	24 Oct 1908	–	Scrapped 1922

AKULA SUBMARINE

This single-hull, saddle-tank design prepared by Bubnov, was an enlarged version of *Minoga*, but with the armament concept of the *Kaiman* class. Although generally considered to have been Russia's most successful pre-First World War submarine design, she nevertheless suffered from a number of troubles, mainly related to her machinery. During the First World War she had a 47 mm gun added on the foredeck.

Displacement:	370/475 tons
Dimensions:	187 ft × 12 ft × 11 ft (56.9 m × 3.65 m × 3.35 m)
Machinery:	3 diesels/1 electric motor; 3 shafts; BHP 900, HP 300; 10.6/6.6 kts
Range:	1,900 nm surfaced, 38 nm at 4.75 kts submerged
Armament:	one 47 mm four (2 bow, 2 stern) 18 in TT (457 mm) 4 Drzewiecki drop-collar torpedoes
Complement:	34

NAME	BUILDER	LAID DOWN	LAUNCHED	COMPLETED	FATE
Akula	Baltic Yard	–	4 Sept 1907	–	Mined Baltic 28 Nov 1915

POCHTOVY SUBMARINE

This design, prepared by Drzewiecki, resulted from a requirement to develop a true submarine, not a submersible. This required a single diesel engine for both surfaced and submerged propulsion using oxygen stored in bottles inside the submarine. However, no suitable diesel engine could be found and petrol engines were substituted which drew oxygen stored in bottles. The experimental installation proved successful, but was not developed further because of the wake resulting from the exhaust gases, and the very high humidity created inside the hull.

NAME	BUILDER	LAID DOWN	LAUNCHED	COMPLETED	FATE
Pochtovy	Metal Works	–	1908	–	Stricken 1913

Displacement: 134/146 tons
Dimensions: 113 ft × 10 ft × 9 ft 3 in (34.41 m × 3.04 m × 2.82 m)
Machinery: 2 petrol engines; 1 shaft; HP 260; 10.5/6.2 kts
Armament: 4 Drzewiecki drop-collar torpedoes
Complement: ?

KRAB SUBMARINE

Krab was the first submarine to be designed as a minelayer. However, she was so long building that when completed the Germans already had minelaying submarines operational. The mines were stored in two horizontal tubes fitted within the hull casing. They were winched aft by an electrically powered chain where they were discharged through two hatches. During the First World War *Krab* carried out numerous minelaying operations. She was seized by the Germans in April 1918 and then by the British in November, subsequently being scuttled to avoid capture by the Soviets.

NAME	BUILDER	LAID DOWN	LAUNCHED	COMPLETED	FATE
Krab	Navy Yard Nicolaiev	–	1 Sept 1912	July 1915	Scuttled Sevastopol 26 April 1919

Displacement: 560/740 tons
Dimensions: 173 ft 3 in × 14 ft × 12 ft 9 in (52.77 m × 4.26 m × 3.88 m)
Machinery: 4 petrol engines/2 electric motors; 2 shafts; BHP 1,200, HP 400; 11.8/7.12 kts
Range: 1,700 nm at 7 kts surfaced, 82 nm at 4 kts submerged
Armament: one 75 mm, two 18 in TT (457 mm), 2 Drzewiekcki drop-collar torpedoes, 60 mines
Complement: 25

Opposite page, top: Diesel-engined submarine *Minoga*. (Author's collection)

Left: The *Akula* seen on the building slip at the Baltic Works, St Petersburg. Engineer Bubnov, the designer and constructor, is seen in the foreground. (Boris Drashpil/US Naval Historical Center)

Right: The minelaying submarine *Krab* seen on a slipway in the Black Sea during the First World War. (Boris Drashpil/US Naval Historical Center)

HOLLAND Type SUBMARINES

These boats were orginally ordered by the Army for defending coastal fortifications. They were taken over by the Navy on the outbreak of the First World War and transferred to the Black Sea and Arctic. They were finally operational on the River Danube.

Displacement: 35/44 tons

NAME	BUILDER	LAID DOWN	LAUNCHED	COMPLETED	FATE
1	Nevski	–	1913	–	Sunk in collision with *Delfin* 26 April 1917
2	Nevski	–	–	–	Constructive total loss 15 Oct 1915
3	Nevski	–	–	–	Captured by Austria-Hungary 12 Mar 1918

Dimensions: 67 ft 4 in × 7 ft 6 in × 6 ft (20.51 m × 2.28 m × 1.83 m)
Machinery: 1 diesel/electric motor; 1 shaft; BHP 50, HP 35; 8/6 kts
Armament: two (bow) 18 in TT (457 mm)
Complement: 4

Left: No. *3* was originally ordered by the Russian Army to defend sea fortresses. She was taken over by the Navy at the outbreak of war and transferred to the Danube. (P. A. Vicary)

MORZH Class SUBMARINES

Developed from *Akula*, this Bubnov single-hull class suffered from a number of faults mainly concerning the hydrodynamic shape of the hull and poor watertight integrity. Further problems arose during construction because the diesel engines had been ordered from Germany, and when the First World War began an alternative source had to be found. Diesels were finally requisitioned from river gunboats serving with the Amur Flotilla. These, however, developed insufficient power to enable the submarines to reach their designed surface speed. As a result of these problems the boats never reached their design surface/underwater speeds of 16/12 kts. Despite the design problems, these three boats proved to be the most active and successful Russian submarines in the Black Sea during the First World War.

NAME	BUILDER	LAID DOWN	LAUNCHED	COMPLETED	FATE
Morzh	Baltic Yard	–	28 Sept 1913	–	Lost May 1917
Nerpa	Baltic Yard	–	28 Sept 1913	–	Renamed *Politruk* Jan 1923
Tyulen	Baltic Yard	–	1 Nov 1913	–	To Bizerta 1920

Displacement: 630/760 tons
Dimensions: 220 ft × 15 ft × 13 ft (67 m × 4.57 m × 3.96 m)
Machinery: 2 diesel/2 electric motors; 2 shafts; BHP 500, HP 800; 10.8/8 kts
Range: 2,500 nm surfaced, 1,120 nm submerged
Armament: one 57 mm; one 47 mm; four (2 bow, 2 stern) 18 in TT (457 mm); 8 Drzewiecki drop-collar torpedoes
Complement: 47

Right: *Tyulen* carried out a number of successful patrols against the Turks in the Black Sea. (Author's collection)

Right: The *Morzh* seen at Sevastopol Navy Yard in the Black Sea during the First World War. Behind the submarine is the hospital ship *Imperator Petr Veliki*. (Boris Drashpil/US Naval Historical Center)

SVYATOI GEORGI SUBMARINE

This Fiat–Laurenti-designed boat was ordered from Italy in 1912 for service in the Black Sea. She was purchased by the Italians in February 1915 and commissioned into the Italian Navy.

Displacement: 255/306 tons
Dimensions: 148 ft × 13 ft 9 in × 9 ft 10 in (45.08 m × 4.19 m × 2.99 m)

NAME	BUILDER	LAID DOWN	LAUNCHED	COMPLETED	FATE
Svyatoi Georgi	Fiat–San Giorgio	–	5 July 1914	–	Purchased by Italy Feb 1915

Machinery: 2 Fiat diesels/2 electric motors; 2 shafts; BHP 700, HP 450; 13.5/8.8 kts
Range: 950 nm at 12 kts surfaced, 100 nm submerged
Armament: two (bow) 17.7 in TT (4 torpedoes) (450 mm)
Complement: 24

NARVAL Class SUBMARINES

These double-hull Holland-type submarines were considered to have been the best submarines built for the Imperial Navy. Among the notable features were watertight bulkheads, a feature previously lacking in Russian submarine designs. As for other Russian submarines under construction at this time, suitable diesels were in very short supply. Hence the original requirement for two 850 bhp diesels had to be changed and instead four 640 bhp diesels were fitted with a consequent reduction in surfaced speed from the designed 16 kts to 9.6 kts.

NAME	BUILDER	LAID DOWN	LAUNCHED	COMPLETED	FATE
Kashalot	Nevski	–	1914	–	Scuttled Sevastopol 26 April 1919
Kit	Nevski	–	1914	–	Scuttled Sevastopol 26 April 1919
Narval	Nevski	–	1914	–	Scuttled Sevastopol 26 April 1919

Displacement: 621/994 tons
Dimensions: 230 ft × 21 ft 6 in × 11 ft 6 in (70.05 m × 6.55 m × 3.5 m)
Machinery: 4 diesels/2 electric motors; 2 shafts; BHP 640, HP 900; 9.6 (*Narval* 10.5)/11.5 kts
Range: 400 nm surfaced, 120 nm submerged
Armament: one 75 mm; one 63 mm (not in *Narval*); four (2 bow, 2 stern) 18 in TT (457 mm); eight (*Narval* four) Drzewiecki drop-collar torpedoes
Complement: 47

BARS Class SUBMARINES

This was the largest class of submarines ordered by the Imperial Navy. The design was a slightly enlarged version of the *Morzh*-class design, and suffered from the same limitations. As with other Russian submarine classes, the acute shortage of suitable diesels led to delays in construction and all except *Kuguar* and *Zmeya* (these two boats were completed with the designed diesels) were fitted with 250 bhp diesels taken from river gunboats of the Amur Flotilla, locally manufactured 240 bhp diesels or diesels purchased from friendly countries. Trials with the first units indicated that the siting of the drop-collars was not satisfactory and gradually these were sited higher up on some boats. The drop-collars were subsequently removed and the recesses plated over. Various other modifications were made to armament during the war. *Ersh* and *Forel* were converted to a minelaying role with two tubes each holding 21 mines sited under the casing aft, the stern torpedo tubes being removed. Gun armament was also modified on a number of units with additional 63 mm added, or 75 mm and 37 mm AA.

After the Revolution *Kuguar* and *Vepr* were used as static training ships while the remaining boats in the Baltic were commissioned into the Soviet Navy. The boats built in the Black Sea were all seized by the Germans in May 1918, but only *Utka* was commissioned as *US 3*. The six boats were all taken over by the British at the Armistice and scuttled off Sevastopol. *Burvestnik* and *Utka* were transferred to the Wrangel Squadron.

NAME	BUILDER	LAID DOWN	LAUNCHED	COMPLETED	FATE
Bars	Baltic Yard	–	2 June 1915	–	Lost 28 May 1917
Burvestnik	Navy Yard Nicolaiev	–	1916	–	Sold 1924
Edinorog	Baltic Yard	–	1916	–	Lost 25 Feb 1918
Ersh	Baltic Yard	–	1917	–	Renamed *Rabochi* Jan 1923
Forel	Baltic Yard	–	1916	–	Stricken May 1922
Gagara	Baltic Yard (BS)	–	7 Oct 1916	–	Scuttled Sevastopol 26 April 1919
Gepard	Baltic Yard	–	2 June 1915	–	Lost 28 Oct 1917
Kuguar	Noblessner Yard	–	1916	–	Hulked 1922
Lebed	Navy Yard Nicolaiev	–	Sept 1917	–	Scuttled Sevastopol 26 April 1919
Leopard	Noblessner Yard	–	1916	–	Renamed *Krasnoarmeets* Jan 1923
Lvitsa	Noblessner Yard	–	23 Oct 1915	–	Lost 11 June 1917
Orlan	Navy Yard Nicolaiev	–	1916	–	Scuttled Sevastopol 26 April 1919
Pantera	Noblessner Yard	–	26 April 1916	–	Renamed *Komissar* Jan 1923
Pelikan	Navy Yard Nicolaiev	–	Sept 1917	–	Scuttled Sevastopol 26 April 1919
Rys	Noblessner Yard	–	1916	–	Renamed *Bolshevik* Jan 1923
Tigr	Noblessner Yard	–	18 Sept 1915	Jan 1916	Renamed *Kommunar* Jan 1923
Tur	Noblessner Yard	–	1916	–	Renamed *Tovarishch* Jan 1923
Ugor	Baltic Yard	–	1916	–	Sunk 27 Mar 1920
Utka	Baltic Yard (BS)	–	1916	–	Sold 1924
Vepr	Baltic Yard	–	1915	–	Hulked 1922
Volk	Baltic Yard	–	1915	–	Renamed *Batrak* Jan 1923
Yaguar	Noblessner Yard	–	1916	–	Renamed *Krasnoflotets* Jan 1923
Yaz	Noblessner Yard	–	1917	–	Deleted May 1922
Zmeya	Baltic Yard	–	1916	–	Renamed *Proletari* Jan 1923

Above: The torpedo room of *Burevestnik*. (Author's collection)

Top right: The launch of the submarine *Ersh* at the Baltic Works, St Petersburg. Originally assigned to the Siberian Flotilla, she was re-assigned to the Baltic Fleet on 12 March 1915. (Boris Drashpil/US Naval Historical Center)

Right: The *Gepard* seen in the Baltic during the First World War. (Boris Drashpil/US Naval Historical Center)

Displacement:	650/780 tons
Dimensions:	223 ft × 15 ft × 13 ft (67.92 m × 4.57 m × 3.96 m)
Machinery:	2 diesel/2 electric motors; 2 shafts; BHP 2,640, 240, 250, or 420, HP 900; 18, 11.5 or 13/10 kts
Bunkers & Range:	40 tons oil; 400 nm at 17 kts surfaced, 25 nm at 9 kts submerged
Armament:	one 63 mm one 37 mm four (2 bow, 2 stern) 18 in TT (457 mm) 8 Drzewiecki drop-collar torpedoes
Complement:	33

Below: This picture of the *Tigr* shows the siting of the Drzewiecki drop-collars for torpedoes in the sides of the hull in the deck casing. (Author's collection)

Left: *Utka* alongside *Blockship 9* in Sevastopol, 1919. (Author's collection)

SVIATOI GEORGI (II) SUBMARINE

This Fiat–Laurenti-design submarine was ordered from Italy in 1916 to replace *Sviatoi Georgi* purchased by the Italian Navy in 1915. She arrived at Arkhangelsk in September 1917.

NAME	BUILDER	LAID DOWN	LAUNCHED	COMPLETED	FATE
Sviatoi Georgi (II) (ex-*F1*)	Ansaldo	–	1916	20 May 1917	Renamed *Kommunar* 1918

Displacement: 260/305 tons
Dimensions: 147ft 6in × 14ft × 10ft (44.92m × 4.26m × 3.04m)
Machinery: 2 Fiat diesels/2 electric motors; 2 shafts; BHP 700, HP 500; 13/8.5kts
Armament: one 75mm; two (bow) 18in TT (457mm)
Complement: 24

AG Class SUBMARINES

Ordered under the 1915 Emergency Programme, these boats were built to a Holland design identical with the boats built for Britain, Italy and the USA. They were delivered to Russia in sections for final assembly. The hull was of streamlined design which resulted in a much better seaboat than previous Russian submarines. The hull was divided into five watertight compartments with escape hatches forward and aft for the crew. The boats differed from the *Bars* design in having internal ballast tanks, and the boats were more stable than earlier Russian submarines. None of the boats under construction in the Black Sea entered service with the Imperial Navy.

NAME	BUILDER	LAID DOWN	LAUNCHED	COMPLETED	FATE
AG11	Baltic Yard	1915	1916	Nov 1916	Scuttled Finland 3 April 1918
AG12	Baltic Yard	1915	1916	Nov 1916	Scuttled Finland 3 April 1918
AG13	Baltic Yard	1915	1916	Nov 1916	Foundered 1916. Raised, renamed *AG16*. Scuttled Finland 3 April 1918
AG14	Baltic Yard	1915	1916	Nov 1916	Mined 6 July 1917
AG15	Baltic Yard	1915	1916	Nov 1916	Lost 18 June 1917. Raised. Scuttled Finland 3 April 1918
AG17	Baltic Yard	–	–	–	Requisitioned by US as *H4*
AG18	Baltic Yard	–	–	–	Requisitioned by US as *H5*
AG19	Baltic Yard	–	–	–	Requisitioned by US as *H6*
AG20	Baltic Yard	–	–	–	Requisitioned by US as *H7*
AG21	Baltic Yard (BS)	1917	1917	1918	Scuttled Sevastopol 26 April 1919
AG22	Baltic Yard (BS)	–	1919	–	Sold 1924
AG23	Baltic Yard (BS)	May 1917	1 June 1920	22 Sept 1920	Renamed *Nezamozhnyi* Feb 1923
AG24	Baltic Yard (BS)	1 June 1920	1921	16 July 1921	Renamed *Lunacharski* 1923
AG25	Baltic Yard (BS)	July 1920	1921	27 May 1922	Renamed *Marksist* Feb 1923
AG26	Baltic Yard (BS)	Nov 1920	1921	11 July 1923	Renamed *Kamenev*
AG27	Baltic Yard (BS)	–	–	–	Requisitioned by US as *H8*
AG28	Baltic Yard (BS)	–	–	–	Requisitioned by US as *H9*

Displacement: 355/433 tons (*AG21–26* 360/470 tons)
Dimensions: 147ft 9in (*AG21–26* 151ft) × 15ft 9in × 12ft 6in (*AG21–26* 15ft)) (45 (46)m × 4.8m × 3.8 (4.6)m)
Machinery: 2 Nelesco diesels/2 electric motors; 2 shafts; BHP 960, HP 640; 12/10 (*AG21–26* 13/11)kts
Bunkers & Radius: 16.5 tons oil; 1,800nm surfaced
Armament: one 47mm; four (bow) 18in TT (457mm)
Complement: 30

B Class SUBMARINES

Ordered under the 1916 Programme for service in the Baltic. The design was based on the Holland design incorporating double hull and watertight subdivision. The design was unusual in that four of the torpedo tubes were mounted broadside within the hull. None of these submarines was ever completed.

Displacement:	971/1,264 tons
Dimensions:	265 ft × 23 ft × 13 ft (80.71 m × 7 m × 3.96 m)
Machinery:	diesel/electric motors; 2 shafts; 17/9 kts
Range:	1,200 nm surfaced, 22.5 nm submerged

NAME	BUILDER	LAID DOWN	LAUNCHED	COMPLETED	FATE
B1	Baltic Yard	1916–17	–	–	Cancelled
B2	Baltic Yard	1916–17	–	–	Cancelled
B3	Baltic Yard	1916–17	–	–	Cancelled
B4	Baltic Yard	1916–17	–	–	Cancelled
B5	Russo-Baltic Yard	1916–17	–	–	Cancelled
B6	Russo-Baltic Yard	1916–17	–	–	Cancelled
B7	Russo-Baltic Yard	1916–17	–	–	Cancelled
B8	Russo-Baltic Yard	1916–17	–	–	Cancelled
B9	Russo-Baltic Yard	1916–17	–	–	Cancelled
B10	Russo-Baltic Yard	1916–17	–	–	Cancelled

Armament:	two 75 mm ten 18 in TT (457 mm) 6 Drzewiecki drop-collar torpedoes 10 mines
Complement:	?

G Class SUBMARINES

Almost identical with the previous class and based on the Holland design. The units were ordered under the 1916 Programme for service in the Baltic and Black Sea.

Displacement:	952/1,289 tons
Dimensions:	265 ft × 23 ft × 13 ft (80.71 m × 7 m × 3.96 m)
Machinery:	diesel/electric motors; 2 shafts; 16/9 kts

NAME	BUILDER	LAID DOWN	LAUNCHED	COMPLETED	FATE
G1–G10	Noblessner Yard	1916–17	–	–	Cancelled
G11–G14	Russud Yard	1916–17	–	–	Cancelled
G15–G28	?	–	–	–	Cancelled

Armament:	two 75 mm ten 18 in TT (457 mm) 6 Drzewiecki drop-collar torpedoes 10 mines
Complement:	?

V Class SUBMARINES

This Fiat design was ordered under the 1916 Programme for service in the Black Sea.

Displacement:	920/1,140 tons
Dimensions:	265 ft × 23 ft × 13 ft (80.71 m × 7 m × 3.96 m)
Machinery:	diesel/electric motors; 2 shafts; 13/10.5 kts

NAME	BUILDER	LAID DOWN	LAUNCHED	COMPLETED	FATE
V1–V4	Russud Yard	1916–17	–	–	Cancelled
V5–V7	?	–	–	–	Cancelled

Armament:	two 75 mm ten 18 in TT (457 mm) 6 Drzewiecki drop-collar torpedoes 10 mines
Complement:	?

Z Class SUBMARINES

Ordered under the 1916 Programme, these minelaying submarines were designed for service in the Baltic.

Displacement:	230/368 tons
Dimensions:	?
Machinery:	diesel/electric motors; 10/5 kts

NAME	BUILDER	LAID DOWN	LAUNCHED	COMPLETED	FATE
Z1–Z2	Russo-Baltic Yard	1917	–	–	Cancelled
Z3–Z4	Baltic Yard	1917	–	–	Cancelled

Range:	2,000 nm surfaced, 90 nm submerged
Armament:	20 mines
Complement:	?

MINE WARFARE SHIPS

BUG Class MINELAYERS

These two small minelayers were originally built as trials vessels to carry out experiments in minelaying in the Black Sea, being converted to a fully operational minelaying role sometime after 1907. *Bug* was caught up in the 1905 mutiny aboard *Potemkin* and was scuttled at Sevastopol to prevent any accidental detonation of her mine cargo. She was later raised, repaired and recommissioned. During the First World War *Dunai* was re-armed with two 3 in, four 3 pdr and four machine-guns.

Displacement:	1,340 tons
Dimensions:	204 ft × 34 ft × 16 ft (62.1 m × 10.35 m × 4.9 m)
Machinery:	reciprocating (VTE); 2 shafts; 4 boilers; IHP 1,400; 13 kts
Bunkers:	265 tons coal
Armament:	six 3 pdr (47 mm) four 1 pdr (37 mm) 250 mines
Complement:	238

NAME	BUILDER	LAID DOWN	LAUNCHED	COMPLETED	FATE
Bug	Lindholmen	–	1891	–	?
Dunai	Lindholmen	–	1891	–	Renamed *I Maya c.*1922

AMUR Class MINELAYERS

These ships, the first purpose-built minelayers in the world, resembled small cruisers. Both carried out a number of minelaying operations during the Russo-Japanese War. On 14 May 1904 *Amur* laid a field of fifty mines which proved to be one of the most successful mining operations in history. In one day the field accounted for two of Japan's most modern battleships, *Hatsuse* and *Yashima*. Both ships were lost during the War, *Amur* from the Japanese siege guns surrounding Port Arthur and *Yenisei* on one of her own mines.

Displacement:	3,010 tons
Dimensions:	300 ft (wl) × 41 ft × 18 ft (91.37 m × 12.49 m × 5.48 m)
Machinery:	reciprocating (VTE); 2 shafts; 12 Belleville boilers; IHP 4,700; 18 kts
Bunkers & Radius:	400 tons coal; 2,000 nm at 10 kts
Armament:	five 3 in (75 mm) seven 3 pdr (47 mm) one 15 in TT (381 mm) 300 mines
Complement:	317

NAME	BUILDER	LAID DOWN	LAUNCHED	COMPLETED	FATE
Amur	Baltic Works	19 May 1898	8 Nov 1898	1899	Sunk 18 Dec 1904
Yenisei	Baltic Works	1898	20 May 1899	1899	Mined 11 Feb 1904

AMUR Class MINELAYERS

As the previous design had proved to be so successful it was decided to build two more minelayers to a similar design to replace the previous two vessels lost in the Russo-Japanese war. During the First World War *Amur* was given eight additional 4.7 in guns and one 1 pdr AA gun. *Amur* was used as a training ship after the war.

NAME	BUILDER	LAID DOWN	LAUNCHED	COMPLETED	FATE
Amur	Baltic Works	May 1905	29 June 1907	1909	Scuttled 27 Aug 1941
Yenisei	Baltic Works	May 1905	18 July 1906	1910	Torpedoed by *U 26* 4 June 1915

Displacement: 2,926 tons
Dimensions: 300 ft (oa) × 46 ft × 14 ft 6 in (91.37 m × 14.01 m × 4.42 m)
Machinery: reciprocating (VTE); 2 shafts; 12 Belleville boilers; IHP 4,700; 17 kts
Bunkers: 670 tons coal
Armament: two 4.7 in/45 cal (120 mm) eight 3 in (75 mm) 360 mines
Complement: 318

VOLGA MINELAYER

NAME	BUILDER	LAID DOWN	LAUNCHED	COMPLETED	FATE
Volga	Baltic Works	–	1905	1905	Used as target *c.*1959

Displacement: 1,711 tons
Dimensions: 213 ft 3 in × 39 ft × 15 ft 9 in (64.9 m × 11.87 m × 4.79 m)
Machinery: reciprocating (VTE); 2 shafts; 4 Belleville boilers; IHP 1,600; 12 kts
Armament: two 3 in (75 mm) two 3 in AA (75 mm) one 3 pdr (47 mm) 285 mines

Complement: 190

Top left: Minelayer *Dunai* *c.*1910–13. (Author's collection)

Left: Purpose-built minelayer *Yenisei.* (Author's collection)

Right: Minelayer *Volga* *c.*1910. (Author's collection)

TEPLOKHOD Class MINELAYERS

Displacement:	80 tons
Dimensions:	68 ft 9 in × 15 ft 3 in × 4 ft (20.93 m × 4.64 m × 1.2 m)
Machinery:	one diesel; 1 shaft; BHP 80; 9 kts
Bunkers:	1.25 tons oil
Armament:	one 3 pdr (47 mm) 80 mines
Complement:	10

NAME	BUILDER	FATE
T1	Pori Yard	To Finland 1918
T2	Pori Yard	To Estonia 1918
T3	Pori Yard	To Estonia 1918
T4	Pori Yard	To Finland 1918
T5	Pori Yard	To Finland 1918
T6	Pori Yard	To Finland 1918
T7	Pori Yard	To Finland 1918
T8	Pori Yard	To Estonia 1918
T9	Pori Yard	To Estonia 1918
T10	Pori Yard	To Estonia 1918

DEMOSFEN Class MINELAYERS/NETLAYERS

This was a dual-purpose design which could double either as a minelayer or a netlayer for service in the Baltic.

Displacement:	320/338 tons
Dimensions:	?
Machinery:	one diesel engine; 8/11 kts
Armament:	one 3 in (*Pripyat* two 4 in) (75 (102) mm) one 3 in AA (75 mm) 90/100 mines
Complement:	?

NAME	LAUNCHED	FATE
Iset	1917	–
Kivach	1917	–
Klyazma	1917	–
Kuban	1917	–
Luga	1917	To Finland 1918
Pripyat	1917	–
Sejm	1917	–
Selenga	1917	–
Terek	1917	–

VOIN MINELAYER

Displacement:	640 tons
Dimensions:	164 ft × 26 ft × 9 ft (50 m × 8 m × 2.7 m)
Machinery:	reciprocating (VTE); 2 shafts; ? boilers; IHP 800; 10 kts
Bunkers:	?
Armament:	two 3 in (75 mm) 150 mines
Complement:	47

NAME	BUILDER	LAID DOWN	LAUNCHED	COMPLETED	FATE
Voin	Kolomna	–	1916	–	Transferred to Finland 1918

MISCELLANEOUS AUXILIARY MINELAYERS/NETLAYERS

NAME	BUILT/COMMISSIONED	TONNAGE	ARMAMENT	FATE
Ayu-Dag	1898/1916	1,765	–	–
Beshtau	1907/1914	1,120	2 × 3 in, 100 mines	–
Bureya	1915/1916	250	95 mines	Seized by Germany 1918
Dikhtau	1907/1914	1,110	2 × 3 in, 120 mines	–
Dyuna	1868/1916	594	–	–
Elborus	1893/1916	1,050	–	–
General Brusilov	?/1916	–	–	–
General Ruzitski	1916/1916	400	–	–
Gidra	1889/1916	300	–	–
Ilmen	1912/1915	2,160	2 × 3 in, 400 mines	Seized by Germany 1918
Irtysh	1916/1916	230	95 mines	–
Khoper	1866/1916	1,100	–	–
Kiev	?/1917	–	–	–
Lena	?	2,400	370 mines	–
Lovat	1912/1915	600	80 mines	–
Mina	1913/1916	180	80 mines	–
Mologa	1903/1915	450	80 mines	–
Monogugai	1891/1911	2,500	7 × 3 pdr, 310 mines	–
Msta	1883/1916	1,955	360 mines	Seized by Germany 1918
Ob	1905/?	780	–	To Finland 1918
Oleg	?/1914	–	–	Mined 24 Dec 1914
Penaj	?/1914	–	–	–
Sheksna	1904/1915	450	80 mines	Seized by Germany 1918
Shika	1897/1911	3,500	4 × 120 mm, 8 × 75 mm, 500 mines	–
Svir	1911/1916	1,800	2 × 3 in, 550 mines	Seized by Germany 1918
Terek	?/1916	–	–	–
Titaniya	1879/1916	128	–	–
Tsessarevitch Georgi	1896/1914	1,130	1 × 6 in, 3 × 75 mm, 1 × 37 mm, 280 mines	–
Ural	?/1915	2,400	4 × 3 in, 360 mines	–
Ussuri	1901/1911	3,200	3 × 120 mm, 4 × 47 mm, 500 mines	Mined 1 Aug 1918
Velikaya Knyazinya Kseniya	1895/1914	2,700	1 × 6 in, 3 × 75 mm, 2 × 37 mm, 160 mines	
Veliki Kniaz Aleksei	1890/1914	2,400	1 × 6 in, 3 × 75 mm, 1 × 37 mm, 200 mines	–
Veliki Kniaz Konstantin	1891/1914	2,500	1 × 6 in, 3 × 75 mm,	–
Zeya	1915/1916	250	1 × 37 mm, 200 mines 95 mines	Lost 1918

Above: Auxiliary minelayer *Irtysh* in the Baltic during the War. (Author's collection)

Top right: Auxiliary minelayer *Svir*. (Author's collection)

Right: Auxiliary minelayer *Ksenia*. (Author's collection)

BEREZINA Class MINELAYERS/NETLAYERS

Displacement: 380 tons
Dimensions: 144ft 3in × 19ft 9in × 8ft (43.93m × 6m × 2.44m)
Machinery: reciprocating; one cylindrical boiler; IHP 500; 8.5kts

NAME	BUILDER	LAID DOWN	LAUNCHED	COMPLETED	FATE
Berezina	Kolomenskaya	–	1917	–	–
Yauza	Kolomenskaya	–	1917	–	–

Armament: two 3.9in (100mm) 90 mines
Complement: 32

INDIGIRKA Class MINELAYERS/NETLAYERS

Displacement: 220 tons
Machinery: one diesel engine; 9kts
Armament: two 3in (75mm) 85 mines
Complement: ?

NAME	BUILDER	LAID DOWN	LAUNCHED	COMPLETED	FATE
Indigirka	Nizhnegorodski	–	1917	–	–
Mologa	Nizhnegorodski	–	1917	–	To Finland 1918

FUGAS Class MINESWEEPERS

With their pre-eminence as experts in the field of mine warfare, particularly in the Baltic, it was only natural that the Russians should also have the first purpose-built minesweepers in the world. Following traditional trawler-type layout, these vessels were built to carry out experiments in minesweeping. The vessels were heavily engaged in keeping shipping lanes open during the First World War, as evidenced by the heavy losses suffered. A mainmast was added to some units during the course of the war.

NAME	BUILDER	LAID DOWN	LAUNCHED	COMPLETED	FATE
Fugas	Izhora	–	1910	–	Mined 22 Nov 1916
Minrep	Izhora	–	1910	–	?
Provodnik	Izhora	–	1910	–	Mined 27 Aug 1914
Vzryv	Izhora	–	1910	–	Mined 26 May 1916
Zapal	Izhora	–	1910	–	Mined Aug 1940

Displacement: 150 tons
Dimensions: 148ft × 20ft × 6ft 3in (45.1m × 6.1m × 1.9m)
Machinery: reciprocating; 2 shafts; 2 boilers; IHP 400; 11.5kts
Bunkers: ?
Armament: one 2.5in (63mm) 50 mines
Complement: 33

Left: *Vzryv*, one of the first purpose-built minesweepers. (Author's collection)

ALBATROS Class MINESWEEPERS

Displacement: 106 tons
Dimensions: 85 ft × 17 ft 6 in × 5 ft (25.9 m × 5.3 m × 1.5 m)
Machinery: reciprocating (VTE); 2 boilers; 1 shaft; IHP 137; 8.7 kts

NAME	BUILDER	LAID DOWN	LAUNCHED	COMPLETED	FATE
Albatros	Bellino-Fenderich	–	1910	–	–
Bakan	Bellino-Fenderich	–	1910	–	–

Armament: two 1 pdr (37 mm)
Complement: 31

PATRON Class MINESWEEPERS

These ships were built in Britain as tugs for service with the Siberian Flotilla. However, they were retained in the Baltic and converted to minesweepers in 1915.

Displacement: 445 tons
Dimensions: 140 ft × 24 ft 6 in × 13 ft (42.7 m × 7.5 m × 3.9 m)

NAME	BUILDER	LAID DOWN	LAUNCHED	COMPLETED	FATE
Iskra	Smith Dock	–	1913	–	Mined 6 Oct 1916
Patron	Smith Dock	–	1913	–	Scrapped 1930s
Plamya	Smith Dock	–	1913	–	To Finland 1918

Machinery: reciprocating (TE); 1 shaft; 2 boilers; IHP 520; 11.5 kts
Armament: one 3 in (75 mm)
Complement: ?

GRUZ Class MINESWEEPERS

Ordered under the major 1912 Programme for the Baltic Fleet.

Displacement: 248 tons
Dimensions: ? ft × ? ft × 4 ft 6 in (? m × ? m × 1.4 m)
Machinery: reciprocating (TE); 2 shafts; 2 boilers; IHP 650; 9 kts
Armament: one 3 in (75 mm)

NAME	BUILDER	LAID DOWN	LAUNCHED	COMPLETED	FATE
Gruz	Putilov	–	1916	–	To Finland 1918
Kapsyul	Putilov	–	1916	–	To Finland 1918
Krambol	Russo-Baltic	–	1916	–	To Finland 1918
Shchit	Russo-Baltic	–	1916	–	Mined 6 Dec 1916

one 1 pdr (37 mm)
64 mines
Complement: ?

ZASHCHITNIK Class MINESWEEPERS

Like the *Gruz* class, these minesweepers were ordered under the 1912 Programme for service in the Baltic.

Displacement: 190 tons
Dimensions: 147 ft 6 in × 20 ft 4 in × 5 ft 6 in (45 m × 6.2 m × 1.7 m)
Machinery: reciprocating (TE); 1 shaft; IHP 550; 12 kts

NAME	BUILDER	LAID DOWN	LAUNCHED	COMPLETED	FATE
Fortral	Ahlstrom	–	1917	–	To Finland 1918
Klyuz	Ahlstrom	–	1916	–	Mined 24 Nov 1942
Udarnik	Putilov	–	1916	–	Mined 2 Oct 1942
Zashchitnik	Putilov	–	1916	–	To Finland 1918

Armament: one 3 in (75 mm)
30 mines
Complement: 35

T 13 Class MINESWEEPERS

This class of minesweepers was built in Britain to a standard trawler design for service with the Arctic Ocean Flotilla.

Displacement: 520 tons
Dimensions: 130 ft (pp) × 23 ft 6 in × 12 ft (39.6 m × 7.2 m × 3.7 m)
Machinery: reciprocating (VTE); 1 shaft; 1 boiler; IHP 490; 10.5 kts
Bunkers: 180 tons coal
Armament: one 3 in (75 mm)
Complement: 32

NAME	BUILDER	LAID DOWN	LAUNCHED	COMPLETED	FATE
T 13	Smith Dock	–	1916	–	To Britain 1918
T 14	Smith Dock	–	1916	–	To Britain 1918
T 15	Smith Dock	–	1916	–	Lost 2 Aug 1918
T 16	Smith Dock	–	1916	–	To Britain 1918
T 18	Smith Dock	–	1916	–	Lost 18 Mar 1917
T 19	Smith Dock	–	1916	–	CTL before completion
T 19 (ii)	Cochrane	–	1917	–	To Britain 1918
T 20	Smith Dock	–	1916	–	To France 1918
T 21	Smith Dock	–	1916	–	Scrapped 1923
T 22	Smith Dock	–	1916	–	To France 1918
T 23	Smith Dock	–	1916	–	Scrapped 1923
T 24	Smith Dock	–	1916	–	Scrapped 1923

MT Type MINESWEEPERS

A small class of motor minesweepers ordered in 1917 for service with the Baltic Fleet.

Displacement:	25/29 tons
Dimensions:	50 ft (pp) × 11 ft 6 in × ? ft (15.3 m × 3.5 m × ? m)
Machinery:	one petrol engine; 1 shaft; BHP 50; 9/12.5 kts
Armament:	one machine-gun
Complement:	8

NAME	BUILDER	LAID DOWN	LAUNCHED	COMPLETED	FATE
MT 1	Andre Rozenkvist	—	—	—	Lost 30 Nov 1917
MT 2	Andre Rozenkvist	—	—	—	To Finland 1918
MT 3	Andre Rozenkvist	—	—	—	To Finland 1918
MT 4	Andre Rozenkvist	—	—	—	To Finland 1918
MT 5–MT 9	Andre Rozenkvist	—	—	—	Seized incomplete by Finland 1918
MT 10	Botnia Yard	—	—	—	To Finland 1918
MT 11	Botnia Yard	—	—	—	Lost July 1917
MT 12	Botnia Yard	—	—	—	To Finland 1918
MT 13	Botnia Yard	—	—	—	To Finland 1918
MT 14	Botnia Yard	—	—	—	Lost 30 Nov 1917
MT 15–MT 18	Botnia Yard	—	—	—	To Finland 1918

A Class MINESWEEPERS

This class of small (13/21 tons) motor minesweepers was ordered from Crichton in 1916–17 for service in the Baltic. Numbered *A10–A45*, records indicate that only numbers *A11, A12, A19–A21* and *A37–A45* were ever completed and these were seized by Finland in 1918.

MISCELLANEOUS AUXILIARY MINESWEEPERS

NAME/NUMBER	BUILT	DISPLACEMENT (tons)	FATE
Aleksandra	1886	288	
Alesha Popovich	1913	350	To Finland 1918
Avans	1884	263	—
Ayaks	—	190	—
Batum	—	1,273	—
Dobrynya	1911	325	To Finland 1918
Dulo	1915	100	To Finland 1918
Garpun	1915	310	—
Ilya Muromets	1910	330	Mined 23 Aug 1917
Kharaks	—	1,324	—
Khersonets	—	1,324	—
Kitoboj	1915	310	—
Kometa	1888	322	To Finland 1918
Kovda	1902	1,225	—
Mechta	—	2,792	—
Mikula	1911	300	To Finland 1918
Namet	1915	310	—
Nevod	1915	310	—
Orezund	1908	195	Mined 20 Dec 1915
Paris	—	—	—
Patroki	—	200	—
Planeta	1858	287	—
Planeta	1893	134	To Finland 1918
Potok Bogatyr	1913	370	To Finland 1918
Rossija	—	1,573	—
Sever	1894	179	Mined 20 Dec 1915
Stvol	1915	100	To Finland 1918
Svyatogor	1911	400	To Latvia 1918
Svyatoi Nikolai	1858	141	Mined 20 Dec 1915
Truvor	—	2,629	—
Tsapfa	1915	145	To Finland 1918
Tumba	1915	145	To Finland 1918
Uliss	—	—	—
Vera	1903	360	Mined 20 Dec 1915
Vesta	—	1,273	—
Vitiaz	—	1,845	—
Yakor	1915	400	—
Yug	1906	191	Mined 10 Dec 1915
1	1892	450	Mined 16 Sept 1915
2	—	570	To Finland 1918
3	1912	600	—
3	1875	245	To Finland 1918
4	—	600	Lost 23 Oct 1915
4	1894	1,100	—
4	1914	200	To Estonia 1918
5	—	580	Mined 27 May 1916
6	1889	700	Lost 22 Aug 1915
7	1890	590	Mined 22 Sept 1914
7	1904	700	Seized by Germany 1918
8	—	600	Mined 22 Sept 1914
8	1910	700	Seized by Germany 1918
9	1911	700	—
10	1911	700	Seized by Germany 1918
11	1898	800	—
12	1901	600	—
14	—	140	—
15	—	140	To Finland 1918
16	—	140	To Finland 1918
17	—	140	To Finland 1918
18	1906	499	To Estonia 1918
19	1906	501	To Estonia 1918
20	1904	450	Minelayer *Sheksna* 1915
21	1903	450	Minlayer *Mologa*
22	—	750	CTL Nov 1917
23	1882	800	—
24	—	150	—
T 1	1909	219	To Britain 1918
T 2	1907	215	To Britain 1918
T 3	1912	242	To Britain 1918
T 4	1912	320	—
T 5	1912	225	Scrapped 1923
T 6	1899	220	To Britain 1918
T 7	1908	104	Scrapped 1923
T 8	1894	351	—
T 8	1912	158	—
T 9	1894	208	To Norway 1918
T 10	1890	170	Lost 14 Oct 1917
T 11	1908	300	Lost Dec 1917
T 12	1908	332	To Britain 1918
T 25	1905	500	Scrapped 1923
T 26	1905	500	Scrapped 1923
T 27	1908	500	Scrapped 1923
T 28	1908	500	Scrapped 1923
T 29	1904	500	Scrapped 1920
T 30	1906	261	Scrapped 1920
T 31	1907	195	To Britain 1918
T 32	1907	195	Scrapped 1920
T 33	1908	270	To Britain 1918
T 34	1908	270	To Britain 1918
T 35	1908	181	Scrapped 1923
T 36	1910	263	To Britain 1918
T 37	1911	276	Scrapped 1923
T 38	1911	275	Scrapped 1922
T 39	1907	270	Scrapped 1923
T 40	1909	251	Scrapped 1923
T 41	1899	191	To Britain 1918
T 42	1899	187	Scrapped 1923
T 43	1905	283	—
T 44	1910	244	—
T 45	1911	244	—
T 211	—	682	—
T 220	—	1,100	—
T 221	1904	894	—
T 222	1905	623	—
T 223	1905	776	—
T 224	1896	783	—

T 225	1897	783	–
T 226	1914	613	–
T 227	1904	644	–
T 228	1891	690	–
T 229	1895	650	–
T 230	1905	671	–
T 231	–	–	–
T 232	1910	579	–
T 233	1883	426	–
T 234	1910	510	–
T 235	1896	472	–
T 236	1904	537	–
T 237	1904	530	–
T 238	1915	519	–
T 239	1911	551	–
T 240	–	295	–
T 242	1887	800	–
T 246	–	215	–
T 247	1872	400	–
T 248	1883	800	–
T 249	–	800	–
T 250	–	515	Lost 10 Mar 1916
T 251	1891	510	–
T 252	–	–	Lost 1916
T 252	–	–	–
T 253	–	500	–
T 254	–	100	–
T 255	–	200	–
T 256	–	100	–
T 257	–	100	–
T 258	–	100	–
T 259	1877	180	–
T 260	1910	590	–
T 261	1910	453	–
T 262	1896	328	–
T 263	1895	328	Removed from list 1917
T 263	–	–	–
T 264	1890	281	–
T 265	1893	318	–
T 266	1902	225	–
T 272	–	–	–
T 273	1913	102	–
T 274	–	82	–
T 280	–	201	–
T 281	1871	100	–
T 282	1883	173	–
T 283	1874	500	–
T 290	1895	470	–
T 291	1895	490	–
T 292	1896	300	–
T 293	1901	480	–

Right: The Estonian minesweeper *Ristna*, formerly the Russian auxiliary minesweeper No. *18.* (Author's collection)

SEAPLANE CARRIERS

ORLITSA SEAPLANE CARRIER

Orlitsa was converted to a seaplane carrier from a merchant ship from 1913 to 1915. During the conversion she was equipped with two hangars to house four seaplanes. Another seaplane was carried in the hold. The first aircraft to operate from *Orlitsa* were the FBA flying-boats, but these were replaced in 1916 by Russian-built *M 9* seaplanes.

Displacement: 3,800 tons
Dimensions: 300 ft × 40 ft × 17 ft (91.37 m × 12.2 m × 5.2 m)
Machinery: reciprocating (VTE); 1 shaft; IHP 2,200; 12 kts
Armament: eight 3 in (75 mm) five seaplanes
Complement: ?

NAME	BUILDER	CONVERTED	COMMISSIONED	FATE
Orlitsa	Caledon	1913–15	20 Dec 1915	Returned to merchant service post-war

Left: Seaplane carrier *Orlitsa* in the Baltic Sea in 1915–16. (Boris Drashpil/US Naval Historical Center)

Left: The forward part of the seaplane carrier *Orlitsa* showing flying boats stored athwartships on the deck. (Boris Drashpil/US Naval Historical Center)

IMPERATOR ALEXANDER I Class SEAPLANE CARRIERS

These two ships were purchased from Britain in 1913 for conversion to seaplane carriers for service with the Black Sea Fleet. The conversion involved fitting a large hangar aft and a flight deck which extended over the stern of the ship. Both vessels were seized by the Germans in April 1918 and then taken over by Britain when Germany surrendered. They were subsequently scuttled when the British withdrew.

Displacement: 9,240 tons
Dimensions: 384 ft × 50 ft × 20 ft 6 in (117 m × 15.22 m × 6.2 m)
Machinery: reciprocating (VTE); 1 shaft; IHP 5,100; 15 kts
Armament: six 4.7 in (120 mm) six 3 in (75 mm) 7/9 seaplanes
Complement: ?

NAME	BUILDER	CONVERTED	COMMISSIONED	FATE
Imperator Alexander I	–	1914/16	29 Nov 1916	Scuttled 1919
Imperator Nikolai I	–	1914/16	29 Nov 1916	Scuttled 1919

REGELE CAROL I SEAPLANE CARRIER

In 1917 Rumania lent Russia the merchant ship *Regel Carol I* for conversion to a seaplane carrier for service in the Black Sea. During the War Russian seaplane carriers carried out a number of raids against Turkish positions.

Displacement: 2,368 tons
Dimensions: 350 ft × 42 ft × 18 ft 6 in (106.6 m × 12.8 m × 5.6 m)
Machinery: reciprocating (VTE); 2 shafts; 6 boilers; IHP 6,500; 18 kts
Bunkers: 500 tons coal
Armament: four 6 in (152 mm) four 3 in (75 mm) four seaplanes
Complement: ?

NAME	BUILDER	CONVERTED	COMMISSIONED	FATE
Regele Carol I	Fairfield	1916	1917	Handed back 1918

RUMYNIYA Class SEAPLANE CARRIERS

Like the previous vessels, these ships were borrowed from Rumania in 1916 and converted to seaplane carriers for service in the Black Sea. Conversion involved building a low structure aft to form a small flight deck. The ships were seized by the Germans in 1918 and then taken over by the Allies on Germany's surrender, finally being returned to Rumania.

Displacement: 4,500 tons (full load)
Dimensions: 356 ft 10 in × 41 ft 10 in × 27 ft 6 in (108.68 m × 12.8 m × 8.4 m)
Machinery: reciprocating (VTE); 2 shafts; 5 boilers; IHP 6,500; 18 kts
Bunkers: 500 tons coal
Armament: four 6 in (152 mm) one/four 3 in (75 mm) four/seven seaplanes
Complement: ?

NAME	BUILDER	CONVERTED	COMMISSIONED	FATE
Dakia	Chantier de la Loire	1916	1917	Seized by Germany 1918
Imperator Trajan	Chantier de la Loire	1916	1917	Seized by Germany 1918
Rumyniya	Chantier de la Loire	1916	1917	Seized by Germany 1918

Right: Seaplane carrier *Rumyniya.* Note seaplanes on deck aft. (NAVPIC)

MISCELLANEOUS WARSHIPS

KOPCHIK Class PATROL VESSELS

Displacement: 450 tons
Dimensions: 168 ft × 26 ft × 10 ft 6 in (51.2 m × 7.9 m × 3.2 m)
Machinery: reciprocating (VTE); 2 shafts; 3 Yarrow boilers; IHP 1,350; 15.3 kts
Bunkers: 38 tons coal
Armament: two 4 in (102 mm)
one 3 pdr (47 mm)
70 mines
Complement: 48

NAME	BUILDER	LAUNCHED	FATE
Kopchik	Sandvikens	1916	Scrapped 1940s
Korshun	Sandvikens	1916	Renamed *Pioner* 1920s

KALMYK Class RIVER GUNBOATS

This class of river gunboats was built in sections on the River Volga and sent to the Far East where they were assembled at Khabarovsk-Ossipovski on the River Amur.

Displacement: 244 tons
Dimensions: 179 ft × 27 ft × 3 ft 4 in (54.5 m × 8.2 m × 1 m)
Machinery: reciprocating (VTE); 2 shafts; 2 mixed firing boilers; IHP 480; 10 kts
Bunkers: 45 tons coal, 36 tons oil
Armament: two 4.7 in/45 cal (120 mm)
one 1.9 in AA (47 mm)
Complement: 63

NAME	BUILDER	ASSEMBLED	FATE
Amuretz	Sormovo	1908	Renamed *Zryanin* Hulked 1914
Kalmyk	Sormovo	1908	Hulked 1914
Kirgiz	Sormovo	1908	Hulked 1914
Korel	Sormovo	1908	Hulked 1914
Sibiryak	Sormovo	1908	Hulked 1914
Ussurietz	Sormovo	1908	Renamed *Votyak* Hulked 1914
Zabaikaletz	Sormovo	1908	Renamed *Vogul* Hulked 1914

GOLUB Class PATROL VESSELS

Displacement: 400 tons
Dimensions: 170 ft 6 in × 24 ft 6 in × 11 ft (51.92 m × 7.46 m × 3.4 m)
Machinery: reciprocating (VTE); 2 shafts; 3 boilers; IHP 1,400; 15 kts
Bunkers: 70 tons coal
Armament: two 4 in (102 mm)
one 1.5 in AA (40 mm)
Complement: 54

NAME	BUILDER	LAID DOWN	LAUNCHED	COMPLETED	FATE
Bekas	Maskin-Brobygnack	–	1919	–	To Chile 1920
Chibis	Sandvikens	–	1919	–	To Chile 1920
Golub	Maskin-Brobygnack	–	1917	–	Seized by Germany April 1918
Pingvin	Maskin-Brobygnack	–	1917	–	Seized by Germany April 1918
Strizh	Sandvikens	–	1919	–	To Chile 1920

FILIN Class PATROL VESSELS

Displacement: 342 tons
Dimensions: 164 ft × 23 ft × 9 ft 6 in (50 m × 7 m × 2.9 m)
Machinery: reciprocating (VTE); 2 shafts; 2 boilers; IHP 1,150; 15 kts
Bunkers: 50 tons coal
Armament: one 3 in (75 mm)
one 1.5 in AA (40 mm)
Complement: ?

NAME	BUILDER	LAUNCHED	FATE
Chirok	Crichton	1918	To Finland 1918
Filin	Crichton	1918	To Finland 1918
Gorlitza	Crichton	–	Scrapped on stocks
Lun	Crichton	1919	To Poland 1921
Sova	Crichton	–	Scrapped on stocks
Vodorez	Crichton	1919	To Poland 1921

GROZNYI Class PATROL VESSELS

Displacement: 1,120 tons
Dimensions: ?
Machinery: reciprocating (VTE); 1 shaft; ? boilers; IHP ?; 10 kts
Armament: two 4.7 in (*Strazh* 6 in) (120 (152) mm)
two 4 in (not in *Strazh*) (102 mm)
one 3 pdr (*Strazh* 1.75 in) AA (47 (40) mm)
Complement: ?

NAME	COMPLETED	FATE
Groznyi	1918	To Italy 1923
Strazh	1920	To Italy 1923

BURYAT Class RIVER GUNBOATS

Built in sections on the River Volga and sent to the Far East where they were assembled at Khabarovsk-Ossipovski on the River Amur.

Displacement: 193 tons
Dimensions: 179 ft × 27 ft × 2 ft 4 in (54.5 m × 8.2 m × 0.7 m)
Machinery: reciprocating (VTE); 2 shafts; 2 mixed firing boilers; IHP 480; 11 kts
Bunkers: 45 tons coal, 36 tons oil
Armament: two 3 in/50 cal (75 mm)
Complement: 66

NAME	BUILDER	ASSEMBLED	FATE
Buryat	Sormovo	1907	To Japan 1920
Mongol	Sormovo	1907	To Japan 1920
Orochanin	Sormovo	1907	Scrapped 1922

Right: A *Shkval*-class gunboat on the River Dvina in 1917. (P. A. Vicary)

SHKVAL Class RIVER GUNBOATS

Powerful gunboats designed for service in the Far East. They were built in sections at the Baltic Yard and shipped to Khabarovsk-Ossipovski on the River Amur where they were assembled.

Displacement:	946 tons
Dimensions:	233 ft × 42 ft × 4 ft 6 in (70.9 m × 12.8 m × 1.37 m)
Machinery:	four diesels; 4 shafts; BHP 1,000; 11 kts
Bunkers:	127 tons oil
Armament:	two 6 in/50 cal (152 mm) four (2×2) 4.7 in/50 cal (120 mm)
Complement:	117

NAME	BUILDER	ASSEMBLED	FATE
Groza	Baltic Yard	1911	Hulked 1914
Shkval	Baltic Yard	1911	To Japan 1920
Shtorm	Baltic Yard	1911	Hulked 1914
Smerch	Baltic Yard	1911	Hulked 1920
Taifun	Baltic Yard	1911	Hulked 1914
Uragan	Baltic Yard	1911	Hulked 1914
Vikhr	Baltic Yard	1911	Hulked 1914
Vyuga	Baltic Yard	1911	Hulked 1914

PULYA Class RIVER GUNBOATS

The class was transferred to the Far East where they served with the River Amur Flotilla.

Displacement:	23.5 tons
Dimensions:	72 ft × 10 ft 6 in × 2 ft 4 in (22 m × 3.2 m × 0.7 m)
Machinery:	2 petrol engines; 2 shafts; BHP 200; 14.5 kts
Armament:	one 3 in (75 mm)
Complement:	10

NAME	BUILDER	LAUNCHED	FATE
Kindzhal	Putilov	1910	–
Kope	Putilov	1910	Scrapped 1940s
Palash	Putilov	1910	–
Pika	Putilov	1910	Scrapped 1940s
Pistolet	Putilov	1910	–
Pulya	Putilov	1910	–
Rapira	Putilov	1910	–
Sablya	Putilov	1910	–
Shashka	Putilov	1910	–
Shtyk	Putilov	1910	–

NICHOLSON Type MOTOR LAUNCHES

This class of small launches was ordered in 1904, the lead ship being built in America and the remainder at Sevastopol. Originally destined for the Far East Fleet, they were transferred to the Baltic following the end of the Russo-Japanese War.

Displacement:	35 tons
Dimensions:	90 ft × 12 ft × 5 ft (27.4 m × 3.65 m × 1.5 m)
Machinery:	petrol engine; 1 shaft; BHP 600; 16 kts
Armament:	one 3 pdr (47 mm) one 18 in TT (457 mm)
Complement:	11

NAME	BUILDER	ASSEMBLED	FATE
1	Flint & Co	1905	Scrapped *c.*1950
2	Admiralty Yard	1905	Scrapped 1940s
3	Admiralty Yard	1905	Scrapped 1920s
4	Admiralty Yard	1905	Scrapped 1930s
5	Admiralty Yard	1905	Scrapped 1940s
6	Admiralty Yard	1905	Scrapped 1930s
7	Admiralty Yard	1905	Scrapped 1940s
8	Admiralty Yard	1905	Scrapped 1920s
9	Admiralty Yard	1905	Scrapped 1940s
10	Admiralty Yard	1905	Scrapped 1920s

SK 311–317, SK 321–327, SK 331–337, SK 341–347 MOTOR LAUNCHES

A series of eighteen fast motor launches was ordered from America in 1915 for service in the Black Sea where they were to be used as submarine chasers. Further boats of the series were ordered in 1916. They were shipped to Odessa where they were assembled at the Revenski Yard. At least one launch (*SK 313*) was lost during the war.

Displacement: 14 tons
Dimensions: ?
Machinery: 24 kts
Armament: one 3 pdr (47 mm)

511–518, 521–528, 531–538, 541–547 MOTOR LAUNCHES

These small launches were ordered from various US boatbuilders in 1916. They were shipped to Russia in sections and an unknown number were assembled by the Revenski Yard at Odessa.

Displacement: 20 tons
Dimensions: 60 ft × 10 ft × 4 ft (18.3 m × 3.04 m × 1.2 m)
Machinery: 2 petrol engines; 2 shafts; BHP 250; 12 kts
Armament: two machine-guns
Complement: ?

BK 1–BK 12 MOTOR LAUNCHES

These units were ordered from the Revenski Yard at Odessa in 1916. *BK* 7 was lost in 1917, and four units were seized by Austria-Hungary in 1918.

Displacement: 25 tons
Dimensions: 50 ft × 10 ft × 2 ft 6 in (15.2 m × 3.04 m × 0.76 m)
Machinery: 2 petrol engines; 2 shafts; BHP 200; 10 kts
Armament: two machine-guns
Complement: ?

RUSSUD Type: Nos 1–50 LANDING CRAFT

These landing craft were ordered in December 1915 from the Russud Yard at Nicolaiev. Their design later became the standard for all landing craft. They were designed to run up on to the beach where a bow ramp was lowered by means of two booms to enable men and equipment to be disembarked. The programme ran into difficulties due to the lack of engines available for powering the craft. As a result, Nos *11–14*, *27*, *30*, *33–36* and *41–50* were completed without any machinery. A number of units was fitted with light armament and some were fitted with heavy guns to operate as river gunboats.

Displacement: 225 tons
Dimensions: 179 ft 6 in × 21 ft 6 in × 4 ft (54.7 m × 6.5 m × 1.2 m)
Machinery: 2 diesels; 2 shafts; BHP 80/100; 5.5 kts
Complement: 8 plus 520 troops below decks and 240 above decks

DOZORNY Class DISPATCH VESSELS

Displacement: 100 tons
Dimensions: 101 ft × 16 ft 6 in × 5 ft 6 in (30.76 m × 5 m × 1.7 m)
Machinery: reciprocating (VTE); 1 shaft; IHP 600; 16 kts
Armament: one 1 pdr (37 mm)
Complement: 23

NAME	BUILDER	LAID DOWN	LAUNCHED	COMPLETED	FATE
Dozorny	Crichton-Vulkan	–	–	1904	Scrapped 1950s
Razvedchik	Crichton-Vulkan	–	–	1904	–

ELPIDIFOR Type Nos *410–439* LANDING CRAFT

In February 1917, thirty troop-landing ships were ordered from the Naval Russud Yard at Nicolaiev. The design was based on a coastal vessel used on the Sea of Azov called the *Elpidifor*, hence the generic name for the landing ships. They were equipped with two long booms for handling cargo from the four holds, while two gangplanks were lowered from a boom at the bows to enable the troops to disembark. A number of units were fitted with minesweeping/minelaying gear during the war. Nos *410–412* were captured by the Germans in 1918; Nos *428* and *429* were scrapped on the stocks and Nos *430–439* were cancelled in 1917.

Displacement: 1,050 tons
Dimensions: 250 ft × 34 ft × 6 ft (76.1 m × 10.35 m × 1.8 m)
Machinery: reciprocating (VTE); 2 shafts; IHP 600; 10 kts
Armament: two 4.7 in (120 mm) 250 mines
Complement: ?

KONVOIR Class DISPATCH VESSELS

Displacement: 211 tons
Dimensions: 121 ft × 20 ft × 6 ft (36.85 m × 6.1 m × 1.8 m)
Machinery: reciprocating (VTE); 1 shaft; 1 boiler; IHP 500; 12 kts
Bunkers: 80 tons coal
Armament: one 3 in (75 mm)
Complement: 20

NAME	BUILDER	LAUNCHED	FATE
Konvoir	Crichton	6 July 1912	Sunk May 1917
Sputnik	Crichton	11 July 1912	Seized by Germany 1918

BARSUK Class DISPATCH VESSELS

Displacement: 168 tons
Dimensions: 100 ft × 19 ft × 6 ft 10 in (30.45 m × 5.8 m × 2.08 m)
Machinery: reciprocating (VTE); 1 shaft; 1 boiler; IHP 350; 11 kts
Armament: one 3 in (75 mm) one 1.5 in AA (40 mm)
Complement: ?

NAME	BUILDER	LAUNCHED	FATE
O.1	Lehtonemi	1915	Renamed *Barsuk* CTL 19 Oct 1917
O.2	Lehtonemi	1916	Renamed *Kunitsa* Scrapped 1950s
O.3	Lehtonemi	1916	Renamed *Khorek* Scrapped 1930s
O.4	Lehtonemi	1916	Renamed *Gronostaj*
O.5	Lehtonemi	1916	Renamed *Laska* Scrapped 1930s
O.6	Lehtonemi	1916	Renamed *Sobol*
O.7	Lehtonemi	1916	Renamed *Vydra* Scrapped 1930s

VOLKHOV SUBMARINE SALVAGE VESSEL

The design of this catamaran-hulled vessel was based on the German *Vulkan*. She was equipped with four enormous lifts with a capacity of 1,000 tons.

Displacement: 2,400 tons
Dimensions: 315 ft × 43 ft × 12 ft (96 m × 13.2 m × 3.65 m)
Machinery: 2 diesels; 2 shafts; BHP 1,200; 10 kts
Complement: ?

NAME	BUILDER	LAUNCHED	COMPLETED
Volkhov	Putilov	30 Nov 1913	27 July 1915

ALMAZ ARMED YACHT

The armed yacht *Almaz* showed very graceful lines with her two funnels close together, three masts, clipper bow and bowsprit. Apart from two destroyers, she was the only vessel to escape the slaughter at the Battle of Tsushima, escaping to Vladivostock. She subsequently transferred to the Black Sea in 1911. During the First World War she was converted to a seaplane carrier carrying four seaplanes and armed with seven 4.7 in/45 cal and four 3 in AA guns.

Displacement:	3,285 tons
Dimensions:	365 ft 8 in (oa) × 43 ft 6 in × 17 ft 6 in (111.37 m × 13.25 m × 5.33 m)
Machinery:	reciprocating (VTE); 2 shafts; ? Belleville boilers; IHP 7,500; 19 kts
Bunkers:	560 tons coal
Armament:	four 3 in (75 mm) eight 3 pdr (47 mm)
Complement:	336

NAME	BUILDER	LAID DOWN	LAUNCHED	COMPLETED	FATE
Almaz	Baltic Works	25 Sept 1902	2 June 1903	Dec 1903	Escaped to Bizerta 1920

Right: *Almaz*. Note the gun mounted in the bows. (Marius Bar)

Right: *Almaz* as a seaplane carrier. The outline of seaplanes can just be made out on the after deck. (Author's collection)

APPENDICES

1. Short Military Chronology of the Imperial Russian Navy

1700–21	Great Northern War
21 July 1711	Treaty of Pruth
1722–3	War with Persia
1725–41	Military forces neglected by succession of weak rulers
1736	Restoration of land to Persia
1736–9	War with Turkey
1741–3	Russo-Swedish War
1743	Peace with Sweden. Russia gains new territory in Finland
1768–74	Russo-Turkish War
6 July 1770	Battle of Tchesme
April 1770	Capture of Navarino
16 July 1774	Treaty of Kuchuk Kainarji
1783	Crimea annexed
1787–92	Second Russo-Turkish War
1788–90	Russo-Swedish War
1806–7	Third Russo-Turkish War
30 June 1807	Battle of Lemnos
1821–9	Greek War of Independence
20 October 1827	Battle of Navarino
1828–9	Fourth Russo-Turkish War
1853–6	Crimean War
30 November 1853	Battle of Sinope. Introduction of explosive shell by Russians
16 October 1855	Bombardment of Kinburn. First appearance of ironclads by French
9–10 August 1855	Bombardment of Sveaborg. Introduction of mine by Russians
April 1877–March 1878	Russo-Turkish War
1880	First systematic construction programme drawn up
1898	Major naval programme drawn up
1901	Russia-China agreement for Russia to take control of Manchuria
April 1902	Russia agrees to withdraw from Manchuria by October 1903
Early 1903	Russia re-occupies evacuated Chinese territory
3 February 1904	Russian First Pacific Squadron puts to sea
6 February 1904	Relations between Russia and Japan severed
8 February 1904	Japanese torpedo attack on Russian Fleet in Port Arthur
10 August 1904	Russian attempt to break Japanese blockade of Port Arthur fails
14 October 1904	Russian Second Pacific Squadron sails from Baltic for Pacific
27 May 1905	Battle of Tsushima
26 June 1905	Mutiny in Black Sea Fleet
April 1906	Naval Staff formed
July 1912	Little Programme of construction approved
1914–17	First World War
12 March 1917	Imperial Russia ceases to exist

2. Russian Shipyards

The full names of shipyards in Russia and overseas that built ships for the Imperial Navy are listed below.

YARD	CITY	REGION	COMMENTS
Admiralty Yard	St. Petersburg	Baltic	Formed from Galernii Island and New Admiralty Yards in 1908
Baltic (Works) Yard	St. Petersburg	Baltic	
Bellino-Fenderich Yard	Odessa	Black Sea	
Car & Macpherson	St. Petersburg	Baltic	
Crichton	St. Petersburg	Baltic	
Franco Belgian Works	Nikolaiev	Black Sea	Renamed Nicolaiev
Galernii Island	St. Petersburg	Baltic	Renamed Admiralty Yard 1908
Izhora Yard	St. Petersburg	Baltic	
Khabarovsk-Ossipovski		River Amur	
Kolomenskaya Yard	Kolomna		
Kolomna	Moscow		
Kronstadt			
Lindholmen Yard			
Metal Works	Petrograd	Baltic	
Mitchell & Co	St. Petersburg	Baltic	
Naval Yard	Nicolaiev	Black Sea	
New Admiralty	St. Petersburg	Baltic	Renamed Admiralty Yard 1908
Nevski	St. Petersburg	Baltic	
Nicolaiev Admiralty Yard	Nicolaiev	Black Sea	Former Franco-Belgian Works
Nicolaiev SB & Engineering	Nicolaiev	Black Sea	
Nizhegorodski Teplokhod Works			
Putilov	St. Petersburg	Baltic	

YARD	CITY	REGION	COMMENTS
Revenski Yard	Odessa	Black Sea	
Ropit (Russian Steam Nav Co	Odessa	Black Sea	
Russud (Russian SB Co)	Nicolaiev	Black Sea	
Society of Metal & Mining Works	St. Petersburg	Baltic	
Sevastopol			
Sormovo Yard	Novgorod	River Volga	
Zolotov Yard	St. Petersburg	Baltic	

3. Foreign Shipyards

NAME	CITY	COUNTRY
Ahlstrom	Bjorneberg	–
Andre Rozenkvist	Abo	Finland
Bekker & Co Yard	Reval	Estonia
Bergsund	Stockholm	Sweden
Botnia Yard	Abo	Finland
Britnev	–	–
Broberg	Helsingfors	Finland
Burmeister & Wain	–	–
Caledon	–	UK
Chantiers de la Loire	Loire	France
Claparede	Rouen	France
Clydebank	–	UK
Cochrane	–	–
Cockerill	Seraing	Belgium
Cramp	Philadelphia	USA
Crichton	Abo	Finland
Crichton	Okhta	Finland
Crichton-Vulkan	Turku	Finland
Fairfield	Clyde	UK
Flint & Co	–	USA
F. & C.	Le Havre	France
Germaniawerft	Kiel	Germany
Krupp	Germania	Germany
Laird	Birkenhead	UK
Lange & Sohn	–	–
La Seyne	La Seyne	France
Lehtonemi	–	Finland
Maskin-Brobygnack Yard	Helsingfors	Finland
Noblessner Yard	Reval	Estonia
Normand	Le Havre	France
Pori Yard	–	Finland
Russo-Baltic Yard	Reval	Estonia
St-Nazaire	–	France
Sandvikens Yard	Helsingfors	Finland
Schichau	Danzig	Germany
Skeppsdocka	Helsingfors	Finland
Smith Dock	Middlesbrough	UK
Thames Iron Works	–	UK
Thornycroft	Southampton	UK
Uleaborg	–	Sweden
Vickers	Barrow	UK
Vulkan	Stettin	Germany
Watkins	–	–
Yarrow	Glasgow	UK
Ziese Muhlgraben Works	Riga	Estonia

BIBLIOGRAPHY

Adams, C. E., 'The reconstruction of the Russian War navy in the years 1905–14' in *Marine Rundschau*, p. 12, 1964.

Dupuy, E. and E., *The Encyclopedia of Military History*. Macdonald & Janes, London, 1970.

Gardiner, Robert (editor), *Conway's All the World's Fighting Ships*, vol. 1 (1860–1905 and 2 (1906–1921), Conway Maritime Press, London, 1979, 1980.

Greger, René, *The Russian Fleet, 1914–17*. Ian Allen, Shepperton, 1972.

Hough, Richard, *The Fleet that had to Die*. New English Library, London, 1969.

Hovgaard, William, *Modern History of Warships*. Conway Maritime Press, London, 1978.

Jane, Fred T., *The Imperial Russian Navy*. W. Thacker & Co., 1904.

— *Jane's All the World's Fighting Ships, 1898*. Sampson Low Marston, 1898.

Macintyre, Donald, *The Man of War*. Methuen, London, 1968.

Moiseev, S. P., *List of the Ships of the Russian Steam and Ironclad Fleet from 1861 to 1917*. Moscow, 1948.

Mordal, Jacques, *25 Centuries of Sea Warfare*. Futura Publications, London, 1976.

Padfield, Peter, *Guns at Sea*. Hugh Evelyn, London, 1973.

— *The Battleship Era*. Rupert Hart-Davis, London, 1972.

Pemsel, H., *Atlas of Naval Warfare*. Arms & Armour Press, London, 1977.

Preston, Antony, and Richard Natkiel, *Atlas of Maritime History*. Weidenfeld, London, 1986.

Warner, Oliver, *Fighting Sail*. Cassell, London, 1979.

Woodward, David, *The Russians at Sea*. William Kimber, London, 1965.

Periodicals:

The Belgium Shiplover, various issues.

Cassiers Magazine, The marine number, 1897.

Transactions of the Institution of Naval Architects, 1911.

Warship International, various issues.

Weapons & Warfare, various issues.

Weyer's *Taschenbuch der Kriegsflotten*, 1914.

INDEX